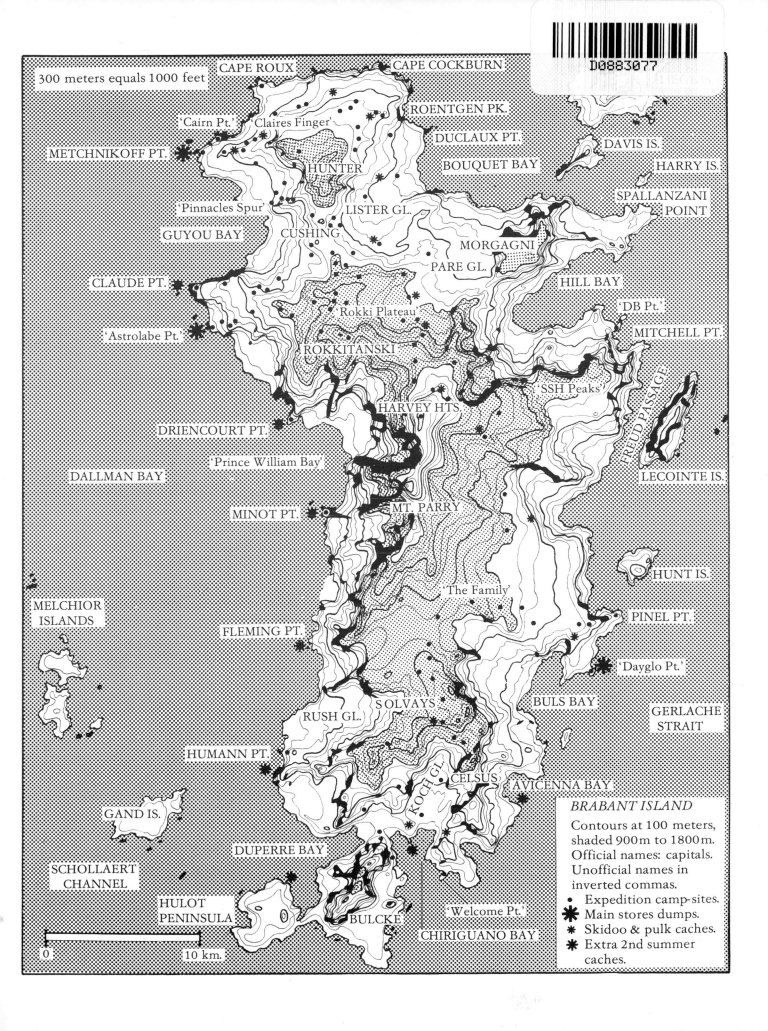

300 meters equals 1000 feet

CAPE ROUX
CAPE COCKBURN
ROENTGEN PK.
'Cairn Pt.'   'Claires Finger'
DUCLAUX PT.
METCHNIKOFF PT.
BOUQUET BAY
DAVIS IS.
HARRY IS.
SPALLANZANI
POINT
HUNTER
'Pinnacles Spur'
LISTER GL.
GUYOU BAY
CUSHING
MORGAGNI
CLAUDE PT.
PARE GL.
HILL BAY
'Rokki Plateau'
'DB Pt.'
'Astrolabe Pt.'
MITCHELL PT.
ROKKITANSKI
'SSH Peaks'
FREUD PASSAGE
HARVEY HTS.
DRIENCOURT PT.
'Prince William Bay'
LECOINTE IS.
DALLMAN BAY
MINOT PT.
MT. PARRY
'The Family'
HUNT IS.
MELCHIOR
ISLANDS
PINEL PT.
FLEMING PT.
'Dayglo Pt.'
BULS BAY
GERLACHE
STRAIT
SOLVAYS
RUSH GL.
HUMANN PT.
KOCH GL.
CELSUS
AVICENNA BAY
GAND IS.
SCHOLLAERT
CHANNEL
DUPERRE BAY
'Welcome Pt.'
HULOT
PENINSULA
BULCKE
CHIRIGUANO BAY

0   10 km.

BRABANT ISLAND
Contours at 100 meters,
shaded 900m to 1800m.
Official names: capitals.
Unofficial names in
inverted commas.
● Expedition camp-sites.
✱ Main stores dumps.
⁜ Skidoo & pulk caches.
✻ Extra 2nd summer
caches.

ANTARCTIC YEAR
Brabant Island Expedition

The Belgica in Neumayer Channel, 1898.
(Courtesy Baron Gaston de Gerlache de Gomery)

ANTARCTIC YEAR

Brabant Island Expedition

Chris Furse

Foreword by HRH Prince Charles

London • Sydney • Dover, New Hampshire

© 1986 Chris Furse
Croom Helm Publishers Ltd, Provident House, Burrell Row, Beckenham, Kent, BR3 1AT
Croom Helm Australia Pty Ltd, Suite 4, 6th Floor, 64-76 Kippax Street,
Surry Hills, NSW 2001, Australia

British Library Cataloguing in Publication Data

Furse, Chris
    Antarctic year: Brabant Island expedition.
    1. Antarctic Regions
    I. Title
    508.98′9   G860
    ISBN 0-7099-1058-4

Croom Helm, 51 Washington Street, Dover,
New Hampshire, 03820, USA

Library of Congress Cataloging in Publication Data applied for

Typeset in 11pt ITC Garamond Light by Leaper & Gard Ltd, Bristol, England
Printed and bound in Great Britain

Contents

Foreword by HRH Prince Charles

Most people probably believe that Antarctic explorers are somehow different from ordinary men, unconsciously associating them with childhood heroes like Shackleton, Amundsen and Scott. In fact, of course, most of them are just ordinary people. This book describes how thirty five 'ordinary' men lived and worked through the adventure of a lifetime after answering a routine advertisement for volunteers. They ranged in age from 21 to 49; most of them were British Servicemen, with three civilians, one a Belgian. Some had never even climbed before.

Most of them had caught the first spark of adventure in their schooldays: one Lance Corporal had been taken climbing at Portland from his East London school; and one reserve had been taught to canoe by his Probation Officer in Plymouth. Others had only taken up adventurous activities after joining the Services. It is immensely encouraging that so many young men (and women too) have this spirit of adventure.

'Ordinary' men these were, but this expedition achieved some extraordinary successes. They were the first to spend a whole winter in Antarctica living in tents rather than huts, showing the way for other light, inexpensive expeditions in the future. The third and last phase of the expedition undertook the first long-distance canoeing in the Antarctic, and incidentally completed a thousand miles of travel in open inflatable boats without any support. The expedition's overland journeys (on skis, manhauling light sledges) also proved exciting, with several serious falls, one man breaking his leg in a crevasse fall, leading to an anxious five-day rescue.

However, all these adventures were merely the means to a more important aim — to study and describe the island's geology and its wildlife. The British Antarctic Survey is analysing the ecology of the region, working with other nations in the unique spirit of the Antarctic Treaty. Realistic quantified information will enable governments to agree measures to control the increasing pressures on the marine food resources of the region. This expedition contributed to that international scientific effort, showing the peaceful side of the British Services, and this book describes the wildlife of the region through one complete year. Antarctica is big enough to swallow much of man's exploitation, but let us hope that it remains a wilderness essentially untouched by man, as it is described here. Let us hope its birds and seals and whales never learn to fear mankind.

The expedition team members will remember Brabant Island all their lives. They were the lucky ones. I know that Chris Furse and his team would like me to thank all those other people back at home who helped to make it possible. Literally thousands of individuals, in hundreds of organisations, were closely involved in raising money, providing food and equipment and helping in countless other ways. I hope that they will enjoy this description of an adventure, which depended so much upon their help.

Charles.

Introduction

Anvers Island stretches across our southern horizon, blue snow mountains silhouetted against the wan sunset. A flotilla of tabular icebergs clutters the sea between, gleaming white on their plane tops, with deeply shadowed indigo walls. A half moon peeps over the glacier at our two tents. The sea is calm, but a recurrent roar of breakers comes up from the rock-shelves down below. Occasionally a thunderous boom echoes round the bay as a piece of the icecliff falls into the sea. Behind the tents the cackle of the nesting Chinstrap Penguins is muted for these two hours of midnight twilight.

The walls of our tent hang idle in this unusual stillness. Ted Atkins sleeps like a seal in his sleeping bag. Between us is the litter of food and cooking. I lie in my own bag, propped against my rucksack, peering out through the entrance. Jeff Hill emerges from the other tent, checks the guys, shovels more snow on the valence, and then walks a little way down the moraine toward the sea.

At last, here I am on Brabant Island. It is 8 January 1984. Earlier this evening four of us were landed at Metchnikoff Point with our main base-camp stores, flown ashore by the two little Wasp helicopters of HMS *Endurance*. The other six team members and remaining gear will be landed elsewhere over the next few days.

This landing, with our 20 tonnes of stores, is the culmination of three years' preparation. As a Joint Services Expedition we enjoy much encouragement within the Services, but we are not officially sponsored, nor managed, so this is really my private expedition, operating within the framework of the Services. We are allowed Service stores and transport, if available, although our priority for them is very low. In practice we have had much Service support, but must also beg, borrow and buy a lot outside. Our expedition budget is £100,000, a third contributed by team members, the rest from widespread fund-raising. No one is required to help us but we have been given marvellous assistance by thousands of individuals in hundreds of organisations. From our tents here we thank all of you, who made this venture possible.

The expedition is in three phases. This ten-man first-summer party will be relieved at the end of March when *Endurance* returns, and a twelve-man winter party will then remain through the long winter, until December 1984, when a larger second-summer party comes out. All but three of the 35 team members are Servicemen, chosen from about 200 volunteers: they range from a 22-year-old Lance Corporal to a 35-year-old Lieutenant Commander, plus me. My brief pen-sketches of them are on pp. 187-91.

I am recurrently asked four questions, which deserve answers.

1. *Why Antarctica?* The white continent was always a dream of mine. It came true in 1970, when I joined Malcolm Burley's team for the first exploration and mapping of Elephant Island. Reality was better than the dream: I was enthralled by the beauty, the power, the isolation; and I discovered another focus for my own all-rounder's interests. In 1976 I led my own 4-month expedition exploring the smaller islands near Elephant Island, and the success of that expedition gave me the openings to materialise my dream again.

2. *Why Brabant Island?* In 1980 I went to discuss my vague plans with the Director of the British Antarctic Survey (BAS); I wanted to explore some piece of the Maritime Antarctic. Dick Laws suggested Brabant Island at 64°S off the Antarctic Peninsula: its geology was particularly interesting, but access on to the island, and movement about it, were both too difficult for BAS within their limited resources. It had never been explored, and indeed I had found records of only three brief landings since its discovery in 1898 (the island's scant history is outlined on pp. 206-8). However a map of the island did exist, produced from aerial photographs: it showed stark relief, with several mountain ranges, one rising over 2,500 metres; it also showed very few (and very small) areas free of snow in mid-summer. Very few photographs of Brabant existed, but people who had seen the island warned me of its inhospitality. These challenges were part of the attraction, so I decided to bring my expedition here.

3. *Why overwinter, without a base hut?* A single-summer Antarctic expedition misses both spring and autumn, so I need the winter to get a full summer. When HMS *Endurance*, the Royal Navy's Ice Patrol Ship, was listed for disposal, no government research institutions would agree to help us, so I planned a very light mobile expedition using tour ships for transport. The lack of a base hut became a source of interest in itself, and attracted a physiological research study. When *Endurance* was reprieved, two little sheds were ordered as meeting places, laboratories and casualty refuges, but not for living in. Thus, by a succession of external circumstances, we find ourselves to be the first expedition planning to overwinter in Antarctica in tents and snowholes, without a hut for living quarters.

4. *What are your objectives?* My overall aim is to explore Brabant Island, and to describe what we discover — its geology and land forms, and what lives and grows here. We have over 60 scientific projects, some large, some small: half involve collecting material for researchers in universities, a quarter are in collaboration with BAS, and the remainder will be analysed and written up by expedition team members. Overwintering will allow us to make several studies of annual cycles and processes, plus research programmes on human physical, mental and social adaptations, and evaluation trials of tents and clothing.

Only five of the team members have worked as professional scientists; a few others have relevant science degrees or are, like me, competent practising amateurs. However, every team member has been given responsibility for some scientific aspect, like Corporal Jon Beattie, a technician and mountain man, who was given terrestrial invertebrates: Jon has arranged to make collections for eleven different researchers. We will not be divided into a party of scientists and a party of mountaineers: every man will do both. The British Services have a long tradition of peaceful scientific exploration around and in Antarctica, and we hope to uphold that reputation. To make their name, professional scientists tend to specialise on esoteric subjects, and Antarctica itself is sometimes treated as the private estate of the research institutes of the Antarctic Treaty nations, but we hope to show that there is still a useful place today for the amateur scientific explorer in Antarctica. Our scientific work will aim to quantify the commonplace, rather than to discover the unusual or unexpected.

However, it would be misleading to imply that we have all come here bent devoutly to the scientific yoke. For most team members the initial impetus was adventure, to set the first footprint on some remote virgin mountain, or discover some unexpected relics of the old sealers. The prime attraction remains adventure, discovering the new and unknown, discovering oneself, and close companionship in hardship and danger — all surrounded by the magic and romance of the last continent.

Books about Antarctica tend to be either stories of human adventure, or descriptions of natural phenomena. In this book I hope to marry these two themes — to show how we live and operate, and also what we discover. My model is of course Peter Freuchen and Finn Salomonsen's classic *The Arctic Year*, with the expedition team taking the place of the north's indigenous Eskimo. In the twelve monthly chapters I will describe the annual cycle as we meet it on Brabant Island, noting how it fits the pattern of the region, based on my own limited experience at Elephant Island and extensive reading. There are also two factual appendices: one covers our expedition and its team, food, equipment, etc; the other outlines our discoveries on Brabant Island, although in most cases it will take a year or two to complete the data reduction and scientific analysis.

For me the adventure has now begun. Here at Metchnikoff Point I have already been chased by some young bull Fur Seals.

Placenames

For convenience of description, some unofficial names coined during the expedition have been used in this book. These are shown in inverted commas on maps and in the text. These unofficial names should not be quoted in subsequent literature.

Since our return, the Foreign Office has discovered some unofficial names given previously by passing ships which have precedence over our names. The following six names have now been submitted to the Antarctic Placenames Committee for adoption as official names:

Lanusse Bay (between Minot and Driencourt Points, we called it 'William's Bay')
Terrada Point (we called it 'Dayglo Point')
Patria Bay (that is what we called it)
Services Point (between Patria and Chiriguano Bays, we did not use any name)
Kayak Bay (between Hunt and Lecointe Islands, we did not use any name)
Cook Summit (we called it 'Mount Frederick Cook').

Research has now shown that three official names were misplaced on the printed DOS map, leading to some confusion.

Roentgen Peak actually applies to the peak we called 'Emery Peak'
Cushing Peak actually applies to the peak we called 'Noddies Hat'
Mount Ehrlich actually applies to the peak we called 'Ben Bangers and Ben Mash'
The peak we knew as Mount Erlich actually has no name.

January

Strangers among the Chinstraps. (Tim Hall)

I dreamt of roaring waters that first night upon our island. Suddenly I realised it was not water, but a helicopter approaching the tent; nine o'clock in the morning, and all of us fast asleep! We scrambled out of our sleeping bags, into cold boots, anoraks and mittens, and emerged into bright sunshine to see the little Wasp helicopter reappearing round the headland from *Endurance*, a red and white toy offshore. Already they seemed an intrusion into our isolated world. For an hour the helicopter flew in and out with more stores, and we rushed to and fro through the penguins carrying cargo nets and boxes. Then they were gone. We were once more alone in our kingdom at Metchnikoff Point. At first the receding roar of engines seemed to leave a blessed silence: then the constant cackle of the penguins and the roar of swell on the rocks below came through the silence, and we were back in our enchanted world.

The four of us (Jeff, Mac, Ted and I) had been landed at Metchnikoff Point to set up our main base. The other six would finish landing the stores at other dumps round the island, and then drive the two boats up from Palmer Base. The sun sparkled on the sea and scattered icebergs, and on the snowslope behind, which rose roundly to 200 metres, hiding the mountains we knew must lie beyond. We arranged the stores in three laagers on the gentle scree platform, each with the plywood cases round the outside to protect the cardboard food cartons, toolboxes, marker flags, fishing tackle, tent valises, etc., from the penguins' mess. Then we started to explore our world.

Metchnikoff Point was one of the largest snow-free areas on the whole island according to the aerial photos — nearly four hectares of rock and scree. The point was dominated by a volcanic butte 110 metres high, its flat top and eastern slope covered by lumpy boulders of red and black lava, many honeycombed by blowholes. Colonies of Chinstrap Penguins covered much of the ground between the snowbanks, forming beaten areas of muddy rock, particularly on the col where our stores were, between the butte and the glacier. A large moraine ridge cut off the whole headland from the glacier behind, which pushed sideways to end in ice-cliffs just below our tents. Around the seaward sides the butte dropped abruptly in little vertical cliffs of crumbling yellow conglomerate rocks, layered by bands of grey basalts. Snow and scree slopes fell from these cliffs, and from the col at 50 metres to the shores. The northern shore was a joyful place in this burst of sunlit weather, offering a series of different delights: at the eastern end was a cobbled beach where the penguins landed; then a flat area of snow and rocks where seals slept; then gravel roadways for penguins between granite ribs where Antarctic Terns nested; next was a beautiful cove, a haven for boats, the opening 15 metres wide between granite bastions, opening inside to a crescent of boulder beach. Immediately west of the cove was a low granite promontory covered with nesting penguins. Penguins landing on the eastern beach marched through the roadways up a slope to the col, and then on up to the top of the butte. Around the rest of the north and west shores the granite formed a complex of little points and bays where the sea surged through narrow channels. Stacks, skerries and islands ran out for over a kilometre into the Bellingshausen Sea.

Here at the north-west corner, that first sunlit day of the expedition, the haunting calls of the nesting Kelp Gulls, and the skerries backlit by the southering sun, were an irresistible reminder of the Hebrides. Weddell Seals dozed on the snow above a tiny cove. Here too we came upon a little party of Fur Seals in the snowy boulder-field: one bull

Metchnikoff Point from the south. The line indicates the base camp col. (Chris Furse)

roared and charged us — this really was the Antarctic, not a summer holiday dream. In the evening the cold drew in and the sun slid slowly round the southern horizon making a blue and yellow stencil of Mount Francais and the other mountains of Anvers Island, clear and distinct over 80 kilometres distant.

That evening of the first day we returned to our tents after eight to start cooking supper, settling very quickly into domestic arrangements which would vary little throughout the expedition. Ted and I shared one of the Antarctic Pyramid base-camp tents: opposite the tunnel entrance we had put a broken box lid on the ground sheet, and on this was our box of food for two days, plus the Optimus paraffin stove and communal oddments like candles, matches and cooking pots. On the left I had laid out my Karrimat, sleeping bag and other gear: as soon as I had crawled in, taken my boots off and placed them between the inner and outer tents with the fuel bottles, I lay on my sleeping bag. On the other side of the culinary altar Ted had arranged his gear in similar fashion, and was starting to cook. I helped by opening compo tins, getting snow from outside the doorway, and making rude comments. Ted was a grand tent-mate with bright sharp humour, twinkling eyes, always thinking of handy practical ways to solve problems and noticing the good things in every bit of life. In the other tent Mac and Jeff were cooking their supper, but for Jeff the lovely warm relaxing evening was interrupted by meteorological readings at 9 p.m.; during this first period he also had daily radio schedules to keep with the boat party at 8.15, and was trying to establish communications with Faraday Base, who would relay weekly bulletins home for us. Two-man tents were the normal, but later three of us would

*South Polar Skua.
(Jed Corbett)*

often share a tent, the third 'camping' in the space below the stove: three was a bit snug for space, but was much better companionship. Two-man tents could tend to isolate the team into couples, so we aimed to change round tent partners about once a week. Hopefully during the expedition each of us would share with all the others — forging mutual understanding and companionship, and making friendships that would last for years.

After supper we talked, wrote diaries, recorded the day's observations or read for a while, then had a brew-up before going to sleep. (When I didn't throw the old teabags away by mistake we made several brews from each bag.) That night we went to sleep late, and while the long summer days lasted most of us ran on like that, going to sleep after 1 a.m. Ted was first to wake and shook me at about 9 a.m. when he had cooked breakfast, finishing his day of cooking. Breakfast, and kick-starting mind and body into life took a bit more than an hour; then we put on boots and outer clothing, and emerged for the day's work.

10 January was another halcyon day. After more work sorting out stores, and routine counts of penguins and seals, we roped up to try out ski-mountaineering bindings and skins. We skied up the snowslope behind, sighting for the first time the mountains beyond, then along to the smaller lava bluff to eastward. Here a pair of skuas had found a typical nest-site in a moss carpet, albeit a tiny patch and rather higher than usual at 200 metres. One waddled about near the nest, raising its wings and quacking; the other dive-bombed us half-heartedly. Some skuas hit our heads with their feet in close bombing, particularly just before and after hatching, but this pair were still brooding two lovely dark olive eggs blotched with dark brown. Two species of skua breed in Antarctica, the Brown Skua and the South Polar (or McCormick's) Skua; at Elephant Island I had only met Brown Skuas, but their ranges overlap near Brabant and the South Polar species is spreading northward. Both species closely resemble the northern Great Skua, and it was immediately apparent that I would often be unsure of separating the two. They are the eagles (and vultures) of the Antarctic, dominating the skies and dive-

bombing rivals who enter their territory: this consists of a nest area and a feeding area, which may be separate, especially where they nest in loose colonies. Brown Skuas usually stake a claim in a penguin colony, though some pairs specialise on Cape Pigeons, or Storm Petrels. South Polar Skuas obtain more of their food, even in summer, by foraging at sea for krill, and so are less tied to penguin colonies. At Metchnikoff Point there was only one breeding pair, plus a dozen birds who did not form the usual batchelor club and may have been failed breeders. One of these non-nesting pairs 'owned' the penguins around our stores dump, taking eggs or chicks left unattended, as inexperienced penguins argued over stones or some imagined trespass. The skuas would carry off an egg in their beak to peck open elsewhere; they also carried off chicks up to a week old. Older chicks were fairly safe unless they left the colony, but the skuas continued to get good pickings from chicks that died of starvation or wet, and from adults hit by falling rocks. One could expect to find skuas timing their breeding season to match that of their main prey but at Elephant Island I had found that hatching dates varied from late December to early February; here on north-west Brabant Island the few chicks found all hatched in the second half of January as the shorter summer reduced the spread. This first pair we found were South Polar Skuas. When their two chicks hatched later in January, one soon died: like eagles, the elder normally gets most food and the younger starves in poor seasons.

For three days we practised roped skiing and man-hauling techniques with our light pulk sledges, putting out some food-caches across the piedmont behind. All our feet got badly blistered and sore from the heavy ski-mountaineering boots, with their plastic outers and soft insulated inners (the latter useable round camp when dry). Jeff's and Mac's feet were really bad, but Ted and I were luckier, so on the 14th we set off in sunshine to climb Mount Hunter. Distances were very deceptive — they looked much closer than the map said, but took much longer to reach. We skied and then trudged through deep snow for three hours to reach the foot of the ridge, then started climbing.

It was a glorious twisting ridge of snow and ice, gashed by a great crevasse at the bottom. On the two steeper sections Ted led, putting in ice-screws as running belays. On the other lovely exposed snowslopes we sat in turn belaying the other on a 'deadman' as he climbed through. Belaying, I sat facing outwards looking past my feet to the edge where the snow dropped exhilaratingly out of sight, to reappear far below on the piedmont. Nearing the top of the ridge we climbed together, both moving at the same time, wending our way up through fantastic snow mushrooms like hugh overflowing dollops of ice-cream, white or creamy in the sun and limpid ultramarine blue in the shadows. These mushrooms are a feature of the tops and ridges in this region: as the moist sea air rises up the hills it condenses and freezes on to the windward side of the crests, creating great rounded masses of toffee-textured snow, often ribbed by vertical thaw-furrows, and sometimes overhanging by nearly ten metres. We reached the undulating summit plateau at 9 p.m. after a twelve-pitch climb of six hours. Being the first human beings ever to step on to these first two peaks gave us a sense of unique ownership of all the mountain, but the climb itself had been the purest joy for both of us. It had been one of my best ever days in the hills, and also Ted's, though he was climbing well within himself. At midnight we pitched our Nova dome tent on the plateau, with clear evening views for 100 km, south to Mount

Adelie Penguin, a visitor.
(Tim Hall)

Francais, north to Smith Island and north-east along the Antarctic Peninsula. Camping on top of a mountain that belonged to the two of us, no others, gave total satisfaction, a sense of uttermost isolation. We drank many brews. We ate hugely. We slept for ever.

Next day we had a long flog in deep snow over another top to Mount Hunter itself (nearly 1500 metres) then down through mushrooms to the slopes below, where Ted fell into a bergschrund, nearly pulling out my iceaxe belay on the steep snow above: 'OK, Ted, I've got you'. Pause. 'This one's a bit deep, Chris'. Another pause. (With both hands and both feet fully occupied in holding him, I was not sure if I could put a deadman belay in to get myself out of the system and help — not at all sure.) 'I can get out myself, Chris'. Great relief! My own expedition rule was never less than three on a glacier and preferably four, for just this situation, and here were the two of us, no one else knew where. 'Footsore Piedmont' was a long walk through mushy snow to our skis: we reached Metchnikoff Point at 10 p.m. to be greeted by Jeff and Mac with many brews and tales of sighting whales and a distant ship.

Their feet recovered, Jeff and Mac spent two days sledging, taking a cache of food and fuel to 'Pinnacles Spur'. Ted's and my feet were now bad so we stayed at Metchnikoff Point. Ted busily and cheerfully got on with mapping the point, and I had several days studying birds. I think perhaps I enjoy working alone on birds best of all, with no leadership distractions or worries, with no fear of letting others down by physical unfitness.

Dominating most of Metchnikoff Point were the Chinstrap Penguins, about 4,500 pairs of them cackling away in their colonies on the scree slopes. Antarctic seas are rich in krill and other food stocks: the whales and seals can mate and give birth at sea, or on the pack-ice, but the birds are limited to the few land areas to hatch their eggs, resulting in these dense colonies. Various species of bird have developed different feeding strategies for the breeding season and their range of foraging varies, from the albatrosses which spend several days away from the nest and fly long distances, down to the Chinstrap Penguin which is limited to a range of less than 30 km.

I knew these tough little creatures well, as about 600,000 pairs bred in the Elephant Island group. Their combined weight of about 6000 tonnes was nearly 98% of the total biomass of breeding birds there, and two to four times the total biomass of seals, so their feeding habits dominated the top end of the local marine food chains during the breeding season. We studied their feeding habits and estimated that they brought home a total of about 450 tonnes of food each day. Through the breeding season they probably ransacked about 30,000 tonnes of krill from a localised area comparable with the inshore fisheries of the Isle of Wight. Penguins are very important units in the Antarctic ecosystem, and breeding Chinstraps are very good indicators of local prey populations.

However, walking through the crowded colonies at Metchnikoff Point it was difficult to think of penguins as ecological units. All penguins have a comical humanity about them so that one instantly thinks of them as people. Ted described one plodding up from the sea, stolidly and solemnly bringing home the wages just as if he were a miner coming home from the pit, getting to his nest at last, saying hello to the missus and inspecting the bairns, before having a few words over the fence with the neighbours. The analogy faltered when the first bairn nibbled dad's beak and then put its face inside dad's throat to gobble some pink regurgitated krill. The scientist must always beware such anthropomorphism: it could equally well be mum bringing home the rations, as the sexes are similar in most penguin species; in general males are rather larger, but there is a large overlap of sizes.

The three Pygoscelid penguins are the archetypal medium-sized penguins and all of them breed on the Antarctic Peninsula. The nervous Gentoo breeds north into the sub-Antarctic and is at the southern end of its range in the Gerlache Strait. The cocky Adelie is typically a bird of higher latitudes, but also breeds north of Brabant in the South Shetlands, South Orkneys and South Sandwich Islands. The Chinstrap used to have a limited range along the Antarctic Peninsula and the islands of the Scotia Arc around to South Georgia; although it now appears to be increasing in numbers in the wake of the vanished whales, Brabant Island is near the southern limit of its range. All three species breed in this region, but so far on Brabant we had only seen the odd one or two non-breeding Adelies and Gentoos visiting. Gentoos need a beach for their large chicks to perambulate around in a creche and Adelies also seem to like flatter moraine areas, but Chinstraps stake out nest claims on any bit of scree at heights of up to 300 metres and slopes of up to 50 degrees. If there were direct competition for nest-sites, I would put my money on the Chin-

Chinstrap feeding large downy chick. (Tim Hall)

straps, which have been well described as 'the most pugnacious penguin'. They are always quarrelling among themselves, and shout and peck at any stray penguin, seal, or human who passes through their colony. As you walk amongst them a cacophony of protest surrounds you, its crescendo moving with you: one feels that some of them actually want you to pass their way to have a chance to peck you. A few do hurl themselves at you from a couple of metres away, a furious cackling little black and white penguin as high as your knee, battering away with its flippers and jabbing at your legs with its beak.

When we arrived, hatching was in full swing. Selecting nests at random I lifted the brooding adults by the tail and recorded the contents of the nest — 2 eggs/chicks or 1 (in about 10% of nests) or just occasionally 3 eggs (3 eggs don't fit well into the bare purple skin of the adults' brood-patch, and I have only once seen three chicks in a nest). Plotting the percentage of chicks produces an **S** curve rising from 0 over a span of about 2 weeks to about 85%; the last 15% of eggs are addled but the frustrated adults continue to brood them for as much as two weeks, before the eggs explode with a quite appalling stench. Curiously these **S** curves showed that the mid-level colony at 50 metres was 4-6 days behind the colony on top of the butte at 110 metres, but ahead of the low-level colony. Hatching at Metchnikoff started early in January and finished by the 24th, about 2 weeks later than at Elephant Island. Now on 16 January many of the downy grey chicks were peering out from under their brooding parent and their plaintive pipings were audible amongst the general gaggle of noise. One or two of the older chicks were sitting up, with their big saggy bellies providing the main support and their feet the balance. Each family clung tenaciously to their little patch of nest-territory, one group still half a metre down in a snowdrift, another on a tiny stable platform halfway down a wet scree penguin ladder between the colony and the sea. In two weeks the older chicks would scuttle about when disturbed, being pecked at by some adults, and tolerated by others: groups of eight chicks would collect temporarily then, but they would go back to their nests after the disturbance, as young Chinstraps do not congregate in permanent creches or huddles like other penguins.

During our first week, a few Snow Petrels visited the cliffs of the butte. Slightly smaller than the dappled Cape Pigeons, they seem to need some overhead protection to help them fend off skuas, and they were entering typical niches as if nesting. Then on 12 January they stopped visiting. At Elephant Island the adults abandoned their chicks in February, and it seemed unlikely that their breeding season was a month earlier 500 km further south at Brabant. I could not sight any of their white chicks, and the crumbling cliffs were dangerous to climb or rope down, so when we saw very few indeed through the rest of the summer, I assumed that our original birds had just been non-breeding visitors.

Mac and Jeff had got back exhausted on 17 January, and with very sore feet. On the evening of 18 January we heard from the boat party: they had arrived at the Buls Bay food-cache that evening after a tremendous five-day journey from Palmer Base, stopping for two nights at Port Lockroy where they explored the old hut (and Bill and Jonathan went swimming!) and for another two nights at Iceberg Point, before the last long stretch through The Waifs. Our own task was to reconnoitre and mark the northern end of the boat party's overland route to Metchnikoff Point. We allowed three more days to recover from blisters while Ted continued mapping Metchnikoff Point by plane table and Jeff fished and worked on stores. I had moved over to share a tent with Mac, a surprising Marine who was always broadening his knowledge and handy at fixing things: he was quiet in the tent, reading a history of the Vikings and letting me get on with this book. Mac fixed up the wind generator, and visited 'Cairn Point' with me one day to census birds.

Then, after an incredibly long spell of sunny weather with gentle zephyrs, the weather turned more typical. At 3 a.m. on 20 January the tent began to rattle in the wind with the sifting sound of snow. We snuggled down for a good night. When we woke in the morning the snow had stopped and the wind eased a little (35 knots gusting 45 our anenometer read at noon). There was a big swell running in from NNW, with the wind from the north-east cutting up a rough cross sea and white water breaking all over the skerries off the north shore. The three grounded bergs offshore were dim white wraiths in a welter of grey. In amongst the maelstrom of the skerries were over a hundred Black-browed Albatrosses patrolling to and fro, and sometimes settling in groups to feed. Kelp Gulls were also actively feeding there, together with a few Giant Petrels, Antarctic Fulmars and Cape Pigeons, but it was the influx of the albatrosses that intrigued me — they foraged a mile or so offshore, but this was the first time I had seen them inshore. Another surprise was an Arctic Tern, rather tired and forlorn, hanging around the fringe of our Antarctic Tern colony, and by contrast emphasizing the dash and elegance of the breeding terns. The albatrosses were clearly in no difficulty, but in two summers at Elephant Island I had only seen them inshore four times (usually after severe storms) although that area is frequented by those breeding on South Georgia. Arctic Terns feed around the pack-ice, so their arrival at the same time suggested some major bad weather out in the Bellingshausen Sea.

The bad weather continued for several days, with mostly north-east winds, gusting up to 50 knots at times, and with snow, sleet and rain making sledging a misery as each foot sank deep into the soft snow, with the pulk sticking all the time. We reconnoitred the route south over the 600 metre 'Wobbly Col' above 'Pinnacles Spur' one day, and relayed a pulk load up on to 'Footsore Piedmont', but by 26 January we were feeling very frustrated. Travel on Brabant Island was much slower than I had expected. That day Ted had finished his map, which I had used to record the breeding bird counts; the four of us ate supper together in our pyramid tent and decided to ski over to Cape Roux for a two-day trip without pulks, leaving next morning.

Wilson's Storm Petrels nested in crannies in the scree all over the point. Each evening they flitted over the screes, rather like large House Martins with their white rumps. That night I went out at midnight to check some of my marked nests, and also to search for Black-bellied Storm Petrels which I had found on the camp moraine the night before, but without any eggs. Mac came out with me, as ever keen to learn more about everything. We didn't find the Black-bellieds, and at 1 a.m. decided to go back to the tent in the dusk. Then Mac noticed a pale shape moving near our stores dump — two pale shapes, too large for penguins. Surely Ted and Jeff had gone to sleep? Then we saw a third shadowy figure. The boat party! It could only be them. We shouted and they replied.

Kevin de Silva came racing over the snow slope and in a minute we were all shaking each others' hands and exchanging scraps of information. They had come by boat all the way from Buls Bay that day, leaving

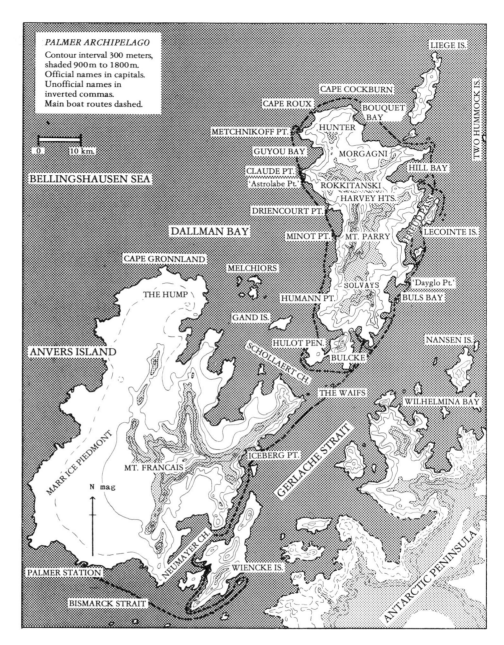

at 3 p.m. in grey claggy weather through brash-ice. After coming through Freud Passage with a headwind and some snow they sheltered in the lee of Davis Island to have a flask and snack. In Bouquet Bay they met thick brash-ice, with Crabeater and Leopard Seals: once a great triangular black head appeared a hundred metres in front of the two boats — they shot to port thinking 'Killer Whale', then realised it was a Humpback Whale (in any case the boats could only push slowly through the brash, and they could not see any landing!). As they rounded Cape Cockburn, they met the three- to six-metre swell of the southern ocean, with a fetch from New Zealand, and the two boats were often out of each others' sight in the troughs. They continued in the gathering gloom past the northern cliffs, through the reefs off Cape Roux and then in through the skerries to the boat haven. They were in tremendous spirits, and rightly so, having completed a 200-km odyssey in the two five-metre Avon inflatables. Bill and Jed were already up at camp, sneakily trying to erect their two dome tents quietly, hoping to startle us next morning. We all gathered round, carrying stores from the beach where they had hauled out the boats, and generally helping wherever we could. What a morning it was! As the grey night gradually paled into a calm dawn they downed their brews of coffee, and we celebrated with the first bottle of whisky of the expedition and a great slice each of Dick's birthday cake from home. Gradually they all slid away to a well-earned sleep and contented dreams. At five I found myself alone in the new day. I took the opportunity to walk round the shore to look at the daily routine of seals, penguins and other birds. To have the whole ten-man team together was a marvellous relief for me — their boat journey (I think the first long open-boat journey this far south) had been an underlying worry. On land one can always just stop and camp if conditions go wrong. In a boat one must get ashore: here the weather and sea could turn foul in half an hour, and we still did not know of one landing in the whole 50 km from Buls Bay! I was happy to muse on good fortune as I walked round the coast. Then at eight I came back up to the sleeping camp. The sun was fighting to pierce the thin cloud over the glacier behind; the Chinstraps continued cackling as ever, totally ignorant of last night's great events, and the surf roared over the rock-shelves south of us. I went into my tent and slept the sleep of the very happy until nearly midday.

The 28th was perfect — sunlit with a gentle drying breeze. People wandered about the point exchanging elated grins and the boat party sorted out their personal stores boxes. That evening all ten of us crammed into one big Pyramid tent and agreed the overall programme until mid-February: first we allowed three or four days for the boat party to find their ski-legs, and for Bill to start his botany and Jonathan his terrestrial invertebrate work; then we would split into three parties to explore the northern part of the island.

We also shuffled tent-partners that day, to meld the two parties who had been apart for three weeks. I put up a little Phoenix Phortress ridge tent and moved in with Jed. It was a small tent, just wide enough for our two Karrimats, but with a reasonable bell at each end between the inner and outer, one to use as porch for boots, etc., and the other for cooking. I needed to try it out, as we wanted to order more backpacking tents for the winter.

Jed was thrilled with his still and cine film taken on the boat trip and enthusiastic about the whole expedition; everything Jed did became a communal activity as he talked his way through it. He proved surprisingly tidy and well organised with his photographic gear in the tent, though after several days we felt it would be too cramped for dry comfort for long periods in winter. The boat party had liked the Super Nova dome tents, with three in a tent; they were big enough to overcome condensation and they had stood up to a couple of gales well, as their reputation promised. We were very pleased with our big MFC Survival Ltd Antarctic Pyramids, but they were base-camp or skidooing tents, not mobile mountain tents. So on the next weekly radio bulletin we asked for eight more Super Novas for the winter. Good tentage was going to be vital through the long winter nights.

My next few days were mostly frustrating work: gutting and skinning a Weddell Seal that we found killed by a rockfall; collecting endoparasites from this seal, and from several Chinstraps found injured by rockfalls; discussing plans and stores problems, etc. Jed on the other hand was having a marvellous time taking still and cine shots of the wildlife on the point. He did not need an ornithologist to show him the penguins or seals, and skuas dive-bombing us in defence of their plaintively squealing chicks were irresistible, but I enjoyed showing him three other good subjects — Kelp Gulls, Antarctic Terns and Cape Pigeons.

Closely resembling the Lesser Black-backed Gulls of Scandinavia, Kelp Gulls breed over a huge range of latitutdes, from subtropical South America down into the Antarctic. They frequent the rocky points and headlands, and are much shyer than their northern relatives: when a colony is approached, all the adults fly up and around, but keep well clear of the intruder, while they fill the air with the same lonesome cries one hears around the cliffs of Scotland. At Metchnikoff Point some granite ribs on the western shore were half-submerged in old limpet shells where the Kelp Gulls had clearly nested for many years. One clutch of two eggs in a lovely nest brooded until late January was probably infertile as most chicks had hatched early in January (a week or two later than at Elephant Island): still largely downy, they hid crouched against the grey rocks.

The lovely Antarctic Terns also rise at the first sign of any intruder; unlike most northern terns their colonies are loosely grouped, whether two or three pairs by a bay, or 400 spread over moraine and cliffs. Most nests are 15 metres apart or more: they are at most a collection of small rock chips, and the one common factor on all sites is a good outlook. Unlike the timorous Kelp Gulls, the terns attack Skuas (or any other intruder) from the moment they appear near the colony, a rolling swarm of dive-bombing terns, calling 'krit krit krit krit-yarr'. Breeding is staggered, both between different colonies and within colonies: at Elephant Island hatching ranged from mid-December to mid-February and on Brabant some chicks were about to fly at the end of January, whilst some eggs were not yet hatched.

The chequer-board black and white markings of the Cape Pigeons are familiar to all seafarers in these southern oceans. Ranging as far north as Brazil in winter, they come south to the Antarctic to breed. At Elephant Island they nested densely on most steeper stable screes where there was enough small material to scrape a little platform backed up against a sheltering rock. On steeper cliffs they were usually replaced by their slightly larger relatives, the Antarctic Fulmar. At Metchnikoff Point about 300 pairs of Cape Pigeons bred around the butte. As you approach, the brooding adult half spreads its wings and 'chitters' melodically at you; as you get close enough to see that the black in the plumage has a plum-coloured blush they are likely to ejaculate orangey oil at you, which your tent-mate can smell for days. Each colony breeds synchronously: here at Metchnikoff Point hatching occurred over the week of 14-20 January, a week or two later than at Elephant Island. At first an adult brooded the grey chick, then, after the chick had established its own thermal regulation but before it was big enough to defend itself against skuas, the adult sat beside it. By the end of January all were in this 'guard stage', the best for Jed to photograph.

January is a quiet month for Antarctic seals: the breeding season is over and they laze around, eating just enough to keep them fat while they moult. The published ranges of the six species suggested we should see three — Weddell, Crabeater and Leopard Seals.

The boat party had seen Leopards and Crabeaters on the ice in Bouquet Bay, and we expected to see more in the winter. Here at Metchnikoff Point there were about 50 Weddells, seemingly always asleep on snowbanks which had melted down to form rounded hollows like a hammock for each seal. Weddells are the Antarctic equivalent of our Grey Seals, living in small sedentary groups around all coasts of Antarctica, as far south as there is open water.

Southern Elephant Seals breed on temperate islands, as far south as the South Shetlands. They dive deep for squid, and come ashore to lie together in great huddles or 'pods'. In the 1820s and 1870s sealers killed out most Elephant Seals, but their populations have since returned to a steady level. A group had been reported in the Gerlache Strait a few years ago, but I was surprised to find three or four ashore regularly.

Fur Seals used to breed in vast numbers in the South Shetlands, and possibly here also, until they were exterminated by sealers within ten years of the discovery of Antarctica in 1819. A few survived the holocaust in South Georgia and over the last 50 years or so that population has exploded until over 100,000 now breed there. They eat mostly krill, so may have benefited from the extermination of whales. In 1970 at Elephant Island we had found the first Fur Seals breeding this century in the South Shetlands, and by 1977 they bred also on Livingstone Island. However it was only when we stopped at Palmer Base that I heard some Fur Seals had been seen in the Palmer Archipelago recently. February would be the most likely time to see them, as the young bulls roam after being driven off the breeding grounds. On 9 January, our first day, we had found five Fur Seals at Metchnikoff Point, and their numbers gradually built up to nearly 200 on 31st, nearly all bulls. The fur seals and sealions comprise the Otarid family of seals, descended from bear-like ancestors whilst the Phocid (typical) seals are descended from otter-like ancestors. The Otarids have small external ears and walk on all fours, with their hind flippers underneath them like legs, and the front half of their body rising vertically from their strong fore-flippers. Indeed they can climb rocks and gallop quite fast. They are also lively and playful, and small sealions are natural circus performers. 300-kg bull Fur Seals are equally playful, but more alarming, as their first instinct is to show their teeth and roar, and often to charge you. The Fur Seals seemed somehow almost our equals, rather than just objects of interest: they were as intelligent as dogs, entertaining, and direct competitors for space along the shore. On land they fought each other playfully, but it was in the water that their true grace and liveliness really showed: they always delighted in porpoising in and out of surf, rolling like corkscrews, swimming upside down or on their sides waving fore-flippers above the surface. Their burst of speed was amazing as they played tag, or raced in and out to tease a somnolent old Weddell floating around nearby. At the end of January I sat on a granite knob looking down through the clear green waters of the boat haven at some Fur Seals disporting themselves: underwater their pelt became distinctly zoned in colour, the pale silvery forebody and pale straw-coloured or chestnut hindbody were separated by dark and russet shoulders and fore-flippers, and tipped by dark head and tail-flippers. As Simon had noticed, their ears stuck out sideways underwater.

Ted had asked why the Chinstraps' hind claw was curled around on top of their webbed feet. Ted had timed Chinstraps taking $6^1/_2$ minutes to climb 50 metres to their nests.

After only a month, innocent amateurs were making worthwhile observations. Long live the amateur in Antarctica!

February

Pulk party coming down to 'Astrolabe Point', its twin promontories directly beyond the pulk. (Jed Corbett)

Blue-eyed Shag defending nest. (Tim Hall)

On the last day of January two groups left base camp to explore southward. Simon, Ted and Kevin took a pulk sledge around the east coast, while Dick, Jonathan, Jeff and Mac sledged to Claude Point. Bill, Jed and I would follow the west-coast party after completing Bill's initial botanical survey of Metchnikoff Point. All of us would return to base camp by 17 February, when *Endurance* was due to visit.

The fine sunny weather that arrived on 28 January continued into February. So far our climate had been dramatically better than at Elephant Island, where weather changed with bewildering frequency and speed. Here, only 500 km further south, we seemed to get blocks of stable weather, with many calm days. Published data did not clearly forecast this difference. Westerly winds circle the Antarctic in the 50s and 60s, driving ocean currents and ice before them, whilst further south easterly winds predominate. The Antarctic Peninsula, about 2000 metres high, is the only landmass to hinder these circumpolar wind systems: eastward the frozen Weddell Sea enjoys a dry continental climate, whilst the west side (Brabant's side) is on the edge of the maritime climate of the Bellingshausen Sea. Depressions move from west to east in the transition zone between the cold polar high-pressure air masses and the temperate air to northward: most depression tracks pass through Drake Passage, but some drive south on to the Peninsula. The whole region is notorious for sudden weather changes and I was worried that the stable weather so far, particularly the two spells of good weather, might lull us into carelessness.

Bill was making the first botanical collection on the island. The Antarctic has a very limited flora, dominated by lichens and mosses, with only two species of flowering plant. Apart from the adverse conditions of the cold, short growing season, and (further south) the surprisingly dry climate, colonisation has been limited by isolation and the scarcity of snow-free areas. Some plants have probably survived through the ice ages on isolated snow-free refuges off the Antarctic Peninsula.

The mosses and lichens grow in various typical communities, or associations, which have been studied and described in most detail by BAS at Signy Island in the South Orkneys. A very few species occur only further south, but in general the richness of vegetation and the variety of plant species steadily diminish down the Antarctic Peninsula. There are few surprises to excite the collector, and scientific effort is now directed to studying in great detail the whole terrestrial ecosystem, which provides a simple model, a natural laboratory.

Crustose lichens provide most of the bright colours on Antarctic snow-free areas: here many rocks were splashed with orange and gold lichens, and some of the crumbling wet cliffs were coated with bright green algae. Bushy lime-green lichens cover the rocks in windswept wet areas: at Elephant Island *Usnea Antarctica* sometimes grew 20 cm long, covering stone-fields like a crop, but here this common lichen was seldom over 5 cm high.

Moss-dominated communities occur in three main forms. In wet areas carpets of green moss form: on Elephant Island some carpets covered a hectare, but so far here we had found only little pockets of moss carpet in places wet with meltwater. In drier areas turf-forming mosses produce the most impressive Antarctic plant communities: with no animals to graze or trample them they build up deep banks over thousands of years. Such moss-banks do occur south of Brabant Island, so we were looking for living moss-banks and also moribund ones which have been overridden by glaciers and then re-exposed by recent glacial retreat; however so far we had only found tiny pockets of some turf-forming moss species, not any accumulated banks. Most of the mosses here occurred in little cushions up to about 5 cm in diameter, which sometimes coalesced to form lumpy soft mats on stones and stable glacial till.

Of most interest to us were the flowering plants. Antarctic Hair Grass *Deschampsia antarctica* and Antarctic Pearlwort *Colobanthus quitensis* are the only two flowering plants found in Antarctica south of 60 degrees. Both species have been found south of Brabant Island, to 68 degrees, but BAS had not expected us to find either on this barren island. So we were very pleased when Bill found two square swards of grass five metres across on the cliff-tops at Metchnikoff Point and also many smaller patches of its spiky green leaves in north-facing sites with per-colating meltwater, free of the trampling penguins. Wading across to a little island at low spring tide he also found some starry pincushions of pearlwort. At home or in the Arctic we would not even notice them: indeed for decades the pearlwort was incorrectly classified as a moss, partly because it seldom flowers this far south, reproducing vegetatively instead. Here both grass and pearlwort seemed very special to us, and Bill marked off his little garden plots to stop us trampling them.

On 5 February Bill, Jed and I set out in one of the boats to join the four at the cache south of Claude Point. After taking our boots off and slipping into waterproof Multifab suits outside everything, we hauled the Avon inflatable down into the water, and loaded on the two outboards and fuel, plus all our survival gear, etc., which nearly filled the boat. Then away we went through the skerries and set course for Claude Point. Visi-bility was good, the swell gentle, and weather looking stable grey, but I never feel comfortable in a small boat alone in the Antarctic, with landing beaches so far apart.

In Guyou Bay we passed a group of Southern Giant Petrels gathered near the floating carcass of a Weddell Seal. These Nellies or Stinkers wander all the southern oceans, and breed in the Antarctic further south than any of the albatrosses, which they resemble in size and flight. They forage for squid, but get much of their food by scavenging dead penguins and seals, tearing into the body cavities with their massive beaks and displaying grotesquely at rivals. The species has two main colour phases, white and dark. The dark phase fledge as uniform dark chocolate birds and disperse north to mingle with the very similar Northern Giant Petrels: they live for 20-30 years and gradually get paler with age, first going white on the face and underparts, and later becoming more and more mottled with grey-white, until they are gener-ally a pale ashy-grey. White-phase chicks have white down and fledge direct into adult plumage, pure white except for a few grey and black feathers scattered asymetrically. There is no truth in the old belief that the percentage of white-phase birds increases further south, and 6% is typi-cal. At Elephant Island we also found a very few leucistic birds, apparently another inherited characteristic: they were pure white without any darker feathers, with dark eyes and pinker bills, and did not appear to have been described before. Over 900 pairs of Giant Petrels bred at Elephant Island, their stone-pile nests in four colonies, on open areas with good winds or natural runways to help their ungainly take off. They breed south to 67 degrees and we had hoped to find some nesting on Brabant Island, but so far we had only seen a few overflying, mostly dark birds, probably too young to breed.

Two hours later we slowly closed Claude Point; a few Black-browed Albatrosses quartering the sea passed close-by our boat with complete disdain, and a Fur Seal leapt out of the water to catch a feeding Wilson's Storm Petrel, as if in play. A band of white water runs out three km from the towering cliffs of Claude Point over a series of reefs and rock platforms but we spied a zigzag through these breakers, close in to the little cobble beach. Yellow, grey and rusty coloured cliffs reared 200m above us, capped with hanging glaciers. Bill was brimful of pleasure steering through the choppy water, while I stood up hanging on to a rope to find the best way ahead, looking down through the clear water to see the shallow rocks below. Safely through, we went on to the cache point.

The point was ramparted with massive basalt columns: there was no landing site. Driencourt Point looked possible but was another hour's journey, so we decided to return to Metchnikoff Point. As we turned for home we sighted two tiny dark rectangles on the snow at the skyline: it must have been the two Phortress tents, but Dick and the others were not in sight.

We went back inside Astrolobe Needle — a great tower of yellow conglomerate rock 80-100 metres high. Its foot was undercut by waves so that its silhouette end-on was like a giant Lombardy poplar.

Around the base of the needle the sea broke over a wide fringe of subtidal rock platforms and several flocks of Cape Pigeons fluttered around the edge of the breakers, landing to feed by plunging their heads underwater. They often feed thus, where the surf stirs up to the surface the Copepods and other small Crustacea they eat. Soon the chicks at Metchnikoff Point would be left alone in the day while the adults foraged, then there would be a week or two when the grey downy chicks were difficult to spot. I had been disappointed to see no Cape Pigeons nesting on the cliffs at the cache point — perhaps they breed here earlier than at Metchnikoff Point and already the chicks were on their own? A little later still the chicks, feathered in the image of their parents, would start exercising their wings, visible from afar.

A few Antarctic Fulmars accompanied the flocks of Cape Pigeons. They often do so, though most feed further out at sea, and at Elephant Island I had found that nesting Fulmars foraged largely at night, whilst Capeys were diurnal. The Fulmars were my favourites, plush grey and white with great dark eyes, sitting confidingly while I lifted them gently to see their white downy chicks. Unlike their coarser descendants the Arctic Fulmars they did not vomit. Here we had only seen a few, mostly flying past Metchnikoff Point in the mornings and evenings; however I still hoped to find them breeding on the island, with their catholic choice of sites from gentle scree to tiny cliff-ledges.

Going back the sky cleared, and we took the boat around to 'Cairn Point' to pick up the skeleton of the Weddell Seal killed on the beach by a falling rock. The week before, after skinning it, I had wrapped it in canvas and left it in a rock-pool: myriads of little amphipods had gathered, and most of the flesh had gone. The skeleton would go to the Royal Scottish Museum. While we had lunch in the sun Jed somehow persuaded an Antarctic Tern to settle on its two eggs while he filmed from a metre away. This pair of terns conducted a running battle with the Kelp Gulls nesting nearby, attacking them whenever they flew. The two young Kelps in their pale mottled grey and sienna plumage scuttled away from us, then sat quiet and helpless when cornered. One then flopped into the water. Kelps defend their colonies weakly, but give communal support to young like this which leave the colony, and several adults settled on the sea nearby. An hour later, as we left, it was still floating happily in the bay, although it would be two weeks before we saw any young Kelps flying.

Coming back through the skerries to Metchnikoff Point we passed under a stack where a few Blue-eyed Shags were each feeding two or three large grey downy chicks. They are striking birds, using their black and white plumage in a variety of heraldic postures at their nests. Like other fish-eaters their breeding season is staggered and these chicks had been hatched within the mid-December to mid-January spread we had recorded at Elephant Island. I was disappointed to have found only this one small colony as they are engaging birds, usually shy, but sometimes allowing a close approach, uttering conversational 'Garrns'.

Next day the three of us set out for Claude Point hauling a pulk sledge in sunshine and at 8 p.m. we pitched our dome tent on the open piedmont. A light breeze had started down the glacier, and we could see the clouds flying down the face of Mount Hunter in little katabatic eddies. An hour later as we cooked supper it began to blow hard and the noise of sifting snow on the tent walls drowned the cheerful roar of the primus. Suddenly there was a bang in the roof. One of the poles had broken near the apex as a gust pushed in the windward side. Jed tried vainly to splint it, working at arm's length between the inner and outer tents. I went out to move the sledge to form a windbreak and found a real hooli blowing, gusting to over 55 knots and filling the air with spindrift. Jed wedged my Karrimat over the broken pole ends to protect the outer tent which had been ripped. We sat with our backs supporting the beating windward

Dome tent blown out on 'Footsore Piedmont'. (Chris Furse)

side. Shouting to hear each other, we decided to sleep as much as we could, and evacuate next morning. I lay curled with my back against the windward side, with the tent walls pushing and beating down on me, while the others found what comfort they could in the rest of the wildly flogging tent. By chance this was the first night I used my Goretex bivouac bag outside my polywarm sleeping bag; cocooned like this I stayed quite dry and warm, and even got some fitful sleep. At first light I woke confused, to hear Jed and Bill shouting above the storm: the outer tent had ripped further exposing the whole inner tent. Jed energetically persuaded us to get dressed and ready to move. When I went out to bring our packs inside, rivers of spindrift were pouring down on the tent, and while digging out the skis from the drift the shovel was torn away and vanished in the storm. We decided to have breakfast, and managed to get the Optimus stove going in the remaining half of the tent. Jed was exhilarated rather than frightened and took cine film of the drift being flung on to the inner tent as patterns of shadow and instantly being torn away. Bill sat calmly reading a book as the windward half of the tent collapsed under the snow: only afterwards did he admit that it was also his first experience of a blown-out tent. By midday we were sitting crammed into the remaining third of the tent which was filling with snow. We ate our chocolate, emerged from the ruins into a maelstrom of white, and collapsed the remaining fragments of tent which drifted over instantly. Jed could not stand up on skis in the hooli, so we left the skis cached beside the pulk with bamboo marker flags. Then we started back in the blizzard, just able to make each other out on the rope, but unable to distinguish between up and down in the snow, nor could we see any hint of shadows at crevasses. After two hours on a compass course I was very relieved to strike a moraine ridge I recognised. From there it was an hour's walk downwind to Metchnikoff Point. We just managed to erect an Antarctic Pyramid tent and went thankfully inside, covered with snow. Base camp was really not much safer: indeed the snow soon turned to sleet and rain, and the wind continued.

The next five days were foul, with almost unremitting rain and sleet, and the three of us spent most of the time in our tent. Camped in the middle like a vagrant between the door and the stove, it was logical for me to cook breakfast. Waking cold I fumbled at the drawcords of my sleeping bag and bivvi bag, then lay in my bag propped on one elbow and lit the metafuel tablet to preheat the stove. The first flare of paraffin flame took the chill off the tent. Then I filled the large pot with snow from the door and kept topping up with more snow as it melted. Jed usually murmured sleepily while I cooked, but Bill (like me in my turn) stayed fast asleep like a papoose until I thrust a hot mug of tea at him. In base camp we ate compo, breakfasting on a potmess of hot meat and beans which we spooned out of the pot soon after the first brew. Washing up was simple — melt a little snow in the pot, wipe it round with Scotchbrite, throw the dirty water out of the door, then wipe out with the J Cloth of the month.

On 8th I found the first Wilson's Storm Petrel chick had hatched in one of my marked nests. Sometimes thought to be the most numerous bird in the world, these delicate little petrels nested in crannies in the scree everywhere we visited. In the evening they flitted like bats over the slopes and their 'chuzz-chuzz' and 'go-go-go' nest calls continued through the gloom of night. Many of the flitters were young non-breeding birds, but some were returning to take over brooding. They change over every 1-3 days, but the large white eggs can remain viable for a day or two unbrooded and one here hatched after at least three days untended. Hatching dates at Elephant Island ranged from mid-January to mid-February. This variation reduces the possibility of a single heavy snowfall at a critical breeding stage trapping whole populations in their nests. Thus, on Brabant hatching dates were compressed into a shorter period over the first half of February. Two days after hatching, this tiny ball of grey down would be left alone in the cold little cranny, visited briefly by one or both parents on most nights.

As they flutter and scramble to and from their nests, these storm petrels are preyed on by skuas. Nocturnal visits are their defence, and often their remains in skua territories are the first clue to their presence. Wilson's arrive through the daylight evenings but their 50g bodies are uneconomical hunting for skuas. Their scarcer relatives the Black-bellied Storm Petrels arrive in a concentrated period after midnight and (weighing 100g) are better hunting. They prefer the steeper broken screes and cliffs, where nocturnal bird-nesting is very sporting. Very few nests had been found by BAS, so I had been delighted to find them nesting in large numbers all around the Elephant Island group, which may well be their population centre. Here on Brabant Island I found a Black-bellied's wing at a skua nest, and heard their ventriloquial nest whistles at several points. I also found adults in nest-crannies, but without eggs or chicks to prove their southernmost breeding. (Later we heard that a colony was found near Palmer Base this season.)

By 12th it was too late to go to Claude Point, so when the weather relented Bill, Jed and I sledged round to Cape Roux. After a day hauling the pulk through heavy snow in whiteout and going chest deep in a few crevasses, we piled into the tent exhausted, for three hours of brew-ups and supper and relaxation. The moraines and clifftop plateaux had looked promising as we arrived, with terns and skuas and Snow Petrels flying, and later that night I heard Black-bellieds in a scree gully, so I looked forward to exploring the cape next morning.

The 13th was a typical day exploring a new area. After breakfast we got out of our sleeping bags, piled our gear into three parts of the tent, and one by one donned outer boots, anoraks, gloves, balaclavas, etc., sitting with our feet in the 'porch' between the inner and outer doors of the Nova tent. Our diets encouraged regular habits, and the urge for the day's constitutional grew while one dressed. Ready, I grabbed the snow shovel and went to find a sheltered spot nearby, then squatted looking east to a spectacular unnamed point, a rock spine dropping 400 metres through icefalls to a little point crowned with giant rock pinnacles. My precept for camping in the Antarctic is: never miss a good opportunity to relieve yourself in comfort.

Through the day we each explored the cape individually — Bill surveying and collecting plants, Jed taking photos, and I mapping breeding birds and collecting rock specimens. This eastern part of Cape Roux comprised granite blocks dissected by gullies to form a complex of plateaux, islands and skerries; a tiny beach right in the middle of the simple eight-hectare blob on the map was connected to the sea in three directions by surging brash-filled channels. Gradually through the day it became clear that here were only skuas, gulls, terns and storm petrels. At Elephant Island, Cape Pigeons and Antarctic Fulmars would have been crammed on to these cliffs and screes in thousands but here there were none. Only a few parties of petrels passed the cape in the morning and evening, plus a westward movement of albatrosses in the afternoon. Colonisation is partly happenstance, usually initiated by wandering young non-breeders; however the driving force is availability of food, as in the spread of the Arctic Fulmar around Britain. The total absence of large petrels from Cape Roux augered poorly for the rest of the island.

The weather deteriorated in sympathy. Sleet that evening turned into continuous rain for two nights and days. We festered in the tent, played scrabble, talked, read, cooked, ate, wrote and slept. Luckily it cleared on 16th and we sledged back. The two groups who left on 1st were due back, so we looked for their tents as we came in sight of Metchnikoff Point at 3 p.m.

No tents were pitched. Neither group had returned.

The wind was beginning to rise, so we pitched three tents ready for the others. I was putting up the radio mast when a heavy gust hit us, and Jed shot out of our dome tent — a pole had broken with a bang and torn the outer exactly as last week. We collapsed the tent to save it and moved into a pyramid; all our gear was sodden wet. The wind rose stronger hurling stinging sleet at Bill and me standing discussing the other parties. I was particularly worried about Simon, Ted and Kevin, who were four days overdue. Next day I could ask *Endurance* to make a helicopter search (it would take us two or three days to reach the area they were exploring). With the rain these last two weeks, snow-holing would be really miserable if their tent had blown out, and they only had the one dome tent, like our two which had broken. I began to think of radio bulletins beginning: 'Deeply regret to report that . . .' We looked up at the sleet and spindrift slicing across the snowslope. There at the top were

East Side Story. Pulk with Liege Island beyond. (Ted Atkins)

three figures skiing on a rope, the middle one harnessed to a pulk! Was it the Claude Point four bringing back one injured man? No. Soon we recognised Simon, Ted and Kevin. Relief was overwhelming.

Half an hour later the six of us were sitting hunched up in our Pyramid tent, all soaking wet, with the primus roaring in the gloom producing brew after brew and the three of them eating compo hard tack biscuits with margarine and cheese and jam like wolves, after two weeks on half rations. Their story poured out in gusts of group high spirits and humour. They were bursting with the joy of two weeks totally alone and self-reliant in unknown land. Three men had become a tight-knit team: now the release of tension overflowed, and they added to each others' tales as we plied them with questions.

Simon cooking in a Nova tent, door open for the photo. (Jed Corbett)

Leaving on 1st, they had sledged along the north coast and then south to Lister Glacier, enjoying four days of superb weather. Once they sat for two hours in stunned amazement overlooking Bouquet Bay and Liege Island, while the sun rose to unravel the mists and to paint glaciers, icefalls, peaks, piedmonts, clouds, sea and icebergs with an incandescent palette. On 5th they climbed Virchow Hill and camped on the piedmont beyond, but that night cloud closed them in, and snow began to fall gently but steadily. They had started with ten days' rations each, and sensibly went on to half rations at once. For six days the snow fell, gradually piling up until the tent sat in a two-metre hole. They called the place 'The Catacombs'. They slept, cooked, ate, played scrabble and mended things. Kevin in particular was always mending or modifying something: the expedition was his element and it was hard to catch him without a beaming smile on his face. When the weather finally cleared, they skied to the col overlooking Hill Bay — a daunting, lonely bay entirely surrounded by steep glaciers and ice-cliffs. From the col they climbed on to the west ridge of Mount Morgagni, until the way was barred by a steep open face with a metre of new snow ready to avalanche. Wisely they withdrew leaving Morgagni for later — a mountain world of its own, a high undulating snowy plateau, protected by rampart cliffs all around. Next day, 13th, they left 'The Catacombs', heading back to base, but were soon caught in cloud and pitched camp. On 14th they pushed on, reaching 900 metres before a blizzard hit them with little warning. They dug into the side of the ridge and then spent two nights and days keeping two-hour watches digging out the tent. On the morning of 16th one of the poles snapped under the weight of spindrift pouring down on to the tent. They struck camp and pushed themselves very hard manhauling the pulk over Cushing Peak and through two completely unknown cols in cloud which lifted only fleetingly and tantalisingly; at last a bamboo marker appeared out of the cloud, which Ted recognised as one we had put out on 'Wobbly Col'. Three hours later they were telling us their adventures, huddled round the roaring primus at base camp. They were elated and pleased to have been entirely self-supporting and to have made their last 20-km dash in time. They had good reason to be proud of themselves — perhaps our strongest three mountaineers this season, they had worked out a pattern of pulk-sledging, tent routine and reduced rations which we would all copy later.

At midnight they went to the other Pyramid tent to spend a wet and uncomfortable night — but a night at home. After they had gone, we cooked supper and settled to sleep at 2 a.m., clammy wet and rather cold. *Endurance* was due that day.

Dawn broke grey but calm. Halfway through breakfast we heard a ship's siren offshore and we scurried out, leaving half-made mugs of chocolate. A helicopter landed and post-office stationery was unloaded. There was mail for us, which we set aside. Then stores started arriving by helicopter and Simon was flown out to the ship to supervise them. A skidoo was landed among the penguins and another was landed on the snow behind the tents, where the first was moved to join it; the third arrived. Kevin, Ted and I rushed to and fro with cargo nets and skidoos. Jed filmed. Bill humped store boxes. I wrote letters to Prince Charles and others in expedition First Day Covers ready for the official opening of our post office. Signals arrived needing urgent answers. Toward midday the Civil Commissioner, Sir Rex Hunt, and Captain MacGregor were flown in, plus Sue the Commissioner's secretary. A woman! We ran broken finger-nails through matted beards. 'Let's have compo lunch,' said Colin MacGregor, brandishing a bottle of whisky to toast the opening. 'Please cook Compo breakfast for nine, Ted,' I said. 'OK, Chris,' replied Ted imperturbably. The post-office opening cortege rolled towards our filthy tent and Jed took photos. While the Captain and Sir Rex posed outside I put my head in and desperately threw breakfast into one corner, gravel and penguin feathers into another, botanical specimens into the third and stoves and cooking gear into the fourth, then threw sleeping bags on top and scattered wet overtrousers about as carpets. They entered. Ted roared two stoves. Sausage and beans were served, and a mug of coffee. The tent was roasting hot. Gary Hunt the observer looked in to say that flying would have to stop due to excessive ship movement. Our guests hurried. Helicopters left and returned. Hands were shaken and the heli-copters left. Quiet returned — just the gaggle of penguins and the roar of the sea below. *Endurance* diminished toward the icebergs off the Melchior Islands.

Life returned to normal — except that we now understood the impact of modern technology and civilisation on a primitive community. The afternoon shone on our little community; sleeping bags and clothes were spread out to dry, new stores boxes were inspected and Ted was already working out how to make skis for the skidoos out of an empty fuel drum, because flying had stopped before the skis were landed. Simon, Ted and I were chain-smoking, having given up for a month and regretted it. We shuffled tent partners and I moved into another Pyramid with Simon. As the evening wore on, each person read his letters from home: mine told of snowdrops and jasmine and pussy willows as spring moved north. Behind us we could hear taped music from Jed and Ted's tent — they were lying cosily reading their letters, with great brews of hot coffee laced with the Captain's whisky.

We waited for the four to arrive from Claude Point, impatient for our mid-expedition feast. Our main rations were standard service tinned 'Compo' rations and dehydrated 'Arctic' rations. In June 1981, when a Defence Review condemned HMS Endurance to scrap, I got 3,900 man-days' rations from good friends in the Naval Stores directorate and shipped them out to Port Stanley. Captain Nick Barker took them on board *Endurance*, and in March 1982 the rations and paraffin were landed at Palmer Base. They sat there in the open for two years, until we arrived and thankfully found them in almost perfect condition, despite sodden outer wrappings. This year we had brought extra 'Booster Rations' provided by the Services, to bring the calorific values up to 5,000 kcal per man-day and the 'booster' included boxes for one full day's feasting. We also had a few goodies donated by helpful firms but so far we had used only the basic rations. In base camp each two-man tent had a four man-day box of compo plus 48 hard-tack biscuits to last two days. Away from base we carried the lighter Arctic rations in one man-day units. A communal box of unused food gradually accumulated in the stores dump, and occasionally we issued no food for a day, using up the accumulated surplus. We had decided to eat the booster rations and goodies (and drink the whisky) only when we were all together, so we waited for the four from Claude Point impatiently, and growing a bit worried.

The next three days were largely foul — windy and wet. We spent most of the time festering in our tents. The Chinstraps also stood looking miserable in their colonies, which were now dirty mires, unpleasant to walk through.

Many Chinstraps were moulting, their usually sleek backs dull and starred white by the insulating down attached to the bases of the strong feather quills, which are arranged in a remarkably regular pattern on their skin. Their shed feathers blew like snow in the wind, landing everywhere like 'penguin toenails' as Mac had aptly described them. These early-moulting birds were the younger non-breeders. Few penguins breed successfully before they are six or eight years old. After two or three years at sea they first return to the colonies and 'practise' breeding, mostly round the disadvantageous fringes of the colony. Usually they give up early, but some failed breeders were still building piles of stones, displaying, fighting and mating, although the last addled eggs had exploded two or three weeks before.

Many chicks were also moulting out of their grey and white down. A few were already almost indistinguisable from their parents, though most had downy mohican hairstyles and some were still all down-covered. The older chicks were mobile and sometimes one or two would chase an adult through the colony, demanding food. The adults were also less territorial now, fleeing before us rather than defending their nests. However, both adults and chicks still returned to their nest-sites after any such disturbance, and late in the evenings most families were together at their nests.

At Chinstrap colonies the evening rush hour is a feature, with parties of 20-50 penguins porpoising back from their foraging grounds. (They swim very fast underwater with their flippers beating several times a second, but when on the surface paddle slowly with their feet; so porpoising is their most efficient way of travel, leaping from the water for each breath.) Nearing shore, the parties often change direction or even circle around, perhaps a defence against Leopard Seals, their main predator. At Elephant Island we had pitched a tent below a colony of 5000 pairs and counted penguin traffic up and down over full 24-hour periods, and together with observations at marked nests and random counts through the colony, these watches confirmed the impression of an evening rush hour, with most pairs roosting together at the nest. However, their foraging routine altered as the chicks grew. When the chicks were young, one parent would depart at sunrise and return around midday carrying 200-500g of krill; after a short turnover one adult (usually the other one, but sometimes the same one again) would depart, to return in the evening with another load of krill. By the time the chicks were five or six weeks old, the foraging routine had changed, one adult spending the whole day away and returning with 400-900g of krill, while the other parent remained at the nest. These half-day and one-day trips severely limit the Chinstraps' foraging range: their colonies must be near good feeding grounds, and are vulnerable to local shortages. Gentoos also forage close to home, but dive deeper (possibly to 250 metres) and feed largely on fish, so they do not compete with Chinstraps. Adelies and Macaronis feed on krill like Chinstraps, but they forage further afield, Macaronis on two- or three-day trips, and Adelies sometimes even longer. Food resources local to breeding colonies probably control the populations of all these four penguins, rather than pelagic food resources in winter. I had hoped to follow up the Elephant Island observations, because BAS still believed that Chinstraps dived for krill at night when the krill approach the surface, but unfortunately the colonies at Metchnikoff Point were unsuitable for traffic counts.

Despite the foul weather we continued the regular seal counts. Fur Seals had steadily increased until on 19 February there were 950 bulls plus three smaller ones which could have been cows (or 'clapmatches'). One of the big bulls was a beautiful pale sandy colour: he moved from one beach to another, and we saw him also in other areas, so there seemed to be no territorial ties, although they maintained a definite spacing in the herd by threats or desultory fighting. Possibly seals moved from the new South Shetland colonies to feed off Brabant in February, but I had high hopes that we would find them breeding here next November. That would be the southernmost breeding record, at least this century. Walking amongst them was tense: their first reaction when disturbed was a throaty, coughing roar like a Leopard, often followed by a threatening advance. We found that clapping our hands frightened them off — (the noise resembled falling rocks) and once frightened they would career away making ludicrously child-like 'nff-nff' sounds. We hoped they would remain through the winter to enliven these desolate shores, but it wasn't likely.

There were fewer Weddell seals ashore now. They are usually resident in specific areas, in family parties or tribes, so I wondered if the livelier Fur Seals were disturbing them. This seemed unlikely — when a Fur Seal blundered over a sleeping Weddell, the Weddell just lay there opening its pink mouth in threat, and seldom moved. Weddells are slow, gentle creatures. When we approached one on the beach it would roll over, stomach up, with one flipper raised, and crane its muzzle toward us, occasionally toppling over backwards into a comical complete roll. Looking down on the rocky bays from above, I often saw them floating idly, letting the waves wash them forward and backward — their somnolent equivalent of the Fur Seals' erratic play.

A whisky bottle stood in the stores dump awaiting the four, an inquisitive Sheathbill pecking dents in the gold top. These white, pigeon-sized scavengers are the only landbirds of the Antarctic, scuttling about on large, dark-grey webless feet. In flight they are lovely, pure white, with a display flight posture just like a Ptarmigan's glide. They scavenge around penguin colonies, like jackals to the skuas's lion, pecking open unguarded eggs, eating dead chicks and licking up bits of krill dropped in the mud. Hopping busily between the penguins they seem like ghosts, immune to the hostile beaks. At Elephant most Sheathbill pairs exploited 200-400 pairs of penguins. They nest under boulders and in dark little caves, with feathers lining a nest of penguin tail-feathers plus oddments like bottle tops. Late in February their ungainly chicks were beginning to moult from grey down to white feathers, and occasionally emerged briefly from their secluded homes. At Elephant clutch sizes ranged from one to four, averaging over 2 eggs, but here the nests contained only one or two eggs or chicks. We found them only close around the penguin colony where pairs defended small nesting territories. We grew to like the Sheathbills for their homely barnyard chicken appearance, and cockney impertinence, with their black diamond-shaped eyes craftily interested in any possibilities of food.

Sharing a tent with Simon was fun: he was like an overgrown grinning schoolboy, enthusiastic over their east-side exploration, Cornwall, mines, climbing and the Royal Marines, laborious in sorting out his kit, and ever-lastingly hungry. For three wet days he talked geology to me, words bursting through like a dyke swarm. Most of the rocks he had found were igneous — basalt lavas overlying some granodiorite intrusions with a clear contact between them on the north shore. He had been more sur-prised and puzzled by the conglomerates which occur widely, in seem-ingly random beds and pockets and interleaved with lavas: their sandstone matrix gives them an ochrous yellow hue; they contain basalt with other fragments, some rounded on the seabed, but most angular as if laid down by rivers or glaciers. Simon's job this summer was to collect basalt samples, for analysis at Nottingham University in time for feedback out to us during the winter.

We had much time in the tent to talk, for three days' bad weather culminated in a storm gusting 60-80 knots on 20th, when 46 mm of rain fell horizontally in 24 hours. The Pyramid tents teetered precariously on metre-high castles of snow sitting on a sheet of melting ice. We had to wear crampons to tend the tent, getting soaked and cold piling on dirty wet boulders from the penguin colony, re-securing melted-out ice-screws on the guys, shovelling on more snow, and using iceaxes to cut channels into the ice so that the crevasse above emptied past us not under us. Rain is far worse than snow. Next day the weather relented a little; so we lashed down the stores, took two pulks up to the skyline and camped down by the beach amongst 650 Fur Seals, ready to leave next day.

Basecamp after rain, with tents perched on snow plinths above melting ice. (Jed Corbett)

On 22nd the six of us set out for the cache near Claude Point, hauling the two pulks across 'Footsore Piedmont'. The snow was wet and sticky, and the pulks were heavy with the radio, still- and cine-camera gear and two spare tents for the others, on top of our fuel, snow-shovels and geological hammers, etc. We settled into the sledging routine developed by Simon, Kevin and Ted, one man leading on a long rope, one on a shorter rope skiing behind over gentle undulations to brake when needed, and the third man as the 'horse' in the bamboo shafts of the pulk harness. Up or down steeper hills, both leader and brakeman slogged ahead pulling, or laid back braking. The three on each pulk rotated daily, so that each man was horse every third day. Each of us carried his own pack weighing 15-20 kg. A pulk carrying 50 kg was quite easy to pull over gentle country, but ours each carried nearly 100 kg and were desperately hard work up hills, and on traverses, where they often capsized. Sometimes on steeper hills we would relay — taking the gear up in two half-loads. How Scott man-hauled a sledge to the pole and back we could not understand.

On the second evening we cached the pulks at 600 metres in cloud and cast about until we found a wide deep crevasse half-filled with drift-snow where we pitched both tents out of the wind. Magically the sun then broke through, and we found ourselves in a fantasy world of caves, and icicles blown horizontal by the wind. We called our crevasse 'The Icicle Works', and everybody gambolled joyfully. Bill, Ted and Kevin climbed 20 metres down into the rich blue caverns of the crevasse, where strangely they did not need lights. We all enjoyed a peaceful night, quiet and silent out of the wind — and were converted to crevasse camping. The sun then shone for two days' sledging, first up to 'Noddies Col' at 900 metres and down to a cavernous crevasse camp, then back over 'Cushing Col' and westward across the long piedmont where waist-high spindrift coursed past us, writhing like smoke before the katabatic easterly winds, piling drifts around the pulks and covering our skis during our short midday snack.

On the evening of 25th we came to the edge of a distinct alpine valley glacier dropping to the sea across our route. We found ourselves in an eerie jumble of great house-sized ice-blocks with streets and alleyways of drifted snow between. Clambering through this giant's maze we found the marks of two tents: the four had passed this way. We also found faint tracks, and argued whether they were coming or going, and how old they were. Feeling like trespassers in this empty town of ice, with its signs of fled inhabitants, we camped in a snowy central plaza and called the place 'The Precinct'. None of us had ever seen an icefall like this. Later we saw that it was formed by two parallel glaciers overflowing sideways over a low separating rib of hidden rock: the big blocks were the ends of the 'roadways' between crevasses, which had been forced up over the rib, then broken off and gradually moved on down toward the sea, while the snow filled the gaps between to form the main street down the ridge crest; the side-streets were the original crevasses.

Next day was stranger still. Halfway up the slope beyond 'Precinct Glacier' we found a snow-wall shelter with a little marker flag and a bag of botanical samples dated 13 February. We dug out the deep drift inside, finding empty food packets, then all the signs of two to four men sheltering for some time in one little ridge tent. The mystery deepened. Late that evening we camped at 200 metres above the cache and Bill and Kevin went down to find out what the four had done. At 11 p.m. they returned, their climbing ironmongery clinking outside the tents: the four

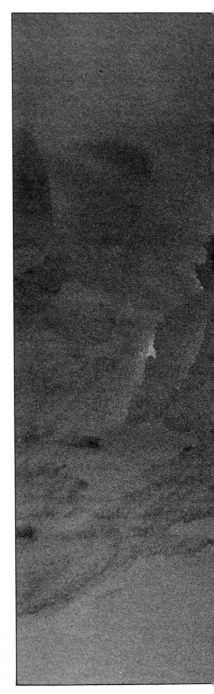

had been living at the cache, but were not there now; they had not left the required message to say where they had gone and we did not even know when. Their pulk had been left at the cache, and we guessed that they had returned to base skiing below 'Pinnacles Spur'. Luckily Ted got the radio receiver working briefly and heard Jeff calling Faraday Base from Metchnikoff Point: so they were safe.

Being split into two groups for so long incommunicado was sad. However, time was passing and this spell of lovely sunlit weather could not continue long. So we decided to start next day to climb Mount Parry, before the March nights drew in too early and the autumn cold bit hard.

The Icicle Works crevasse camp, Kevin at the gateway. (Jed Corbett)

March

Our second pulk arrives at the Eagles Nest. Mount Hunter and far away Smith Island wade in a sea of cloud. (Jed Corbett)

In the last three days of February we hauled the two pulks up toward Mount Rokkitanski. A hooli blew up the first night, and all next day spindrift blasted the tents. In the evening Jed and I had to get food from the pulks cached above on the open ridge, leaving the tents to walk a compass course in the blizzard. Behind us our tracks were instantly obliterated. We reached the pulks after 342 paces, and after returning 327 paces I was very relieved to glimpse the two green domes, our only security in the storm. 29 February was a laborious haul up in cloud and soft snow until in the evening we pitched camp exhausted under an ice-cliff, at 1500 metres. Then the cloud dropped, and from the lip of our windscoop we enjoyed superb outlooks over cloudscapes racing between the white tops of other mountains.

We were stuck in the 'Eagles Nest' for the first three days of March by continual cloud, a gale and a metre of snow falling, scarcely leaving the tents except to dig them out, and once to relay the pulks up past the ice-cliff. By now we were experts with 'pissbombs' (pee into a polythene ration bag and throw the bag through the door). With temperatures ten degrees lower at 1500 metres the zips often froze, causing a comic struggle to open the door with one hand, holding the full pissbomb in the other, without spilling any in the boots. We had started with 9 man-days Arctic rations each, but after the first day holed up we had reduced to two-thirds rations, giving us until 10 March to return to 'Astrolabe Point'. 3000 kcals a day was enough, but we were always hungry. Simon spent hours working out which tent had most chocolate; he licked the inside of every packet and, after his turn for scrapes of the hoosh [stew], finished off with all four fingers in the pot like Pooh Bear. We festered, thinking about the next meal and playing scrabble: the loser only got two Rolos from the packet of eight, the winner could have the sugar off Simon's beard.

On 4th the cloud thinned and we sledged on up. On the shoulder of Rokkitanski we emerged from cloud to be hit by the dramatic sight of Mount Parry and its western ridge dropping 2500 metres in fantastic toothed arêtes to the dark grey sea below, where icebergs lay like little white chips. No one had ever before looked down at this glorious bay from our towering mountain cirque with icefalls tumbling below; we named it 'Williams Bay'. Naming places here is controlled by an international Antarctic Placenames Committee and we would submit this for official adoption. Of course we also gave names to many other nameless places, but those remained our private unofficial names. Beyond into the distance fell the western glaciers and ridges of Brabant, beyond again Anvers, and further beyond again the Antarctic Peninsula lay starkly clear. At sunset we completed the first ascent of Rokkitanski (1,800 metres) hauling one of the pulks. After minutes of quiet amazement, looking out over an endless sea of soft grey cloud which smothered our route up, and lapped at the white islands of the highest peaks, we hurried on to pitch camp on the ridge beyond as stars tingled in the darkening sky.

Next morning I was surprised to find an awkward narrow col that the map disguised. Returning to the camp as clouds enveloped us, I was relieved when all four climbers counselled stay — I always worried that I would hold the tigers back. Later, when I was black from stripping and cleaning our stove, Bill and Ted took advantage of a clearance to reconnoitre the route. They returned at dusk, tired and very cold, having climbed and named 'Per Ardua'.

As breakfast cook, Jed woke at 6 a.m. Cooking, eating and packing up

Ted & Bill on Mount Rokkitanski. (Jed Corbett)

inside took nearly two hours, before Simon and I booted up and emerged to clear the packs and valences of snow, while Jed filled thermos flasks, rolled up our Karrimats and packed his rucksack in the porch. Then with all three outside we struck the tent. Two hours was the fastest time from the cook waking to moving off, in good conditions. We cached the pulks in the empty campsite and set off in three roped pairs over 'Unexpected Col'.

By lunchtime we were in thick cloud above a steepening icefall, on the unknown ridge beyond. We felt our way cautiously on skis past the shadowy rim of a great crevasse, then set off hopefully on a compass course. I was unable to distinguish anything but white beyond my ski tips. Slowly we skied up into sunlight on a broad whale-back of snow breaching from the soft cloudbed. The wind and spindrift were now biting cold and our progress slow, so we pitched camp at 1800 metres under the hanging eaves of a great mushroomed ice-cliff that cut like a turquoise swathe across the north ridge of Harvey Heights. (When ice falls off, the fresh scar is distinctly blue or green, sharply contrasting with the otherwise unnoticed mauve tinge of old snow.)

On 7th we broke camp in a lovely dawn, looking out at creamy sunlit heights, while cloud laid a soft grey pall over the nether regions. We skied up the long ridge to the north summit of Harvey Heights, taking five hours to reach 2400 metres. Bill and Ted arrived exhausted and dizzy, as Kevin had been the day before: we felt sure it was carbon monoxide poisoning due to dirty fuel in their stove. We looked along the ridge to the summit block of Mount Parry, beautiful, lonely, attainable, ours. We were on the end of a long logistic chain, like a Himalayan peak, except that we sledged and packed our own food with no support. We had two days' food each, plus four man-days between the six of us back at the pulks. We would need another camp on the ridge. I wavered, then decided that the equations of health, speed, distance, height, food and time did not allow for the likelihood of bad weather. We looked again at Mount Parry, misleadingly close, and then skied back down to the campsite under the eaves. The others took it remarkably well, though they were all bitterly disappointed to turn back when so close after ten days' ascent. The wind felt more bitterly cold despite the low sun.

Next day we made good time skiing down, and sat dividing our snackpack for lunch at the whiteout crevasse of two days before. We looked out over a breathtaking view of the east coast: clouds played hide and seek in the icefalls dropping off the ridge, trailed a chequer-board of grey shadows over Paré and Lister Glaciers far below, and wavered below the cliffs of lonely, beleaguered Mount Morgagni. Everywhere, unknown new peaks and icefalls showed through the drifting clouds then vanished into mystery again. Collecting the pulks we skied down to a flat snow-shelf on top of the Eagles Nest ice-cliff. Far below us Astrolabe Needle stood silhouetted, where a katabatic wind poured down the slopes to clear a pool of sunlight in the sea of cloud that stretched to the horizon. We still had one days' rations left and felt safe, so we ate a full supper ration, with a pudding of chocolate, milk and biscuits.

Overnight it snowed, and all next day, and the following night, finally stopping as we woke at 6 a.m. It took four hours to dig out the tents and packs and pulks, all buried under a metre of snow. Then in five glorious sunshine hours we skied the pulks downhill and arrived at the cache on 'Astrolabe Point'. Offshore a pair of Humpback Whales greeted us with lazy flaps of their vast flukes. It was good to see birds again, after three weeks in the lovely, sunlit, lifeless mountains.

'Astrolabe' was really twin points, with two ramparts of massive basalt columns jutting out from the ice-cliffs. Between these twin points ran a seven-metre high seawall of black basalt, with a moat inside it, filled by occasional waves expiring over the sea-wall. The heart of the point was a gentle slope of clean gravel and boulders running down from the icefall behind to the moat. It was our first campsite off snow: the snug gravel would not melt into troughs below our Karrimats and we could go out in our socks for a pee, and the calm muggy weather conspired to create a seaside holiday atmosphere. We all ate ravenously. I fell fast asleep on top of my bag, full at last after two weeks' hunger, physically tired after three weeks' sledging, and mentally relaxed from our safe return.

The 11th was a holiday. We ate vastly, laid out gear to dry, and explored the point. I found five pairs of South Polar Skuas defending territories on the southern ridge. Loose colonies and clubs of non-breeders are typical of skuas, but on Brabant I had seen no clubs, and this was the first place where more than one pair bred, despite the seawall preventing penguins breeding. Most of their chicks were now a patchwork of down and feathers, either slinking away when approached, or freezing immobile against some rock. One was just flying, calling querulously for food: it would remain around the nest territory for another two or three weeks.

In one skua territory I found the grey wing of an Antarctic Prion. These wild-flying petrels, called 'whalebirds', feed off the South Shetlands and in March 1971 I had seen hundreds just north of Smith Island. However the southernmost known colonies in this half of Antarctica are three small groups we had found at Elephant Island. That night, hoping to find a new southernmost colony I searched the point listening for their murmuring underground calls, but I heard none. Perhaps the wing had come from a floating corpse.

In the bay around Astrolabe Needle a flock of 2000 Cape Pigeons fed daily at the tide jobbles. They flew in each evening to roost on the cliffs of 'Astrolabe Point', but surprisingly only one small breeding colony appeared to exist.

On 13th we talked at last with the four at Metchnikoff Point, after six weeks incommunicado. They were all well, and sounded in good spirits, but I determined to return there as soon as possible.

We also passed a radio bulletin to Faraday Base. BAS allowed us a 100-word bulletin each week, with news for our families and sponsors, etc. My home and family were in my thoughts a lot this wet day. It was my mother Polly's 85th birthday. I pushed my love out into the Antarctic night, and hoped it arrived in Smarden, Kent, where celandines would be bursting up below the hedges, lambs playing, and small birds singing of spring.

Pale sandy bull Fur Seal from Metchnikoff Point. (Chris Furse)

On 14th Simon, Jed and I started off for Metchnikoff Point, but Simon's awful cough over the last week had left him very weak and we returned to 'Astrolabe'. Bill, Ted and Simon would stay there until *Endurance* arrived. They had plenty to do. Ted prepared a map of the point, Simon mapped the varying basalts, which warranted a paper in themselves, and Bill had hit the scientific jackpot here. He found both grass and pearlwort growing profusely (much more richly than anywhere on Elephant Island). Both were in flower, and setting seed. The pearlwort flowers were insignificant little pinheads of dull pink, cupped in tight green calices, less bright than the shiny green cruciform leaves: but flowering and seeding are rare at this latitude. Bill and I felt a bit smug that BAS could not land a botanist here by boat — we amateurs had something to offer! The two plants grew together on many damp flats and north-facing slopes and buttons of pearlwort starred cracks in the basalt. Bill started a vegetation survey preparing for a more detailed statistical study next summer to determine the factors affecting their growth. Absence of penguins, northern aspect, local weather conditions, moisture retention by the rocks, base-rock chemistry and the rotted limpet shells he found 15-20 cm down were all possibilities (we hoped to get these shells radio-carbon dated to determine how long ago Kelp Gulls fed or nested here, when the point must have been snowfree).

Kevin, Jed and I set off for Metchnikoff Point on 15th. It was the first goodbye of the expedition, as we might not see each other when *Endurance* came on 24th for the team changeover — a strange, poignant almost feminine sadness clutched us after adventures very close together.

We cached our pulk on the ridge, and skied down to Claude Point to collect rocks, pitching the tent on a hectare of flat earthy moraine on the clifftop. Then we got rather wet exploring in the rain, but found some nice surprises.

From the moraine we looked down carved yellow cliffs to a pebble beach 200 metres below, with Fur Seals and only the second Chinstrap colony found so far. At last here was clear evidence of Antarctic Fulmar's breeding, plus numerous Cape Pigeons. All their chicks had flown, but adults of both species patrolled the cliffs, and sat at obvious nest-sites.

Kevin found both grass and pearlwort at the clifftops. I found a way down the northern cliffs and just below the black lava cap was a narrow ledge of sloping scree almost covered with grass swards, and pearlwort buttons. This corner of the island seemed to be an eldorado for the two flowering plants. (Later we learnt that the 200-metre site equals the highest record of pearlwort in the whole Peninsula region, though grass has been found at 275 metres.)

The rocks fascinated me even more, though I knew so little about them. The thick slab of very black lava capping the cliffs was a prominent landmark. From the grassy ledge below it I looked up at a 40-metre vertical cliff of shiny black blocks, large hexagonal columns at the bottom changing suddenly to curvilinear patterns of brick-sized blocks above. This lava cliff sat directly upon the top surface of a friable orange sandstone, containing lots of tiny rounded stones arranged conspicuously in parallel bands just as they had been laid down (slowly) underwater long ago. Brabant's geology is of regional importance as 40 million years ago the island may have been a key point in crustal movements. The Pacific tectonic plate had then virtually stopped being subducted under the continental crust of the South Shetlands, but the islands were still separating from the Peninsula by back-arc spreading of the trench under Bransfield Strait. (Igneous activity in the Bransfield Trench is still evident today at Deception Island.) We hoped that petrographic analysis and potassium–argon dating of the pleistocene basalt lavas on Brabant would help to explain the sequence and timing of the opening of the Bransfield (and Gerlache) Straits. Even to my untutored eye, this great black lava cliff, frowning in the murky cloud and sitting just as it had flowed over the neat sedimentary sandstone, was very impressive geology.

We set off in cloud next morning, following our ski tracks until they vanished under falling snow. On the plateau we had to make a box search for the pulk, skiing on compass courses to and fro, until after an hour Jed sighted the friendly orange silhouette waiting for us 30 metres away floating in the enveloping whiteness. We got lost in an unexpected icefall going down toward 'The Precinct', pitched the tent in a crevasse at lunchtime, and waited for a brief clearance — until the following morning. Then we worked the pulk through 'The Precinct', now much changed by opening crevasses, eerie in the whiteout, no longer a friendly ice township. Traversing 'Terrace Piedmont' the wind strengthened in our faces. The stinging spindrift made skiing a compass course difficult: once, stopping to check my compass, I looked back to see Kevin in the pulk harness calmly cutting his hair with his Swiss Army knife scissors. After two hours the slope steepened. It got steeper and steeper, until we were floundering hopelessly in thigh-deep snow, our arms dug in beyond the elbows, unable to move the pulk. The windborne spindrift was now hurtling downslope into our faces. It was cold, and rather unpleasant. We dug a ledge for the pulk, marked it with our skis, and ploughed on upward hoping for a sheltered campsite. A dim shadow appeared to our right below us, and at the third attempt we climbed down the mushroomed upper wall of a crevasse, a sanctuary from the wind. Half an hour later we were inside our 'Lucky Nova', with the stove melting snow for a brew, and the wind rattling the tent in frustration. The snow turned to rain and overnight the tent grew still, though the gusts still roared around our sanctuary. It was still blowing and snowing at breakfast, but the whole outside of the tent was a rigid dome, case-hardened by a centimetre of dappled ice. We stayed there all day (two-thirds rations again), talking about the impending end of the first-summer expedition.

We broke camp on 19th still in thick cloud, relayed the pulk on a compass course up over Cushing Peak (we thought) and down the east side to 750 metres using our altimeters, which were invaluable in these conditions. Then we contoured north. It was the route we knew, but our way was barred by a large crevasse curling away downslope. Before deciding which way to turn it, I unclipped for a short recce, walking slowly down on skis, keeping the faint shadow of the crevasse lip just in sight in the cloud.

WHOOMP! At the noise I looked down to see grey cracks arrowing under my skis. Christ!

As I dropped I could only think: 'How deep is this? Down to a black grave?'

Bang! I landed on my back, spreadeagled, stunned, the breath knocked out of me. Another big block of ice landed on my chest. God. My back was broken. I was jammed amongst big snow blocks. 'Help,' I shouted plaintively and uselessly. In a mindless panic, somehow I heaved the blocks off my body. There was grey light: I was not down a cavernous hole. Oh, thank God!

Gradually I came to my senses and took stock. One by one I released my rucksack, tried sitting up, released my feet from the buried skis, and tried all my limbs. My back was not broken but hurt like hell, probably some ribs. Nothing else broken. Then I coughed, a great gobbet of bright red blood. The lip of the crevasse was about eight metres above me. The whole side had dropped bodily. I had come down on a car-sized block and the bottom of the crevasse was covered with icy snow blocks like the rubble of a house. I shouted again and again: no answer. Snow absorbs sound so well that you cannot hear each other with one in a crevasse and one just outside it, but this one was so wide open — were Jed and Kevin buried under the rubble 30 metres along the crevasse?

Finally, Kevin's face appeared above. The edge had gone beside his boots and they had moved the pulk away first to put in a safe belay. Twenty minutes later we were together by the pulk, Jed giving me a whole chocolate bar and offering a thermos, but I was still spitting some blood and wondered where inside my battered torso it came from.

Looking east over 'The Precinct' to Mount Hunter in fine weather, showing the 'Milk Run' between basecamp and 'Astrolabe Point': over 'Pinnacles Spur' (P) and 'Wobbly Col' (W), then up left of 'Noddies Hat' (H), down onto Lister Glacier, reappearing over 'Cushing Col' (C) and dropping down to 'Terrace Piedmont' (T). (Howard Oakley)

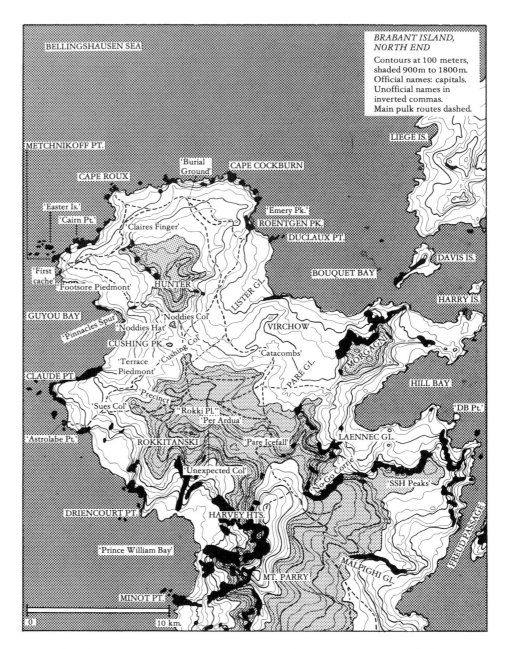

BRABANT ISLAND,
NORTH END
Contours at 100 meters,
shaded 900m to 1800m.
Official names: capitals.
Unofficial names in
inverted commas.
Main pulk routes dashed.

BELLINGSHAUSEN SEA

LIEGE IS.

METCHNIKOFF PT.

CAPE ROUX

'Burial
Ground'

CAPE COCKBURN

'Easter Is.'

'Cairn Pt.'

'Emery Pk.'
ROENTGEN PK.

'Claires Finger'

DUCLAUX PT.

DAVIS IS.

'First
cache'

BOUQUET BAY

'Footsore Piedmont'

HUNTER

HARRY IS.

GUYOU BAY

'Noddies Col'

LISTER GL.

'Pinnacles Spur'

'Noddies Hat'

VIRCHOW

CUSHING PK.

'Cushing Col'

'Catacombs'

MORGAGNI

'Terrace
Piedmont'

PARE GL.

CLAUDE PT.

HILL BAY

'Precinct'

'Sues Col'

'Rokki Pl.'

DB Pt.

'Per Ardua'

'Astrolabe Pt.'

ROKKITANSKI

'Pare Icefall'

LAENNEC GL.

'Unexpected Col'

'No-Go Corrie'

'SSH Peaks'

DRIENCOURT PT.

HARVEY HTS.

FREUD PASSAGE

'Prince William Bay'

MALPIGHI GL.

MT. PARRY

MINOT PT.

0   10 km.

With a four-man party, one can stay with an injured man while two go on a rope for food, medical supplies and help; alternatively the three can sledge him back. Neither is possible with a three-man party. Gradually I was feeling less shaky, and I could walk: so we set off again in the whiteout. As dusk fell we breasted 'Noddies Col', exhausted, and found a little pothole crevasse to camp in down the west side. I slept badly and woke almost unable to move, with my whole trunk stiff and aching — but now I was only worried that they might send me home in *Endurance*.

At last, after four days' whiteout, some sun broke through the clouds. We made good time over 'Pinnacles Spur' and across 'Footsore Piedmont' on hard névé. At five we sat on the pulk looking down at Metchnikoff Point, changing to crampons, drinking a flask of coffee, savouring coming home after a month away, and anticipating our meeting with the other four. Seven weeks apart was too long, for over half the expedition we had been split in two parties. Rivalries, jealousies,

1

2

1 **January.** HMS *Endurance* and Wasp in Gerlache Strait (Johnny Morris)
2 **January.** Ted halfway up Mount Hunter (Chris Furse)

3   **January.** Boat party in brash ice (Jed Corbett) Opposite
4   **January.** Boat party on the journey to Brabant Island (Jed Corbett)
5   **February.** Fur Seal playing in the Boat Haven (Jed Corbett)

6 **February.** Chinstrap Penguin with chicks (Jed Corbett)
7 **February.** The Icicle Works crevasse camp (Chris Furse) Opposite

8   **February.** Underneath the Icicle Works (Ted Atkins)
9   **March.** First view down the west coast (Jed Corbett)
10   **March.** On top of Mount Rokkitanski (Jed Corbett) Opposite

11

12

11 **March.** A day's snow halfway down from Harvey Heights (Kevin de Silva)
12 **March.** Pearlwort at 'Astrolabe Point' (Jed Corbett)

suspicions and even antagonisms can develop between parties separated so long.

As we came down the glacier it was grand to see Jeff coming to meet us, with Mac and Dick (unrecognisable with long hair, and fibrepile undertrousers). As Jeff carried my pack down past the empty icefield of our old camp we were all talking fifteen to the dozen. It was good to be together again.

Four Nova tents were pitched in line near the stores dump. The site was exquisitely chosen for shelter, but was a dirty area of wet penguin scree, very different from the pristine trackless snow in the hills behind us. Johnny emerged from the 'Bugs' tent grinning, as ebullient as ever. We pitched our tent at the end of the row, then all crowded into the 'Mess' tent with our boots scattered in the muddy entrance. Jeff sat making us many brews and a huge supper, while we talked and talked, bringing each other up to date. They told us their adventures.

Late on 31 January, Dick, Mac, Jeff and Johnny had left Metchnikoff Point with a pulk. They travelled mostly at night for good snow conditions and enjoyed glorious weather. Breaking camp at 'Pinnacles Spur' Johnny lost his sleeping bag, so slept cold for three weeks. They climbed 'Noddies Hat' and (going the same route as us) reached 'Astrolabe Point' at 1 a.m. on 6 February, after negotiating the maze of crevasses behind — then still concealed by new snow.

For two weeks they were pent up at 'Astrolabe' by rain, feeling very frustrated with little to do, and on 17th they were bitterly disappointed when *Endurance* passed by without a helicopter visit.

On 20 February they broke for home, leaving the pulk and carrying only three days' rations. That evening they were caught on an exposed slope by a blizzard and all four piled into one Phortress outer tent. During the overnight hooli the tent was completely buried in the 50-metre long drift behind their protective snow-wall. After two more days' travel, largely in whiteout, they reached the halfway point at 'Cushing Col' and camped there with only one main meal left, deciding for some reason to go down to Lister Glacier and around east of Mount Hunter. Next evening they ate their last food camped near Roentgen Peak, praying for a better morrow. On 24th contouring at 650 metres in cloud they were stopped by the mushroomed drop north-east of Mount Hunter and had to backtrack, then traverse the long low piedmont route, now desperately thirsty in roasting sun. Finally they reached Metchnikoff Point late in the evening, very hungry indeed, having skied 30 km on unknown glaciers in one day.

For the last month they had stayed at Metchnikoff Point. Twice this last week they had taken a boat out. First Dick and Johnny tried to take anti-biotics to 'Astrolabe' for Simon's bronchitis, but were turned back by a steep nasty swell in Guyou Bay. Then Jeff and Johnny went to 'Cairn Point' to collect bugs, but broached on landing and nearly capsized. However for most of the month they were again frustrated by rainy weather. I think they felt imprisoned in the muddy base camp.

Meanwhile Johnny had accumulated a grand collection of over 300 'bug' samples. There are no large land animals in the Antarctic, only an impoverished fauna of tiny invertebrates. On sunny days we had occasionally found some wingless midges (first described by Racowitz from the Belgica expedition) crawling about on the surface of moss patches. The only other Antarctic higher insect is a rare winged midge seldom

Young bull Fur Seal at Metchnikoff Point, with the route to 'Cairn Point' beyond. (Jed Corbett)

49

found this far south. There are however other, smaller arthropods, the largest of which can be found by turning up stones. In slightly damp patches (often near penguin colonies), dense black swarms of 300-400 springtails are common, like tiny 2 mm long tealeaves. In drier and mossier patches brown mites, like shiny 1 mm diameter eggs, cling to the stones in clusters of 100-200 just below the moss surface, while a few, slightly larger, red, predatory mites run about frantically. These midges, springtails and mites, plus a free-living tick, are the only macroscopic land animals in the Antarctic, but smaller arthropods and other groups also live in the vegetation and organic debris.

Ours was taxonomic and biogeographic 'stamp collecting'; nowadays BAS are working more on quantitative studies of the whole terrestrial ecosystem on Signy Island. The Antarctic provides a good model, simplified by the absence of any larger predators or herbivores, so the inter-relationships of the lower orders and the vegetation can be more exactly defined. Collecting these tiny animals could be very tedious, particularly when lengthy extraction processes were needed to concentrate the organisms before preserving them. However, organised amateurs can do the task well, and Johnny had got a lot of satisfaction from doing it well, helped by an extractor made by Peter Stuttard from a plastic dustbin. It could have its scientific excitements too. Our similar collections from Elephant Island had proved unexpectedly rich and varied, possibly because it is the bit of Antarctica closest to South America. We had collected some enchytraeid worms and terrestrial crustaceans never recorded in Antarctica — and still unidentified 14 years later. Here, we only expected to fill in, define, or extend the known ranges of various species, but already Johnny and Ted had found some brown mite-like creatures free-living around a Chinstrap colony, with 5 mm bodies plus 3 mm legs; they were larger than anything described in the literature, but Johnny was not sure that he would want these gruesome little creatures named after him.

In the three days before *Endurance* arrived I was too busy to look at wildlife, except the Chinstraps around camp. All their chicks seemed to have gone, but the colonies were still nearly full of adults, now mostly through the moult. The morning and evening rush hours seemed even busier than before. Most nests were still occupied throughout the day, with penguins going about busily stealing each others' stones, either practising or preparing for next year. (There is a strong tendency for individuals to return to the same part of the colony or even the same nest, and pairs quite often mate two years running.)

One day Johnny and I walked over to 'Cairn Point' to collect rocks. Coming back we witnessed a superbly appropriate end-of-summer-expedition sunset, spreading shimmering copper-green and gold across the waters off Metchnikoff Point, with the skerries casting deep purple shadows that raced across the sea to the glacier below us. Arriving back at 8 p.m. in gathering darkness we joined the others for our much delayed 'Christmas' feast of chicken, tinned potatoes, cake, biscuits, toffees and other mouth-watering goodies. We radioed the three at 'Astrolabe' to tell them what they were missing. Otherwise I spent the three days on expedition paperwork in the 'Post Office' tent, servicing philatelic covers, accounting for £5,000-worth of stamps, writing letters to the second-summer party back in England and writing Service reports on my nine friends of the first-summer party. I collapsed into my sleeping

Erecting the Triwall Hut at basecamp. (Jed Corbett)

bag at 4 a.m. the first night, at 5 a.m. the second, and not at all the last. Jeff brought me a steaming mug of tea as a chill dawn broke on 24th. HMS *Endurance* was offshore. By that evening only Ted, Jed and I would remain of our little summer team. There would be nine new faces here, nine newcomers in smart new gear. They were all visiting the Antarctic for the first time in their lives, having left Britain together nearly six weeks before, in RFA *Fort Austin*.

The first helicopter chattered in to land, blowing over and wrecking my Post Office tent to start a hectic day. Over 50 loads of food, fuel and other stores followed pell mell, slung in nets below the two shuttling Wasps. Halfway through the afternoon the first new faces arrived: John Kimbrey (Kim) and Jon Beattie (JB) in orange immersion suits stumbled across the penguin colony carrying their rucksacks, grinning hugely and continuously, while we all shook hands and banged backs and exchanged four months' news. After that, people came and went in a whirl. Suddenly I was saying goodbye to the last of the summer people, and a strange new gang were rushing to and fro carrying stores. Kevin and I grasped each others' shoulders and said goodbye for a year: yes, of course we would meet again, the whole team would; how could we do otherwise after hardships and happiness together here; yes, he would phone Carole from *Endurance* and she would phone Faye. As we finally shook hands, Kevin pressed his precious Swiss Army knife into my hand. It was a symbolic farewell. They were gone.

However I was flown out to the ship to say farewell and thank you to Captain Colin MacGregor and his men, and goodbye to the seven standing in the hangar, looking strangely clean, and gazing for the last time at their island home and kingdom with a mute tearing feeling of ending something great. Then I was flying back. Momentarily my spirits capsized, wishing I were going home also. Then the black and white crossword pattern of Metchnikoff Point rushed up at us, and the little figures round the landing site grew tall.

Fur Seal Confrontation:
1. Newcomer François.
(Jed Corbett)

Minutes later the twelve of us stood waving as the last helicopter roared close overhead — the last outsiders we would see for nine months. The Wasp flew away to the little red ship out beyond the skerries.

After a stunned pause the penguins resumed their cackling.

It was after six; it would be dark by eight; tonight a blizzard could strike us. So I gathered all twelve around a bottle of Hankey Bannister whisky to say: 'Welcome. Tonight just settle in domestically as quickly as possible, but first collect the scattered stores (against snowdrifts), and put rocks on all loose gear (against wind). Snow for water is on the glacier behind; gash [rubbish] goes into the crevasses below the old camp; the heads area [toilet] is down the south-western gully. Tomorrow we will start erecting the hut and sorting out the stores'.

The camp was a mess, but everyone set to, cheerfully hurrying to settle themselves into a new world, finding and erecting tents and collecting fuel, stoves, compo rations, Karrimats, cooking pots, etc. As darkness fell, people lit stoves, talking quietly. I settled in with Howard. I was exhausted. Sometime about 3 a.m. I fell asleep amongst a sackful of letters from another world.

When I woke next day, late and feeling guilty, I found the whole team working away with cheerful gusto in sunlit weather. For three vital days the weather smiled on us. Spotts, Ted and Peter (with nine helpers) erected, sealed and reasonably secured the little cardboard hut.

On 27th we all gathered in the hut at 8 p.m. and celebrated the first gathering of many with a bottle of Pusser's Rum. The little windowless house, three metres by two, was built of folded Triwall cardboard. Entering through an oval door, a gothic table built by Peter almost filled the far end. Ted fitted ski-rafters to stiffen the roof, with a central shelf of skis head-high over the table. The Tilley lamp lit our twelve faces as we sat along the sides, each on a little wooden box of personal gear; the lamp chased the shadows to the corners, enclosing us in a capsule of humanity and comradeship. We could lay out maps and use the microscope there, but the greatest advantage was to have a place where we could meet and

*Fur Seal Confrontation: 2
Old hand Ted. (Jed
Corbett)*

laugh together at the wind outside. Living in two-man tents, group cohesion is difficult in this climate: here in the hut we would meld into a family. It was a priceless boon.

That same night it rained: the hut had been sealed just in time. Peter built a marvellous porch, a gloryhole store, where cameras, books, climbing ropes, tools and repair materials crowded the shelves and nails around the walls, instead of lying in snow-filled boxes on the moraine.

Most of the newcomers snatched a day out on the piedmont getting used to skiing on a rope. The ologists began to settle in. On the sloping grass sward above the northern cliffs, JB found a little cluster of brown toadstools, each about a centimetre across. A few toadstools do occur in the Peninsula region, but hitherto we had found only patches of mould on mosses and lichens. Perhaps, as in Europe, autumn is the season for fruiting fungi — a brief interlude before the winter snows.

The rain continued for the rest of the month. Metchnikoff Point was nearly bare of snow, with fields of naked scree, where snow had lain through summer. On melting ice, the mud from penguins' feet was concentrated on the surface with their moulted feathers. Below our camp the glacier was breaking into cavernous crevasses, with old yellow and blue ice like giant trellis-work between.

When would the winter snows begin, we asked ourselves. The nights were closing fast, but we longed for snow — to clothe the muddy campsite in clean white, hold down tent valences softly and evenly instead of tearing rocks, and make snowholes possible — but most of all to let us brush dry snow off our clothes, instead of being soaking wet, with fog filling the tent as we lit the stove.

April

JB outside the porch door into the hut. (Jed Corbett)

After a week settling down, the winter expedition really began now.

It rained.

Sometimes it snowed, usually it froze at night, but the first week of April was dominated by a continuing thaw and low cloud, and barren flattened slopes of glacier till appeared around the butte. I began to get itchy feet again; so did Kim and the other mountaineers, though the inexperienced men hung back, waiting to be led out. However everyone was busy — improving the hut, repairing tents and other gear and making short roped ski forays. The great benefit of the enforced stay was that all the scientific programmes were started quickly.

Nick tended the tide gauge that Mac had installed in March. Tides round the Peninsula are less regular than in Europe — usually there are two high and two low tides each day, but some days there is just one long high, and one low tide. Tidal predictions are prosaically based on those for Fort Galveston in the Gulf of Texas. Our tide gauge was showing a range of nearly two metres — three times that predicted. However the timings roughly followed the predictions for nearby Nansen Island.

Later we planned to measure iceberg drifts to gauge tidal streams and prevailing currents. Already, from fishing, we knew there were strong currents to and fro through the skerries. Flotsam is rare in the Antarctic (except for the remains of 19th-century sealing and whaling in the South Shetlands) but we regularly found bits of wood — dull, modern, but useful. An old whale jawbone was probably ancient flotsam and we found no relics of human activity. Due to ice-scour, little seaweed grows on Antarctic shores, but small bits from lower depths were often cast up. That week I found a frond with four fingers seven metres long like brown rubber hoses 4 cm across: little white and black barnacles clustered like butterflies at various lesions.

Francois loved animals, and enjoyed his daily seal counts. The number of Weddells continued to fluctuate without apparent pattern, as if groups went away fishing for a few days at a time. There were usually one or two Elephants, but no more Crabeaters, and still no Leopards. The boat party had seen several Leopards in the Gerlache Strait and Bouquet Bay; they are lone wanderers and I had expected to see them occasionally here. They catch penguins by lying in wait at bottlenecks, or by a startling burst of acceleration in open water. Sometimes they play a ghastly cat-and-mouse game with wounded penguins before the grim final scene when they shake them out of their skins in the water, with Giant Petrels, Cape Pigeons, Wilson's Storm Petrels and Kelp Gulls gathering for scraps. At Elephant Island one large Chinstrap colony suffered about 10% predation by Leopard Seals in a season, five seals each eating four penguins in an hour, then hauling out with an obscene smile on their heavy heads. Leopards also eat other seals: a BAS friend had a Crabeater snatched from him while he was butchering two on the ice-edge for the dogs. Faraday told us that a Leopard Seal had attacked one of their inflatables this summer, but usually they just inspect boats or canoes with impersonal curiosity. About 600 Fur Seal bulls still rested ashore and played in the water. This was less than the peak of 950 in February, but they seemed to have spread out to other beaches. We learnt that there had been a krill famine in South Georgia this season: half the albatross chicks had starved, and many Fur Seals had emigrated, being seen in unusually large numbers in the South Orkneys and South Shetlands. A beautiful pale sandy-coloured bull (the fourth we had seen) came ashore, which suggested a South Georgia origin as that colour phase occurs there. Another recognisable old yellow one had moved from Metchnikoff Point to Claude Point, supporting the general impression of a wandering non-territorial population. At last on 2 April I saw one with a tag on its right fore-flipper, which was almost certainly applied at South Georgia. Perhaps we were just the southern fringe of this season's unusual emigration.

There was an air of impending departure among the birds.

After breeding, penguins go to sea for a spell to build up fat reserves, then come ashore to moult in their colonies. The latter part of their breeding season is confusing because of the non-breeders and failed breeders moulting early, and with Chinstraps this is complicated by the juveniles being virtually indistinguishable from adults. By the first week of April most of the Chinstraps had nearly finished moulting, except for regrowing their 'brush' tails. The morning and evening rush hours seemed as busy as ever, and on 4th a random check of homeward commuters showed 64% still with the last white stars of body moult. By 7th only 30-40% of nests were occupied by day, and even at night the birds' cackling was no longer continuous. Overnight roosts had built up below the colonies, but possibly these were mainly visitors from elsewhere, because later in April we caught two with flipper bands.

The occasional individual juvenile Adelies were certainly visitors. In contrast we had seen no Macaronis since early February.

Few Wilson's Storm Petrels now flitted over the scree, and their frog-like chorus of nest-calls ceased in the first week of April. Chicks still sat in eight of my nine marked nests (the ninth had died, of starvation or possibly soaking cold): all were well feathered, with a little duvet of down on their bellies. Like most petrels, the adults stop feeding them about a week before fledging: the chicks live off their fat, and then find their own way to sea, and north across the oceans to Nova Scotia and Cape Clear. On 8th the first chick had fledged from the marked nests. Their breeding cycle (38 or more days' incubation plus a 60-day fledgling period) is longer than the Cape Pigeons (45 plus 49 days) and they start later, because they cannot dig down through spring snow to their underground nests. The Black-bellied Storm Petrels need even more time (46 plus 70 days), and at Elephant Island most of their nests contained the sad mummified bodies of chicks entombed by previous autumn snowfalls. However here, as at Elephant, the Wilson's largely escaped.

The Southern Giant Petrel is the only Antarctic species to fledge later than the Storm Petrels, their chicks sitting like geese upon the snow until early May. Perhaps the autumns on Brabant were too harsh for them (or too wet).

Groups of up to four Shags were present, including the first brown and white juveniles that I had seen. I was sad not to have found more and larger colonies, because they are local residents, who would have enlivened our winter days.

Juvenile Kelp Gulls form gangs, flying together around the coasts local to their colony, occasionally with a few adults attached. Here at Metchnikoff Point the main gang was only about 16 strong; even with some extra individuals this was a low output for the 30-odd breeding pairs. There were rather fewer adults around now: having completed their wing moult gradually through February and March, perhaps some had left to winter elsewhere. At Elephant Island we saw flocks of 50-60 roosting remote from colonies after mid-March, and suspected they were migrants passing through and waiting for good conditions to cross Drake Passage. Perhaps some of our Brabant Kelps were there now?

Migrant Sheathbills had also collected in flocks of up to 60 at Elephant Island from mid-March onward, making their last landfall before the long crossing to winter in South America. I had expected them to leave earlier from Metchnikoff Point, but their numbers seemed unchanged, and we saw some dispersed to other points for the first time. Here they still scuttered about, pecking at everything interesting, round the seals, in the penguin colonies, and around our tents.

On 4th Howard began his physiological research into adaptation to cold. We offered a unique group of subjects exposed to adequate cold for a long time in the field: unique, because Fids* are too warm in their BAS bases, and Royal Marines are not in Norway long enough. For over a year Howard had prepared to seize this opportunity with typical efficiency and enthusiasm. We approached some of the data collection with rather less enthusiasm, but this first 'fluid-balance' 24-hour day was easy — recording all we drank, bottling all our urine, and giving a blood sample. Next day Howard weighed us, and measured skinfold thicknesses: on average, people had lost 5.7 kg (9% of initial weight) since leaving UK, but I was staggered to find I weighed only 67 kg, 20 kg below my steady weight for the last 25 years. No wonder I was hungry!

During the summer expedition we had suffered few medical problems. Most of us had blistered feet, some severe, and some continuing. Most also had numb big toes (a cold injury) and Jed's camera fingers were also numb. Our nails were rather soft and frangible and grew slowly, and most had footrot from constantly wet feet. Occupants of two tents had recovered quickly from carbon monoxide poisoning. Three of my fillings and a tooth had lost battles with frozen Rolos. Lying in our tents after a hard day most of us got cramp, which Howard ascribed to dehydration. The one serious illness had been Simon's cough — probably caught on board *Endurance* in February when he alone flew on board. Bill had suffered the only real injuries, needing nine stitches in his head in Valparaiso after being nearly killed by a falling craneload, and two stitches later in a cut thumb. I hoped the winter would be as trouble-free.

I decided to take an eight-man party to Duclaux Point, partly for a geological survey, but mainly to get the newcomers out, learning the arts of pulking and living on the move. We planned for a five-day trip and took seven days' rations, and we finally broke camp on 9th. It was good to move the tents from the dirty base camp penguins' promenade, and that night we pitched three tents in the clean peace and stillness of a snow-filled crevasse above the north coast.

Waking in the dark at 7 a.m. we managed to get away about 10 a.m., but the shortening days drastically reduced our travelling time. Because of the short day, and the cold, we only stopped very briefly for lunch, sitting together on the pulks with our backs to the wind having a cup from a thermos flask and a bite of chocolate or biscuit, and then harnessing the horse, roping up, and away. By 6 p.m. the light would fade and the cold would quickly grip, so we started looking for sheltered crevasse campsites at latest from 4 p.m. That second day, pulking along the open windswept north coast piedmont, enveloped in cloud, I started peering for crevasse shadows at 2 p.m. because some of the party did not even know how to pitch our tents.

*BAS staff have kept this nickname, originally given to the staff of the Falkland Islands Dependencies Survey.

Sighting a small mushroomed face, we parked the pulks and skis nearby and dropped our packs, harnesses and ropes. Nick and Francois, sharing a tent with me, now learnt the standard routine that could get everyone warm and cosy inside within half an hour, in any conditions. First we made a quick roped recce for hidden crevasses, then set to work digging level tent platforms in the sheltered snowdrift. Leaving one to finish the platform, two of us erected the tent below, then moved it bodily on to the platform. Once guyed there, Francois (who was cook) went inside. Then Nick and I passed in our three Karrimats, followed by the stove, the three cooking pots and the rations, our three Sigg fuel bottles, thermos flasks, sleeping bags, bivouac bags and individual stuff-sacks with tent gear. While Francois sorted out the interior and got a brew going, we two outside men put snow on the tent valence, built a protective snow-wall, stocked the back porch with snow for cooking, put the rucksacks into polybags in the snow, secured the pulk and skis properly (planting bamboo marker wands), and generally sorted out the campsite. I then had a chat with the other tents giving Nick five minutes to sit inside the tent removing his boots and brushing off snow into the porch. Finally I followed, to get into my sleeping bag, feeling frozen feet and hands began to thaw out, and hoping that Francois had the first brew nearly ready. That second night the tent was a bit of a mess both inside and out, but Francois cooked a delicious hot sloshy chocolate and biscuit pudding.

For the next three days a deep depression (960 mB at sea level), sat over us. At this latitude the atmosphere directly affecting cloud formation and weather is only 5-8 km deep. The old sledging plateau, running at 2 km height along the length of the Antarctic Peninsula, acts like a partial

Three-man pulking is very frustrating. Righting Peter's capsized pulk for the seventeenth time traversing the north coast. (Jed Corbett)

Duclaux Point party digging out the tents on 11 April. (Jed Corbett)

Opposite. Working down through the icefall at Duclaux Point. (Jed Corbett)

dam, deflecting weather systems like this or holding them up. For three days a pool of blue sky sat over us, but a big west wind blotted out the sun with smoking spindrift the first day, while we dug out drifts over the tents, and went on to the familiar two-thirds rations. The second day we moved up 300 metres on to the ridge and camped on the floor of a huge crevasse wider than a tennis court. It was bitterly cold at night: our nostrils crackled, fingers stuck to fuel bottles, tent zips froze solid, ice inside the outer tent fell with the sound of shattered glass as we banged the tent walls, and my inner boots froze hard inside my bivouac bag. On the third day of depression we sledged over the broad ridge, to overlook Lister Glacier at midday. A curtain of grey cloud trailed across Bouquet Bay, shrouding first the black gothic towers of Davis Island, then the cluster of grounded icebergs. The curtain swirled clockwise around our pool of sunshine like a meteorological demonstration, then abruptly swallowed us. In snow and rising wind we felt our way eastward, and three hours later pitched camp in an icefall somewhere under Roentgen Peak.

On 14th we woke to the heavenly light of a full moon, poised to drop below the dead white snowline opposite. Beyond, the mushrooms of Mount Hunter blushed already at the sun rising behind our perch. Three Snow Petrels flew swiftly past, then around our camp as welcome talismen, showing pearl grey underwing-coverts. In glorious weather we left the tents and skied down to Duclaux Point, gliding through untouched powder snow: Francois saw the indigo waters of the Gerlache Strait for the first time. Below us in Bouquet Bay the moored bergs glittered white and liquid blue against the slatey sea. Under the glacier snout a mauve tracery of brash-ice calmed lagoons between, which reflected the cerulean blue of the sky. Behind us, our three little green tents peeped over the roof of a great iceblock just below the summit of Roentgen Peak. Brabant Island had produced a perfect day again, and our spirits sparkled too: one day like this was worth a week of bitter pulking.

Duclaux Point is a narrow rib of vertical black rock crowned by a knife-edge snow arête sticking out from Lister Glacier. It may be one of

Snow Petrel. (Chris Furse)

the feeder necks where the basalt lavas surfaced, before flowing out to Metchnikoff Point and elsewhere, but Mike needed three days with three good climbers to survey it, and once again our rations were running out. So, after investigating the tortuous route down the icefall toward the shore, we skied back up, and on to the snowy pate of Roentgen Peak, to stand quiet in wonder at the silent white mountain islands and empty seas spread all around us. A cold winter sunset crept in.

Next day in continuing sunshine we hauled the two pulks 12 km back to Cape Roux. Arriving at the iceslope above the cape everyone was tired and hungry. I was weary of continually teaching Nick and Francois elementary camping and ropework, and I was irritated by the length of time it took unloading the pulk, cacheing the skis, roping up, and putting on crampons. Then several things went wrong: JB fell waist deep in a crevasse and Nick froze with the rope slack; someone kicked one of our two precious Bulldog snow shovels, which slid irretrievably down over the ice-cliff and into the sea; five minutes later Nick tripped over his crampons, and one of our three remaining good sets of tent poles followed the shovel (we had started with five sets). I had a total sense-of-humour failure. Having run out of cigarettes at Roentgen Peak, my temper remained foul that evening and next day, and Nick got the brunt of it as he did various slipshod or clumsy things around the tent. Poor Francois suffered, as even my normally sparse conversation and Nick's monosyllabic responses died into silence. The total breach of communications between Nick and me became a cold, hard, silent object, filling the tent with palpable antagonism.

Mike's feet were in an awful state after the day's heavy sledging: he could scarcely walk, let alone ski to Metchnikoff Point. After visiting Cape Roux West next day, Peter, Mike and I stayed with six man-days rations, while the other five set out for Metchnikoff Point with two pulks and just two man-days' rations between them.

While we had been in the hills, winter had arrived on the coast. The mossy plateau was drifted over, the rocks along the shore were thickly glazed with ice, and the skerries were cold, white and unwelcoming. We also noticed great changes in the bird life.

Antarctic Terns usually depart their nesting areas as soon as their own chicks fledge, or their nest fails, although occasionally they will lay a second clutch elsewhere. At Elephant Island we seldom saw Terns after fledging, but here at Brabant Island small parties often overflew the coast. As we pitched camp on 15th, Terns were passing east over Cape Roux almost continuously, perhaps a hundred in the hour. I assumed this was migration from more southerly breeding or foraging areas to their winter quarters, wherever they may be. Nearly all were mixed parties of juveniles and adults and the great majority of adults were now in winter plumage with white foreheads, and their underparts pure white or mottled with summer grey. Then on 17th I saw several flocks moving slowly west past the cape, one flock of 30 resting awhile on an ice-covered skerry, so perhaps these were all just local feeding movements. (Later in April, parties continued to overfly Metchnikoff Point, mostly but not all headed north-east.)

One very welcome sign of winter was the mass arrival of Snow Petrels. As we arrived, parties of 2-20 were coasting westward, flying along the ice-cliffs and over the cape past our tents, rather than low over the sea like the Cape Pigeons and Fulmars. The movement continued for three days with 373 per hour on 17th, before tapering off the next day.

Possibly this was just the visible part of a great circular feeding movement; it might on the other hand be a southward migration to the pack-ice of the Bellingshausen Sea — but where from? Snow Petrels breed in South Georgia and the South Orkneys, but I would expect those to winter around the Weddell Sea. The only known colony in the South Shetlands is the small group of 50 pairs we found on Elephant Island, although they do breed along the Peninsula. We had seen very few during the summer but since the end of March we had seen them more often and after 7 April a handful had begun to frequent the cliffs at Metchnikoff Point. We saw them also over the glaciers, wildly swooping and tumbling down the icefalls like joyful katabatic spirits. They are lovely birds: their pure whiteness, set off by the black bill and gentle curious disinterested black eyes, gives them the pristine aura of doves of peace. If dead sailors do become petrels, I would like most to be a Snow Petrel (later). We prayed that they would stay with us through the dark months to come.

After three days Mike's ankle was still bad, and we were running short of food, so on 20th Peter and I left him with three days' rations to fetch more. I did not like leaving anyone alone here, but Mike was relaxed, cheerful and unworried as always. Halfway back we met Ted pulling a pulk, with JB as brakeman. Ted gave me a smoke: 'Well, Chris, there's been quite an epic here. The others are up by the snowhole. Nick went into a big crevasse three days ago.' Then Ted and JB went on to Cape Roux with rations on the pulk, to camp with Mike. We joined the three above: they had a story to tell.

After his crevasse fall Nick lies in a bivouac bag by the packs while JB and Spotts dig a snowhole on the right. (Jed Corbett)

Spotts had led the five leaving Cape Roux on 17th, he and Jed on one pulk, and Nick as horse on the heavier pulk with JB and François.

On an innocent snowslope Nick suddenly fell through up to his shoulders, and shouted. As he struggled to get out, the pulk slowly upended 'like a torpedoed ship', and vanished, taking Nick with it. Francois was jerked off his feet and slid helplessly toward the hole. JB dropped into the snow and fought with iceaxe, ski-sticks, skis, arms, legs and body to stop the fall as he was dragged back. Anguished determination written large across his face in the snow, he finally held the fall when he was himself almost at the edge. With Nick and the pulk's weight on him, dug deep like a snowy octopus, he was unable to move. Spotts dug frantically putting in deadmen to belay first JB, then Francois who was frozen with shock, lying across the wide crevasse bridge, shouting to Nick who did not answer. Belaying himself to a third deadman, Spotts crawled over to look down the hole: Nick was about 13 metres down, hanging suspended from the pulk in a cavernous crevasse with one hand jammed in the harness, but he was uninjured. Spotts lowered the second rope to him, and gradually Nick cut himself clear of the pulk and found a snow-ledge where he freed his skis and sorted out his harness, before starting the climb up the vertical rope to the patch of sky above. Jumaring up with his rucksack on the growing bight of rope below was heavy work: two hours later Nick emerged from the grave, exhausted, half expecting Wagnerian music, but getting something better — a cup of coffee.

Francois was still shocked, and Nick appeared hypothermic. Their tent and all but one rope were still down the crevasse. Leading them quickly to an open crevasse, Spotts and JB dug like furies into a big drift. In only an hour and a half all five were lying cramped up in a snowhole, wet and cold, but alive and secure.

Next morning Spotts and Nick stayed in the snowhole with the one remaining main meal to share. JB, Jed and Francois skied to Metchnikoff Point to get help, losing their way in the blowing snow, but eventually homing in on the faint cackle of penguins as evening approached.

Kim and Ted prepared the skidoos, but the powder snow and ice on the slope behind was too much for them next day, so Ted, JB and Jim set out with a pulk, and reached the snowhole at 4 p.m. on the 19th. Spotts and Nick were very glad to see them (and the food!). That evening Ted climbed down into the crevasse with a cyalume light in his mouth and they hauled up the tents, ropes, rock specimens and cine camera, then the emptied pulk. All five spent that night in the snowhole, and next morning Ted climbed down again, recovering Nick's skis from 25 metres further down the crevasse. An hour later, as perky as ever, Ted went on to Cape Roux, greeting us with his laconic: 'There's been quite an epic up there'.

Without JB holding the fall magnificently, and without Spotts' experience, speed and superb leadership after that, there would have been three dead men. Anyone could fall into a crevasse like that: the hard fact was that if it had been either JB or Spotts who had fallen, the others would have lacked the mountaineering skill and experience to hold and rescue them. Over the next few days we talked a lot about this, and I laid down a tighter set of rules for the composition of parties travelling, raising the minimum size of party from three to four, except for local day-trips. I also ranked the team in three mountaineering grades: Leaders (Kim, Spotts, Ted, Peter and me), Seconds (JB, Howard and Jed) and Beginners (Mike, Jim, Nick and Francois). Each party had to include at least as many Leaders as Beginners, and the numbers of Beginners in any party were limited. The price of this improved safety was our flexibility and mobility. The Beginners in particular needed to improve to avoid our being hamstrung: Mike would soon qualify as a Second, but I feared that Nick and Francois would take a long time.

Spotts and I skied down to Metchnikoff Point with his pulk. After

Opposite. Basecamp in late April. (Jed Corbett)

eleven days away we felt like coming home. Across a scree sclope, drifted snow traced a path with white, a symbol of human occupation. Arriving at the foot of the glacier we came upon a little house built out from the moraine: a skidoo stood inside with the other two outside. One day Ted and Kim had started digging out a small wind shelter: at 5 a.m. six days later they had finished, fixing the Union Flag over the door of this story-book garage, with a stove burning, bright with the tilley lamp and, with all our tools and repair materials ranged neatly to hand in the plywood box walls. Howard had continued his physiology and the four at base camp had been very busy. Kim had developed blood poisoning from a badly bruised ankle, but was now chafing at the bit to move.

Now the skidoos had their first job, collecting Mike from Cape Roux. For two days Kim, Spotts and Peter attacked the slope behind Metchnikoff Point. The 22-degree iceslope was covered in powder snow and the machines bogged down, or slid sideways down the awkward traverse to half capsize in snowed-up crevasses. Once, in hurtling spindrift, Peter careered down backwards a hundred metres and turned his machine over just before hitting the moraine. Driving skidoos here needed controlled dash and courage and the skidoo drivers quickly became a cheerful club, an élite bunch of self-styled cowboys. By the evening of the second day, they were up on the skyline; sunset lit the snow mushrooms along Mount Hunter with saffron, rose and gold, offset by shadow blues and pallid white — a perfect backdrop for the two skidoos parked triumphant on the twilight piedmont.

Next morning Kim, Spotts and Peter, with Howard, roared off across the piedmont towing the heavy sledge. They expected to be back by evening. Dark fell. Then at 8 p.m. Ted and JB arrived out of the pitch blackness and quietly unloaded their pulk by the hut. Mike's foot was improving, after going badly septic; he was coming back with the skidoos, but they had got stuck halfway and camped.

The skidoos arrived back in cloud next evening, 24th, Mike limping down the last slope with Howard. Spotts cried for a whisky. Kim said the brief love affair with skidoos was over. They were fast over open undulating country, but very limited going up slopes with deep snow, and towing loaded sledges was difficult or impossible on any steeper slopes, whether up or down or traversing. Journeys would have to be done in sections, ferrying to and fro. Safety was also difficult — any good roping system for the drivers made operation much more awkward. On the journey back, both skidoos had broken through big crevasse bridges, just clawing their way forward by keeping speed up (Kim's with Mike riding pillion). As always, going downhill was most dangerous. That morning, bringing down the sledge (with the chain brake wrapped round its runners), Peter had careered down sideways uncontrollably towards a bergschrund, luckily stopping just as he was about to abandon the machine to the drop.

The slopes and hazards of Brabant Island were not really suited for skidoos, but Spotts, Kim and Peter were full of enthusiastic energy. They at once began preparing for the next trip, a longer one to Lister Glacier and beyond. They worked out loads, lashings, safety roping and techniques in detail in discussion, and then tried out ideas on the awkward traverse behind the base camp. They were bursting with ideas: for years BAS have had trouble with the rear skidoo overrunning the tow-rope, but Peter solved it by rigging a rope with bungee elastics which pulled it together when the load came off.

The 24th was Easter Tuesday. That evening we had a short service outside the hut, giving thanks for Nick's safety and Mike's recovery, and thinking of spring at home, with children hunting Easter eggs among the daffodils and birds singing in the hedges. The Wednesday was declared a Sunday and the weather was calm and peaceful, in keeping with our mood. On quiet days like this in base camp, one almost forgot that a blizzard could blow up in an hour or two. In fact 25th was the last good weather in April, for the rest of the month was bitterly cold, with snow and cloud.

Francois had been badly shaken by Nick's crevasse fall, but he recovered his spirits and restarted the seal counts on 20th. There had been a dramatic reduction of Fur Seals at Metchnikoff Point, from 600 on 7th to only 80. A beautiful surprise was one very pale bull with pink eyes — the first true albino we had seen. At the end of the month 50-80 still remained, their coats hoary-white with snow, but surely soon they would be leaving for the winter.

The Chinstraps were also leaving. It seemed to be a gradual thinning out. The evening rush hour had reduced to a trickle and the overnight beach roosts were almost empty, though penguins still cackled in the colonies near the tents. The colonies on top of the butte had hatched earliest, and by 25th there were only 30 penguins there, from nearly 600 nesting pairs. The lower colony had been last to hatch; on 23rd it was still nearly 40% full, with birds stone-gathering and holding territories, and one pair even trying hard to mate.

A cold northerly blizzard on 26th and 27th raised metre-deep drifts running 50 metres from the lee of the tents. Howard's Fjellravn Pyramid centre-pole broke, and he and Nick became refugees in other tents. During the blizzard the Chinstraps went to sea; and they did not return. All the colonies were suddenly empty — 10 days later than they had left Shackleton's men at Point Wild in 1916, the same lag as their hatching dates, so their breeding season here was merely later, not compressed.

In late March a few Gentoo Penguins had started roosting overnight on the beach. The roost had built up to 30 early in April and now about 100 came ashore each evening. Their orange beaks and feet were splashes of colour, and their rich braying calls made a nice change from the pugnacious Chinstraps. Surprisingly some returned from sea in company with parties of Chinstraps — waiting longer, swimming to and fro, until they found an easier landing. At first I assumed they had stopped here on a leisurely migration from their southernmost breeding colonies near Palmer Base. Then on various dates we caught four Gentoos all banded at Admiralty Bay on King George Island, 300 km to the north. This reverse migration must have evolved to exploit some local autumn food resource. They would not stay long: Gentoos and Chinstraps have seldom been recorded in the winter pack-ice, only Adelies and Emperors.

The Wilsons' Storm Petrels had left while we were away. After returning from Duclaux Point I only saw two tardy individuals. All my nine marked nests were covered with snow and most of the nest-crannies themselves were also snow-filled, but seven of the chicks had fledged just in time.

Only the Cape Pigeons seemed oblivious of winter coming. They had vacated their colonies in March when the chicks were fledging and spent a period at sea, moulting. At the beginning of April the cliffs round the butte had again been full of these clown-patterned petrels. Now many still circled around and fluttered to land, while pairs courted and chittered on their snow-covered nest-sites, for all the world as if spring were about to return. In the dire gloom of late April their bustling activity and noise was cheering, amongst all the signs of impending winter.

The cold weather and snow encouraged the lethargy which seemed to creep over me at base camp. I kept putting off the personal repair jobs which were a continual load on all of us. (At the end of April my own list was typical: sew failed main straps back onto rucksack; mend torn rucksack pocket; patch and darn four pairs of mittens; sew up failed breeches seams; put braces buttons on spare breeches; patch burns on mountain jacket and bivouac bag; modify snowgaiters to fit boots; patch torn trouser legs used as makeshift snowgaiters; remove and stiffen my ski binding uphill fitting and rivet the footplate in lieu of missing screws; shorten footfang crampons, loose after bedding in; sew torn guy becket back onto tent; strip and clean stove; sort out and dry my boxed up spare clothes; make up new prussik slings; oil and free all my karabiners, etc., etc.). Apart from personal gear there was communal expedition gear to keep in good repair — skidoos, pulks, generator, hut, boats, returned tents, etc. Ted, Kim, Spotts, Peter and JB were always working, fixing things. These five were forming a very strong core to the team. Howard, Jed, Mike and I were each clearly fully occupied with our individual projects, but Jim, Nick and Francois were general supporters, without major individual tasks. It worried me a little that these three groups corresponded so closely to mountaineering strengths. I had left the

Jim taking readings at the Met. Station. (Jed Corbett)

*Ted and Kim beside the
half-built garage.
(Howard Oakley)*

workload to sort itself out, and the loads had become unbalanced. I
dished out some extra individual jobs to equalise the effort on general
quartermastering and repairs: Jim took on radio and general camp stores,
Francois tent repairs, and Nick fuels.

The routine met. readings that Jim went out to take daily at 10 a.m. and
10 p.m. confirmed the increasing cold. At the end of April temperatures
were generally about −5°C, and for the first time the monthly mean was
below freezing, at −1.6C. The wind had reached or exceeded gale force
on twelve days, so effective temperature due to wind-chill was much
lower. During the day my hands and feet now usually felt cold, and
several others felt the same. Some also felt cold at night, but I was cosy in
my bag (fully dressed as always, except for anorak and boots, with my
wristlets and balaclava on). Only Howard was genuinely pleased that it
was growing colder.

Because early man was a tropical animal, our physiological reactions to
cold evolved to protect the body's core against the real threat of
exposure (hypothermia), sacrificing resistance to frostbite of the extremities, which was not a threat to survival in the tropics. On 26th, Howard
gave us all a second fluid-balance day. We showed the standard response
to cold — urinating more than we drank ('cold diuresis'), thus dehy-
drating the body, particularly the blood. Normally packed cell volumes
(PCV) of red corpuscles are constant for any individual at 40-45% of the
blood volume. The team's mean PCV had risen from 43% to 48% in three
weeks: this more viscous blood conserved heat in the core, starving the
extremities, so we were more susceptible to frostbite now than three
weeks before. Howard hoped that we would adapt over the long winter
— we would obviously balance our fluid intake, but no such long-term
studies had been done before, and no one knew whether our PCVs
would return to normal after a time — or even whether they would stabi-
lise at all.

In our three-month summer on Brabant Jed, Ted and I had not
adapted (my PCV rose from 46% to 52% over those three weeks of
April). Howard explained that we had only recently had conditions
regularly colder than the vague threshold which triggers cold diuresis.
With cold-injured toes and now my fingertips also numb and tingling, I
hoped that we would adapt, and soon.

Winter was now upon us.

May

François crossing avalanche track on 15 May
(Chris Furse)

The bad weather continued into May, with heavy snow and drifting on 3rd. We worked around base camp. Nick produced the first monthly edition of the Chinstrap Chronicle — mostly humorous contributions about life here in a tent. Francois had his 23rd birthday party in the hut — presents from his family, a sewing kit made by Spotts, and a bottle of whisky between the twelve of us. Palmer Station offered to send home some 250-word messages for us — one personal letter each per month, a marvellous unexpected bonus. Then radio conditions around the Peninsula deteriorated due to a big 'maggy storm' in the ionosphere. Magnetic storms cause aurorae, so we watched each evening, but in vain: the Southern Lights only reach this far from the magnetic pole about three times a year.

The wind and snow continued through 5th, but next morning we woke at last in quiet tents — it was calm and sunny! The skidoo party dug out the two-metre drifts across the garage and accelerated their preparations, although the drifts on the iceslope behind still proved impassable. The two weeks' bad weather had delayed their planned one week initial depot-laying trip, so this would now be the last long journey before midwinter, going to Lister Glacier and hopefully 'Astrolabe Point', and taking two or three weeks. On 8th and 9th Peter dug a motorway up through the drifts and the skidoos fought their way up, ferrying over a tonne of gear to the skyline. They left on 10th, Kim leading our strongest mountaineering team with Ted, Spotts, JB and Peter, plus Jed looking for cine-film angles. The sun shone, and they left in great excitement, but realising this would be a very, very hard journey, as winter conditions deepened.

After waving them a last farewell as they crossed the skyline, the six of us left behind were fully occupied with general work, as well as sciences. Francois in particular worked tirelessly mending tents in the garage, as well as the seals work which he liked best. He was visibly growing in maturity and self-confidence as his English improved (now laced with Service slang). On 12th, like a schoolboy on holiday, Howard went to 'Cairn Point' for five days with Jim and Mike for geology. Nick, Francois and I went with them carrying rations (and Howard's homework — physiology), then we returned to Metchnikoff Point.

In this spell of glorious weather I spent afternoons on the butte photographing the Snow Petrels which had joined the Cape Pigeons about the cliffs. Pairs of these lovely white birds sailed around in close company, played in the updraughts, and flew out together on circuits over the glacier. They were clearly pair-forming, courting at likely nest-sites, and sometimes sitting in the snow. Their harsher creaking calls mingled with the Cape Pigeons' titters on the cliffs. The Snow Petrels also called in flight, pairs hovering together with heads extended and black legs lowered — the legs a display signal rather than preparation to land. They seemed to enjoy their mastery of the air, and their flight was more varied and flexible than most medium-sized petrels. Parties of 5-20 coasted past, often diverting to overfly us curiously, and a few now foraged around the skerries, sometimes gathering to feed with the Cape Pigeons.

Apart from snow on 11th the superb weather continued from 6th to 20th. This was what is often called 'Peninsula weather' with a big high (reaching 1018 mB) pinned against the Peninsula giving us crisp sunshine and cold breezes. Perhaps the stable polar high was already extending north, as it tends to do in winter. The Cape Pigeons largely forsook their cliff colonies by day, but at dusk they flew in, not in the

The Skidoo Party leaves basecamp: JB fully geared. (Chris Furse)

flickering flocks of summer, but quietly and singly from foraging at sea, silhouetted against the gorgeously rich orange and red sunset skies north of Anvers. Pairs greeted each other at snow-covered nest-sites as the cobalt eastern sky darkened, making the glaciers appear an almost luminous white. In the middle of the month a glorious full moon sailed up over the moraine to cast sharp shadows on the snowy campsite, where our dome tents glowed green with the tilley lamps inside. Turning off the warm hiss of the lamp, we could hear a few Cape Pigeons chittering quietly at their roosts.

Snow Petrel, legs lowered in display. (Chris Furse)

Most Antarctic bases are sited on bays giving sheltered anchorages for supply ships. Here at Metchnikoff Point we were on a headland jutting out into the sea — a classic site for observing migration, or feeding movements of seabirds in and out of Dallman Bay. This was good weather for migrants to depart, however some species which I had expected to leave still lingered on. The skuas had dwindled to none at the end of April, though I saw odd stragglers until mid-May. There were fewer Sheathbills at Metchnikoff Point now: about 17 scavenged around the shorelines (from a summer population of about 40), but food was scarce and on 17th Francois found one frozen on the beach, apparently starved to death. However twos and threes were now present on other points where none had been in summer, so possibly the Metchnikoff Point population had simply dispersed, and at the end of May, 16 were still gathered to roost on the east beach. We saw parties of Antarctic Terns coasting and feeding almost every day; some of the adults were almost back in summer plumage and couples often performed pair flights as they passed over the colony sites at Metchnikoff and 'Cairn' Points. Their calls over our wintry tents sounded out of place, so evocative of summer holiday beaches.

Adult and juvenile Kelp Gulls were still present, and one (second-year?) bird, was the first subadult seen here. In April and early May fresh limpet shells were scattered on the new snow covering the colonies at Metchnikoff Point, and at feeding areas at other points. I collected samples of these shells in mid-May: most were in the size range 9-15 mm, with reducing numbers in two distinct ranges of larger sizes up to 50 mm (either three year-classes, or juveniles, adults and post-adults). By the middle of May the limpets had migrated down to avoid ice-scour: there were none between the tidemarks, and the Kelp Gulls foraged offshore much more.

Icebergs were increasing again, with tabulars offshore drifting up from the south-west. Among the grounded bergs in Dallman Bay was one staggeringly beautiful one — a castle with two towering keeps above complex ravelins and battlements. It seemed to dwarf the low white shapes of the Melchior Islands where an old Argentine base was now abandoned. Of all the wonders here, I think I love the icebergs best, for their purity and serenity, their ethereal power and unknown impersonal journeying. The contrasting slabs of colour on the big tabulars sharpen sunlight and shadow; the cavernous arches washed out of grounded tabulars glimmer with entrancing blues and greens; the marvellous variety of old eroded bergs never ceases to amaze; then, as they finally diminish, the sea washes out lagoons of limpid blue, where seals sometimes laze.

Sea temperatures were now below −1°C. Frazil-ice began to form like grease on the surface of small coves. Beach cobbles remained coated with ice as the tide covered them. Ice banded the rocks and skerries with white, alternating with bare rock at and above high tide, and tantalising me with visions of chocolate cake and layers of cream. Nick had mapped the cobble beach, measuring levels down six transects, and he would repeat these transects monthly to determine the effects of ice. Brash-ice from the last storms now remained frozen into the storm-beach level above high tide. Large bergy bits and growlers appeared offshore among the necklaces of brash-ice and on 15th the first fleet of little icefloes sailed in among our skerries, followed by some small icebergs and the first Crabeater Seal of the winter.

Flat rock platforms just below low-tide level stretched a kilometre out into Guyou Bay from the three little points south of Metchnikoff Point. Similar intertidal platforms are a feature of the South Shetlands, with old ones inland marking periods when the relative sea-level was higher. We planned to record movements of boulders and abrasive gravel upon the landward end of these platforms over the year, with particular reference to the effects of sea-ice. This information would help Jim Hansom at Sheffield University to estimate the rate at which such platforms are cut, and so to estimate the lengths of earlier sea level 'still-stands' in the South Shetlands. On 15th, Francois, Nick and I walked round to the next point to start these measurements.

Behind the beach there I found a boulder of lovely banded gneiss. We had found no outcrops on Brabant, though gneiss occurs on the Peninsula. Perhaps this was evidence for the mainland icecap extending across Brabant, with a glacier flowing north-west in Dallman Bay? We had been asked to look for striations or moraines that might indicate that, but this boulder could have been transported by an iceberg.

Coming back we crossed the debris of a slab avalanche which had swept the route the day before. A sunlit band above us marked the break-line, where the lee-slope drift had parted. Blocks of snow, many over a metre thick, littered the slope of summer ice down to the ice-cliffs. Surprisingly I had seen very few slab avalanches on the island before, only falls of seracs and hanging glaciers, and small powder-snow slides. Slab avalanches are the most dangerous because most difficult to predict, and they can occur on any slope from 15 to 70 degrees, though commonest on 25- to 50-degree slopes. Our protection was prudence, digging snowpits to check the layering on every risky slope we had to cross, and remembering recent weather. This one had fallen nine days after the last heavy snowfall and high winds: evidently in these cold winter temperatures we would have to beware of fresh snow avalanches for much longer than the standard no-go period of 48 hours after falls over 40 cm deep. Perhaps we had been lulled into carelessness, and I worried a bit about the skidoo party. We each carried a little Pieps II transceiver with a range of 50 metres, switched to transmit: if some of a party were caught and buried, the others would switch their Pieps to receive, and start searching. However some of these were already defective.

On 15th over 70 Blue-eyed Shags had arrived to roost on one of the stacks, giving the Sheathbills another scavenging site. Individual Shags still fished in small bays, but the flock fed further offshore, apparently on the reefs off Cape Roux. At first their movements to and from the roost appeared to be tidal, but they soon settled into a diurnal routine, leaving just before sunrise, and returning to roost in the half-hour after sunset. During the last week of May the roost built up, with counts of 1,255 to 1,662 returning from Cape Roux at sunset. Big birds flying in formation are always impressive, and the straggling lines of 10-80 shags flying low through the skerries fighting a westerly gale, with the swell crashing up around them from the ice-crusted rocks into the dour sky, reminded me emotively of Brent Geese flying low over stormy surf in a northern winter.

Two days later we went over to 'Cairn Point' and I swapped with Howard, who went back from his camping holiday to base camp with Nick and Francois, all three laden with rock specimens. Mike, Jim and I went over to the eastern half of the point, cramponning up a loosely frozen scree slope. Mike triggered a two-tonne rock avalanche rumbling off down the access gully on to the beach, and Jim felt his honeymoon was getting quite adventurous, having fallen head-deep into his first crevasse a few days before. We found complex faulting of the granites underlying the confused basalts and conglomerates, then went back to Metchnikoff Point on 19th with another load of rock specimens, planning to return later for a week's detailed geological mapping.

On 21st the good weather broke. For three days snow and strong easterly winds piled drifts over the camp, and the rest of the month was unsettled, with snowfalls, and days with clear skies but pillars of spindrift smoking off the ridges in big westerly winds. We kept putting off the second week at 'Cairn Point', but got over twice to the intermediate bluff, where Mike was surprised to find the lavas were andesite, not basalts as at Metchnikoff and 'Cairn' Points. (Andesite wells up to the surface of continental crust further inland, from the same basaltic oceanic plate, after it has been subducted deeper.) Then Mike's ankle turned bad again.

Since mid-April, Francois' counts of Weddell Seals at Metchnikoff Point had fluctuated daily between 8 and 40. Plotting all our counts we found more consistent numbers (between 22 and 54) during the post-breeding moult in January and early February. Totals had dropped to 5-15 in late February then rose to 16-30 through March, when immatures tend to come ashore more often. Now something seemed to be stirring the dozey Weddells. They normally mate in December and January with delayed implantation of the blastocyst, and one female at 'Cairn Point' bleeding from her vulva may well have completed her oestral cycle after a failed conception. On 20th I watched two playing under brash-ice close under the rocks, rolling around like yin and yang, biting each others' chests and grunting under water. They continued for half an hour, the first social behaviour by Weddells that I had ever seen. Soon such rolling couples became a regular sight. They were finding it increasingly difficult to get ashore over the snow-step forming at high tide, humping them-selves painfully up over the cobbles and rocks, using their teeth as iceaxes on the step, and then shovelling the loose snow aside with side-ways sweeps of their heads. In the high Antarctic the Weddells would now be dispersing, each keeping breathing holes open in the fast ice by constant gnawing with their specially adapted forward-pointing teeth. Perhaps our Weddells playing were feeling the urge to defend their own breathing hole — their own fishing territory. From mid-May the counts stabilised at 20-30 possibly due to territorial behaviour.

Howard used an infra-red sensing 'gun' to measure surface tempera-tures. With an air temperature of $-2°C$ Weddells' skin surfaces were $+4$ to $+5°C$, compared with Fur Seals' $+1$ to $+2°C$ and Gentoo Penguins' 0 to $+1°C$. This shows high heat loss, but the Weddells' blubber would be better than the others under water. The 50-odd Fur Seals left at the beginning of May gradually dwindled to about ten at the end of the month. The evening roost of Gentoo Penguins also diminished, but two or three hung on into June, by when the last Chinstrap stragglers had left. Surprisingly, up to six Elephant Seals continued to come ashore, most of them youngsters under four years old.

On the afternoon of 29th we were working around the stores dump, when there was a shout from the col. Peter appeared on skis, followed by Kim and Ted. We all shook hands; it seemed appropriate after nearly three weeks apart. They had quite a story to tell.

Above 'First Cache' Kim watches another skidoo start the traverse toward 'Claire's Finger' towing a sledge. (Jed Corbett)

They had left in sunshine on 10 May with Spotts, JB, Jed and the three skidoos. In two days they ferried the two big steel ex-Transglobe sledges, two pulks, 317 man-days rations, 29 jerrycans of petrol and paraffin, and about 400 kg of general equipment round to 'Claire's Finger'. Once Spott's skidoo (in the middle) was rolled two and a half complete turns — fortunately he was not tied on to anything and leapt clear.

They snowholed below 'Claire's Finger' for four nights while Kim, Spotts and Peter ferried gear to 'Roentgen Ridge', marking the cache with an upended sledge. The loaded sledges went well along the flat, but going up the 400-metre slope from the piedmont to the ridge, the skidoos had to ferry the loads, and then haul each unloaded sledge up with all three machines. The weather was worse than at base camp and once a katabatic gust blew over a parked skidoo.

After a day's hold-up, drying out an iced-up magneto, the whole party crossed the ridge, and camped halfway down the steep 600-metre descent to Lister Glacier. They cautiously made their way on down next

Ted, JB and Kim spend six days in an igloo below 'Noddies Hat', on short rations. (Jed Corbett)

day in bitter cold (night temperatures were down below −21°C). Filming the descent, Jed got both feet frostbitten and thawed them out on Kim's stomach that evening. As the only inexperienced mountaineer in the party Jed was being stretched, and Kim decided to spend a day at the cache on Lister Glacier. Jed recuperated, and Ted repaired the two ex-Transglobe skidoos, which had been losing power with leaking cylinder-head joints. This sort of skidooing was very hard work and slow in the deep snow and mountainous terrain; it was also impossible to always rope up for complete safety. However in one week they had proved the value of skidoos, cacheing over 200 man-days of stores well beyond the limit of our pulk journey in April. At night the glorious scenery around Bouquet Bay was luminous white, lit by the full moon over the Peninsula.

On 18th they set off for 'Astrolabe Point' with the three skidoos and 7 days' rations on one sledge, but were stopped by whiteout at 700 metres near 'Noddies Col'. There they were held for six days by typical Lister Glacier cloud and bad weather, apart from one day when they skied up to the ridge to mark the best skidoo route. Kim built one three-man igloo the first day, and later a second. Heavy snowfalls covered both igloos, and made skidoo travel impossible. After being on two-thirds rations for several days, food was getting short, so on 24th they marked the skidoos with bamboo wands and set off on skis, heading for Metchnikoff Point by the direct route over 'Noddies Col'.

Ten minutes after they left camp, a cornice fell from 'Noddies Hat'. There was a heart-stopping crack, and the whole half-kilometre-long side

The Skidoo Party break camp the day after the sledge fall. The 'tent' is actually a jury rig porch over a snowgrave. (Jed Corbett)

of the mountain avalanched toward them. The two roped groups started skiing clear, but Jed fell, and he, Spotts and Peter watched helplessly while the snowblocks swept past only 30 metres away, the debris ending up even closer than that to the skidoos and igloos. The route over 'Pinnacles Spur' was clearly unsafe, so they turned to ski the long way back. They arrived that evening at their Lister Glacier cache, backs aching from their 30-kg packs, exhausted from ploughing through deep soft snow.

A blow then consolidated the powder snow, allowing them to recover the skidoos. It took three days, camped at the cache, with skidoos and sledges scattered over Lister Glacier, bogged down in drifts, and hidden in recurrent cloud. Snowfalls continued and a blizzard hit them one night. At 3 a.m. Ted and JB woke as their Phortress ridge tent collapsed and filled with snow, burying JB's boots and breaking a pole. Ted managed to squeeze out through the tiny space at one end into the howling night. Digging furiously, they replaced the pole and covered the tear, and gradually got some order into the chaos of snowed-over gear inside. By 7 a.m. they were thawing out in sodden sleeping bags. Then, as the wind eased, they heard Spotts waking the four in the Vango tent, two hours before sunrise, as he always did.

On 28 May the whole party made a remarkable journey of 15 difficult kilometres, over 'Roentgen Ridge', climbing and descending 600 metres in dense cloud, navigating between the bamboo wands they had planted two weeks before. Half an hour after sunset they were approaching 'Claire's Finger' in falling snow. Spott's and JB's skidoos were in line ahead towing the sledge (loaded with two full pulks, etc.), and Jed was driving the brake skidoo, while Kim, Ted and Peter were ski-joring [being towed on skis] behind Jed, roped together ready to recce the route ahead. Without warning the sledge fell out of sight. The two lead skidoos stopped dead, but held the weight. The sledge was hanging a couple of metres down into a wall-sided crevasse. As they stopped the engines, they could hear the groans and rumbles of ice in motion all around them in the gloom. This was the moment when Kim's leadership and each individual's experience bore fruit. Within 20 minutes they had driven in two dead-giant belays, eased back on the tow-ropes so that the belays took the weight, and driven the skidoos clear of the minefield. It was cold and dark, they were tired, and two of their tents were down the crevasse. Kim and Peter set off into the night looking for their old snow-holes below 'Claire's Finger', but in vain. They found their way back to the others at the skidoos, and all set to work erecting the Conquest Snowline box tent and digging two snowgrave bivouacs down into the glacier. Finally at 9 p.m., 5 hours after sunset, they were all safely inside their shelters, tired, cold and soaking wet, but safe, and brewing up before supper.

Next morning they woke like frozen carcasses. Emerging from their silent snowgraves they found it blowing hard and snowing, but prepared to move, leaving the sledge for recovery later. The wind eased and they traversed round in whiteout. Ted had to make a one-hour track repair, then they raced down to Metchnikoff Point, with Kim, Ted and Peter each ski-joring behind one skidoo.

Chris and Spotts enjoying basecamp luxury (the Tilly lamp). (Jed Corbett)

We had erected the four Pyramid tents on the drifts covering the camp flat, and new tent pairs quickly settled in. Spotts moved in with me in a Nova. After many brews and much talk, he made a rum punch. Then we all celebrated in the hut, and many tales were told.

The winds blew and it snowed for the last two days of the month. We did another fluid-balance day for Howard, and after hand-centrifuging blood all next day he emerged from the hut with muted cries of 'Eureka'. Five of us had reversed our dehydration, with blood PCVs down to normal values, the first-ever scientific evidence of physiological acclimatisation by Caucasians to central cold stimulus, but six PCVs were still rising, and Nick's had hardly varied. Mean temperature in May had been −4°C at sea-level, and June would be colder.

June

Midday in midwinter — looking north from the beach below basecamp. (Jed Corbett)

Our first priority was to recover the sledge load — particularly the three pairs of skis, without which travel was impractical.

The clouds cleared on 2nd and next day Kim, Spotts, Peter and Mike took 2 skidoos over to 'Claire's Finger', while Francois, Jim and I followed with a pulk. Arriving shortly before sunset Francois and I pitched the tent, but thick cloud held us all in camp next day, so we spent three hours leisurely digging a snowhole in the big drift.

It was a standard two-man snowhole, in plan view shaped like a young mushroom with the entrance tunnel along the stalk. Our sleeping benches stretched along each side of the mushroom head, with space for the stove between us in the crown. First we dug a narrow head-high tunnel into the steep side of the drift, then Francois dug out the sleeping benches from waist-height up, domed to a comfortable height, while I shovelled the debris out and started cutting snowblocks from a quarry outside. When he was nearly finished we put our packs inside, before I walled up the outer end of the tunnel to make a low doorway, with the lintel block just below the sleeping bench to keep the warm air in.

Inside was complete peace, utter silence. We could not hear the wind, only see the spindrift wisping in, to coat our rucksacks in the doorway. The sense of total security was beautiful after the flapping tent. One candle lit the whole cave with soft yellow light. We dug alcoves in the walls as shelves, and stuck iceaxes over the stove to dry gloves, while knives, spoons and toothbrushes were stuck handily into the walls. We got straight into our sleeping bags — Karrimats and Goretex bivvi-bags have made snowholing comfortable, but it is still colder than a tent. Cooking supper was easier than a tent — just scrape snow from the sides, and throw the gash into the cold pit of the entrance. Here in this limitless drift of dry, well-packed fresh snow we could fashion a convenient home — a far cry from cramped snowholes dug as emergency bivouacs in wet Scottish snow.

We emerged next morning to another day of wind and whiteout. Francois mended the tent, then struck it; I extended our tunnel with snowblocks, as the drift had overwhelmed the entrance. Next day was the same miserable weather, but Kim and JB skied out, found the sledge crevasse and marked it. The rest of us skied up to 'Claire's Finger', a 20-metre rock spire, which Mike found was granite, much altered as if by the pressure of a major fault.

The weather continued too bad to recover the sledge. First Francois, Jim and I skied back to Metchnikoff Point, after four nights holed up, then the others followed with the skidoos, reaching base on 9th.

Base camp was heavily drifted, and all four Antarctic Pyramids had been re-pitched on the deep snow. I spent two luxurious nights in one with Peter: he had dug a central trench between the two sleeping benches, and built a kitchen range and larder using biscuit tins and packing cases. It was like a cosy railway carriage: we could sit like passengers and entertain visitors, or recline along the sleeping benches, propped up by our bags against the end walls of the tent. When the skidoo party returned, Spotts and I dug out our Nova tent from its two-metre deep windscoop and repitched it further along the drift.

It was my birthday on the 10th. We gathered in the hut after supper for a special two-bottle meeting, with whisky spliced into real coffee. Francois gave me a beautifully bleached Chinstrap skull, the black sheath of the upper mandible sliding on and off like a pen-top. I had cards from Faye, and from the whole team. I managed the 49 candles (planted in a

Ted and JB in a snowhole at the 'Claire's Finger' cache. (Jed Corbett)

bucket of snow) in one blow. Then Ted and Spotts started singing and we went on until 3 a.m. while JB plied us with coffee and more whisky. A big moon shone as we went back to our tents in crisp calm; it was −11°C.

Now another glorious spell of calm clear Peninsula weather began, but the cold kept the snow powdery, frustrating Spotts every morning as he tried to get the skidoos up the slope behind. The sun now rose at 10.45 a.m., north of Hoseason Island, slid along the northern horizon, and at 3.30 p.m. set behind 'Easter Island' just offshore. Often the low bank of cloud offshore shadowed us, although above us was Brabant's private pool of clear sky. Despite an hour's cold twilight each end, the days were now so short that much of our time was taken up with simple domestic logistics. It took me a day to dig out six folded Triwall packing cases, and another two days making them into two kennels for skidoo parks. Ted was carefully improvising the repair of a track sprocket shaft on one of the old skidoos — building up the shaft journal with Araldite, machining it on a homemade lathe, fitting it to the bearing, and reinforcing the damaged bearing housing. The garage was totally buried by snow: Ted strengthened the ski rafters of the roof, and Peter spent eight days making the biggest igloo in the world as a porch above the garage door, using 70 cm thick snowblocks quarried by Mike and others. Kim led preparations for Mid-winters Day, and scattered about in secret places everyone was making a present for the team member they had drawn out of Kim's hat. There was a definite feeling of base-camp inertia about. We discovered the Breadmix: the dough rose beautifully when fried — our first taste of bread for months.

On most days I found time to visit the beach and keep an eye on the birds. Two lonely Gentoos lingered until 16th and a last (lost?) Chinstrap stayed symbolically until Mid-winters Day. Otherwise it seemed that the winter populations had settled down into regular routines. More species remained to keep us company than I had expected.

Kelp Gulls constantly flew to and fro along the coast and could sometimes be seen offshore and, in the middle of June an evening flock of about 80 tended to gather — roughly corresponding to all the breeding adults and juveniles from Metchnikoff Point. Then on 19th a mass of nearly 400 appeared from nowhere to feed greedily in the shallows below the ice-cliffs; about half were juveniles, and there were also a few older sub-adults. Later that day the flock rested on the sunlit glacier, while others wheeled in a soaring gyre above the bay. Next day the big flock had gone, and the evening flock did not reassemble. It could have been a pre-migration flock, but I hoped it was merely local populations concentrating (together with Terns, Cape Pigeons and Crabeater Seals) to exploit a wreck of plankton blown in by two days of big westerlies.

Most of the Shags left the roosting stacks in the gloom before sunrise. They returned at varying times in the hour after sunset, but not in the big battalions of late May — the highest count was 522. I could not distinguish any brown juveniles, but it was difficult to see them at all in the half-dark. The Sheathbills stayed around Metchnikoff Point, and dispersed at nearby points, scavenging disconsolately on the Shag roosts and round the beaches, where sometimes there were as many Sheathbills as seals. Weddells in twos were now regularly circling in their ponderous underwater dance; perhaps this behaviour was a means of keeping breathing holes open? Surprisingly a few Fur Seals remained, and Elephant Seals came ashore twice.

At the beginning of June a roost of Antarctic Terns gathered at Metchnikoff Point. At sunset small parties arrived from foraging in lee-shore bays, or among the skerries and necklaces of brash-ice. Flocks of 30-70 flew to and fro in the dusk, and gathered in a fluttering swarm over one or other exposed moraine slope. Some pairs sailed over the colony site in slow-beating noisy display flights, often with one carrying a small fish. Sometimes pairs landed near known nest-sites, and territorial rivalry was seen. There were no juveniles now, and 80% of the adults were again black-capped and grey-bodied, in summer plumage except for their darker, duller red beaks, white chins and shorter tail-streamers. Long after dark we could hear Terns calling in flight over the tents, and it was difficult to estimate total numbers roosting. Big winds on 17th and 18th bared the moraines again, and when new snow then fell the pink and ochre droppings and tiny footprints suggested over 150 Terns roosting, tallying with the largest evening count, and far exceeding the local breeding population.

A few Giant Petrels sailed past the point and some roosted on the snow overnight; lines of their giant footprints (as wide as my mountain boots and half as long) marked their ungainly take-offs. They were the only large petrels still around, for I had seen no albatrosses since mid-April.

The Snow Petrels continued to soar around the butte, with sometimes a few Cape Pigeons. Both species foraged around the skerries, and numbers coasted in and out of Dallman Bay, passing both round the point and over the col so that they were difficult to count. The evening roost of Cape Pigeons reduced, and the only Snow Petrels roosting locally seemed to be the few resident pairs.

Spotts fitted metal toe and heel pieces to Mike's leather Dolomite boots, so that he could ski without wrecking his ankle yet again in the plastic Vallugas. On 17th the three of us skied halfway to Cairn Point to look at the shoreline granite. A big westward movement of petrels and

Terns was concentrated over the foot of the snowslope there, and a ten-minute count gave hourly rates of 744 Cape Pigeons and 456 Snow Petrels. The sun broke through as I watched. As the Snow Petrels swept along, less than a metre above the snow, their sharp blue shadows raced below them.

Several Antarctic Fulmars also passed west; apart from occasional individuals these were the first I had seen since mid-April. All were now in winter plumage, with grey on their faces, darker brown upperparts, and grey smudges on their bellies. In April 1971 I had seen flocks moulting in the Magellan Straits: perhaps unlike Cape Pigeons they go north to moult in temperate waters at the end of the breeding season, and then return to winter. Since they feed further offshore than the Cape Pigeons we would not expect to see many, except in movements like this.

This movement of petrels included greater excitement. There were several petrels the same size as the Cape Pigeons but immediately distinct by their bolder flight, more-angled wings, and blocks of white and chocolate markings — Antarctic Petrels. They breed in the High Antarctic (up to 400 km inland in the Theron Mountains) and their only known colony on the Peninsula is somewhere south of Brabant Island. We had seen them flying around Gibbs Island in summer 1977, but these were the first seen at Brabant. They winter in the pack-ice, and more in the days following raised our hopes for pack soon, to help us explore the offshore islets. The sea temperature was now almost freezing (about −1.7°C); several small bergs had grounded in the skerries, and brash-ice gathered thickly offshore, breaking the low sun's orange track into splashes of flame on the pale blue patches of open water. However it was in vain that I searched the horizon daily for iceblink, the white reflection of ice on the undersides of clouds.

Three days later there were other promising visitors to Metchnikoff Point — two skuas, and some whales close inshore. The brief glimpses suggested they were Killer Whales, the first we had seen, although we had been told they frequented bays in Gerlache Strait during the summer.

Crabeater Seal on the beach, with Weddell beyond. (Howard Oakley)

I also saw two Crabeater Seals feeding in the bay, wallowing near the surface and poking their nostrils up to breathe like snorkels, then diving lazily where a cloud of Terns, Gulls and petrels were busily feeding. One bore a pair of great circumferential scars on its back: Crabeaters frequently have such scars, previously believed to be from Killer Whales, but now attributed to Leopard Seals, which prey on the youngsters. Crabbies are the typical seal of the pack-ice, living scattered wherever there are open leads: unlike the land-based territorial Weddell, Elephant and Fur Seals they form pairs during the breeding season. Based on aerial strip-surveys of small percentages of the pack, estimates of their world population have varied from 13 to 50 (and now 30) million: they are far and away the most numerous seal in the world, outnumbering the populations of all other species combined. They are known to feed mainly on krill, expelling gulps of water through their interlocking crenellated teeth, which sieve the krill like the whalebone of baleen whales. However, numerical data on their food is lacking, because in summer they need little food and, like other seals, their digestion is very rapid. Nearing the breeding season they need more food, so we had been tasked to collect five stomachs a month until good food samples were obtained, and then to increase the sampling. Crabbies now began to visit more often, and Francois shot our first: its stomach was empty, but Howard dissected the gut for parasites for Hull and Oslo Universities. We were sad to kill these neat little fawn-coloured seals, but found they yielded over 40 kg of red, tender meat that fried like prime fillet steak. Giant Petrels, Kelp Gulls and Sheathbills gathered around the carcass, and after a week Francois was able to clean the skull and skeleton for the Royal Scottish Museum.

Mid-winters Day, 21 June, dawned gloriously calm and sunny. Howard went swimming among the brash-ice in the cove. Wearing an orange Multifab drysuit, he stayed in for 20 minutes, saying he felt comfortable, but looking apprehensive. Jed filmed him playing with the Weddell Seals, until one objected fiercely and chased Howard out. Through the afternoon we all enjoyed Kim's Winter Olympiad — knockout shovel races and snowball fights, then an obstacle race in tent-pairs. Howard beamed receiving the winner's gold compo-tin lid; Mike was second, and Jim third. We spent the evening in the hut overeating for seven hours — a seven-course dinner (soup, Kaviar, pilchard-and-cornflake cakes, tinned chicken, Crabeater steak, rummy fruit duff, and trifle). Sods Opera acts, forfeits, Howard's Brabant Island ballad, and Spott's punches drowned our slight disappointment at being omitted from the Falklands Mid-winter broadcast to Antarctic bases.

For me the best part of the evening was opening the presents we had made for each other. The parcels disclosed some marvellous ingenuity and craftsmanship. Among various sewn items and driftwood carvings three stood out: JB gave Mike a schooner sailing a blue sea in a whisky bottle; Peter gave Nick a sheathknife, beautifully fashioned from a broken hacksaw blade with a polished driftwood sheath, bound with soldered and burnished bands of copper wire; Ted gave Kim an engraved tankard cut from a Pusser's Rum bottle, encased in stitched leather with a Karabiner handle. Gradually people slipped away to their tents, the last four at 7 a.m. — four hours before the first earlier sunrise.

While most of us recovered from the feast, Spotts and Peter worked two skidoos up to the skyline, and ferried food and fuel to 'First Cache'. Clear calm weather continued. On 24th, JB, Jed, Jim, Nick and I took two pulks away, taking two days to reach the cache below 'Claire's Finger', where Peter and Mike caught us up on skis. JB was now a Leader, as his skiing had improved and another superb clear day allowed him to lead the first ascent of the ridge above 'Claire's Finger'. While collecting rock samples halfway up, Jed, Mike and I watched the other four climb up into gold and blue sunshine. The low midday sun also lit the coast, but half-way up we were shadowed by the thin band of cloud far out at sea. Kim and Ted arrived with the skidoos and put a route up 'Claire's Finger' which they graded Severe, climbing the glazed granite in crampons. (Our rigid Footfang crampons were simple to put on, and stood up to all sorts of rough useage like this — we all vowed never to go back to old-fashioned jointed ironmongery and frozen straps.)

At sunset the colours of the spectrum glinted in high western clouds, first in horizontal bands and then bands radiating toward us from the clouded sun. They were 'nacreous clouds'; probably 15 km high, above normal clouds, the mother of pearl effect caused by refraction in fine ice crystals. They are a rare phenomenon, but we saw them several times through the winter.

The seven of us were now ready to recover the sledge. First we spent a day holed up in bitter spindrift, but two perfect days followed. On 28th Kim and JB climbed down into the crevasse: the old bridge had fallen and the sledge was now vertical, and totally buried except for the front towbar held by a dead giant. A new bridge had formed and they dug in the cave below it, while Ted and Peter belayed and heaved from the lip above. Exactly a month after the accident we got the first pulk out, and next day they recovered the second pulk and the 120 kg sledge using our little Tirfor winch. The need to recover the sledge-load had dominated June: it was an exhilarating relief to be free of it. Jed filmed the quiet teamwork of the climbers during the two-day recovery, but a planned crevasse rescue sequence next day was abandoned in a gale of spindrift, after Jed had himself joined the (involuntary) Head-Under Club in the same crevasse.

The clear nights at the cache were bitterly cold. Nick and I ate, read, wrote and played chess or scrabble until midnight. Each morning I woke cold around 6 a.m., then dozed fitfully, moving about trying to get warm. While dozing I dreamt. Most of us were finding that we remembered our dreams more often than at home. Mine had usually been prosaic, of real and imaginery people back in Britain, but now I enjoyed a series of erotic dreams, triggered by I knew not what. Frozen though I was, I looked forward to those three hours before Nick shook me at 9 a.m! Lighting the candle to start cooking breakfast, ice crystals on the tent walls glittered like stars in a dim planetarium, the water melted the night before had frozen to form a skirted piston in the pot. By sunrise, at 10.45 a.m., we were ready to emerge.

The last day of June started with a starry dawn, but at midday spindrift began to rush down the ridges, and driven snow was silhouetted grey-blue against the fading promise of clear skies above. Kim and Ted just managed to get the skidoos up the slope behind the cache, capsizing several times in the soft and deepening snow. Then they set off for Metchnikoff Point, while the five of us settled in for a night of heavy snow, to round off a month of mostly fine clear weather. The mean temperature in June had been −4.4°C. July and August would be increasingly cold, and possibly also September.

July

Pyramid tents in basecamp, looking east to Cape Roux.
(Jed Corbett)

Digging for stores boxes: the food cache is buried behind the digger, so is the hut porch. (Jed Corbett)

We woke on 1st to find the tent completely drifted over. To light the stove I had to push an airhole up through feathery snow above the door. It was too deep to pull the pulks, so we cached them after striking camp, and skied back to Metchnikoff Point, arriving at dusk. 80 cm of snow had fallen there overnight, with a gale that we had scarcely noticed, buried in our snowdrift.

Next day in glorious sunlit calm I walked out to the west end, watching birds, dawdling, and thinking. This was my expedition's midpoint, a time to take stock.

First and foremost, I was delighted with my team. The self-starters were all pushing along with preparations for our move in September, and both Jim (on 'met' and radio) and Francois (on tent repairs) now filled real niches in the team. People were enjoying the mixture of scientific projects and mountain adventure. I had always expected July and August to be frustrating months, bringing a nadir of our spirits, but we started July strong and busy. Our health was good, and the only serious threat to progress was Mike's feet: the plastic Vallugas had brutally injured his ankle, and in his modified leather Dolomites his toes had been bruised and mildly frostbitten returning from 'Claire's Finger'.

Snow was inexorably accumulating, but winds kept some moraine screes exposed, and orange crustose lichens splashed the northern sides of rocks on the butte. Temperatures had dropped noticeably since Midwinter's Day, but only my hands and feet were often cold, and the promise of lengthening days was a constant encouragement. Swathes of ice offshore now littered the flaming reflections of sunset. The intertidal rocks were thickly iced, and sea temperature nearly −2°C, but the bays were still not frozen over. Nor was there any sign of big pack-ice floes, though Faraday had been firmly packed in for three weeks. The arrival of the pack, bringing colder winds, would be the only further major change as winter deepened.

More bird species remained than I had expected, probably because our exposed headland was on the fringe of pelagic ranges, and also offered open water for the inshore feeders. As I stood ruminating at the far point, great flocks of several hundred Blue-eyed Shags flew low overhead in straggling skeins, and next day they fished a reef near the grounded iceberg, in a busy rolling carpet, attended by several Kelp Gulls. The Kelps were now thinly scattered and mobile, sometimes disappearing for a day or two but then reappearing, with adults and juveniles in roughly equal numbers approximating to the total summer population. The local Sheathbills were also more mobile, scavenging the shores but seldom visiting our camp at 50 metres; 23 around the second Crabeater carcass indicated stable numbers. Giant Petrels regularly patrolled inshore, and for a week up to two dozen had gorged themselves on the Crabeater until they could scarcely lumber into flight, roosting on the snow near their dinner. The Antarctic Terns continued to gather in from offshore at dusk, changing their actual roost sites in the fickle manner of their family. They expended much energy flying to and fro along the shore calling: perhaps collecting small returning parties had survival value. Snow Petrels still flighted around the butte; others coasted past, and increasing numbers foraged around the skerries among the necklaces of ice. Occasional Antarctic Fulmars coasting after a blow suggested that more were still feeding offshore. Probably some Cape Pigeons were also feeding pelagically out in the Bellingshausen Sea, but most range northward into subtropical waters, and only a few now returned quietly to roost. Far off in the North Atlantic the little Wilson's Storm Petrels would now be starting to move southward again — God speed their four-month journey!

When the pack arrived I expected the Fur Seals to depart, but it should bring other species — Crabeater Seals, Adelie Penguins, Antarctic Petrels and the first Leopard Seals. We hoped just possibly to see a few Ross Seals and Emperor Penguins, pack-ice specialists at the limits of their ranges.

Logistics for the move south, and preparing gear, were now our top priorities. We planned to take the skidoos round by Lister Glacier, hauling scientific stores and a dwindling pyramid of fuel and food to the 1000-metre plateau below Harvey Heights. Then, after collecting more fuel and food from 'Astrolabe Point', and delivering some stores, the skidoos would be worked up over Harvey Heights and down to 'Dayglo Point' in October. Our first estimates suggested we would reach the 1000-metre plateau with less than 20 jerrycans of gasolene, so I reduced everyone's initial bids for load space; Howard's physiology gear and Jed's photographic kit were the largest loads, and most heavily pruned. We discussed various compromises, revolving mostly around the time people spent at 'Astrolabe Point', constrained by our stocks of food at Metchnikoff, 'Astrolabe' and the other caches, and totally dependent on the weather and snow conditions. I aimed to keep a steady pressure on our environment, with flexible plans.

I had naively expected fields of large icefloes to drift up from the Bellingshausen Sea. Instead, scattered sea-ice accumulated almost unnoticed. By the 6th, after a week of lovely, clear, still, cold weather, bergy bits were scattered offshore as far as the eye could see, and mushy strings of pancake-ice had drifted into many of the bays.

Mike, Spotts and I skied over to 'Cairn Point' to start a week's detailed geological survey. For two days the sun shone, but the west wind was bitter cold so we worked along the coast, ploughing through thigh-deep soft snow from outcrop to outcrop, looking up from shelter at spindrift pouring over the clifftops. Fresh grey-brown pancake-ice filled the bays; the turquoise shadows of a few old icefloes gleamed in brilliant contrast.

We spoke with base by walkie-talkie each evening and parties skied over at intervals, bringing rations and returning with rock samples. On 10th Ted and Jed came over bringing Nick to do a trig survey, establishing ground control for aerial photography. Spotts returned with Ted and Jed to Metchnikoff.

All that day petrels were sailing over into the teeth of a strengthening westerly wind. At 300 an hour there were now almost as many Antarctic Petrels as Snow Petrels, with only a few Cape Pigeons, Antarctic Fulmars and Giant Petrels. The Antarctic Petrels were a joy to watch, strikingly plumaged with broad, chocolate boxer's shoulders, they whooshed past me on the point at speeds that made even the agile Snow Petrels look pedestrian.

That night the wind rose to a serious south-westerly blow, but we felt quite snug in the Nova tent, with double poles, storm guys and a protective snow-wall. Next evening over the radio we heard that gusts of 100 knots had hit the camp at Metchnikoff Point: all four Antarctic Pyramids and the Conquest Snowline had survived without snow-walls, but three other tents were blown out and wrecked. Kim and Ted tried to check the skidoos, but up by the garage the wind was even fiercer: belaying each other, they tried to crawl through the blasting waves of stinging snow but were blown over, and got back with difficulty to comparative shelter at the tents. A big moon lit the whole wild scene, and fleeting stars glimmered where the spindrift parted.

By morning the wind had backed southerly, and the sky was still clear. Unaware of the devastation at base camp, we plodded up the 'Cairn Point' ridge again. While Nick set up survey marks on top, I went with Mike to a little cliff of graded yellow conglomerates. Mike was proving a natural mountaineer, and was now a Second. I enjoyed helping him: clearly he knew his geology, working patiently and logically, unworried by cold or exposure; also he was always willing to explain and discuss what he found, so all of us felt involved and wanted to help. How hard to measure is that gift, and how invaluable because it multiplies results. Great icicles hung like curtains above us, the rough rock was plastered with grey crusts of lichen, and little buttons of moss enjoyed the sun.

After dark that evening wet heavy snow began to fall, The Falkland Islands Dependencies Survey's sledging logs from Anvers Island in the 1950s described occasional winter thaws, but this was our first since mid-April. Snow continued falling all next day, and all the following night, and all the day after. On the third night it changed to sleet and rain. We went out seldom: returning soaking wet we filled the tent with gloomy fog and a skin of white vapour poured down the inner tent walls wherever the snow-laden outer touched and cooled them. We loafed about inside the tent. The roar of avalances above us in the dark stopped us six times, silently looking at each other, wondering. Once the roar was followed by the clatter of scree just behind the tent: it was hard not to flinch, even though reason said our site was safe.

THIS MONUMENT WAS BUILT
BY FRANÇOIS DE GERLACHE AND OTHER MEMBERS
OF THE JOINT SERVICES EXPEDITION 1984-1985
TO COMMEMORATE THE FIRST LANDING ON BRABANT ISLAND
BY THE BELGIAN ANTARCTIC EXPEDITION 1897-1899
ADRIEN DE GERLACHE (BELGIUM) LEADER
ROALD AMUNDSEN (NORWAY)
HENRYK ARCTOWSKI (POLAND)
FREDERICK COOK (U.S.A.)
EMILE DANCO (BELGIUM)
CAMPED NEARBY FROM 30 JANUARY TO 6 FEBRUARY 1898

*François and Chris with
the Belgica plaque, 21 July.
(Jed Corbett)*

Filling the stove while lighting it on Friday 13th, flames suddenly flared across my Karrimat. Nick slept, while Mike and I beat out the fire. The same day they had two similar fires at base; all three fires were due to petrol in a jerrycan marked for paraffin. Luckily none were serious. By coincidence the BAS base on Bird Island, South Georgia, had a bad fire that day also. Fire is one of the feared dangers of Antarctica.

On 14th three Leopard Seals were resting on a tiny icefloe just below our tent. Their great ugly reptilian heads, disproportionately large for their tapering bodies, looked malignant and cruel. We had seen one or two daily since the sea-ice arrived the week before, but three so close together is unusual. There were still no penguins nor Crabeaters for them to prey on: diving among the pancake-ice they were probably feeding on krill, as they do surprisingly often. Four Sheathbills soon arrived from east and west to feed on the pink stains around the Leopard Seals.

That night, in bright moonlight again, a stronger storm hit us, from the north-west. Our tent nestled in its windscoop sheltered by the 70 cm of snow that had fallen, but shook furiously in the blasts and fusilades of spindrift. The noise was like sitting in a kettle drum under volleys of shotgun fire, punctuated by sudden cracks as plates of icy snow-crust hit the tent. We could not progress with geology or survey because of the

*Man's inhumanity to man:
Kim wears the dreaded
rucksack and Howard
measures humidities.
(Jed Corbett)*

avalanche risk, so next day we dug out and skied back to Metchnikoff Point, passing several fresh snow slides and one deep slab-avalanche scar. All the tents at base had weathered the storm, but Spotts and Francois had been up most of the night digging out their dome tent, and then sewing up a rent caused by a flying object. Overnight the thermometer had dropped to −31°C, the coldest yet. Windblown scraps of green terrestrial algae and particles of rock were scattered on the snow: no gravel remained exposed, only rocks, so this suggested rapid erosion of the rocks by frost and wind.

Gusty unsettled weather continued for the rest of July. Whirligigs of snow chased around the base-camp flat in the lee of the butte. Snow was first drifted deeply in one place, then torn off and drifts formed elsewhere, but the general level mounted inexorably, up to the eaves of the hut. One or two brief clear days offered unfulfilled promises, but snow conditions underfoot were very difficult: this and avalanche risk delayed our planned three-week geology journey to Cape Cockburn, and finally we postponed it until late August. We continually discussed our plans for the spring and a better strategy evolved, with six based on 'Astrolabe Point' and six going south in September, then interchanging early in December.

Logistics were repeatedly reviewed: Nick revealed that paraffin at Metchnikoff Point would run out early in September, so useage was rationed to one litre a day per tent. We were also becoming increasingly concerned about the safety of the food and fuel cached at 'Dayglo Point'; if that cache had fallen into the sea in the autumn thaws, or been buried under deep winter drifts, five weeks living on seals and penguins would restrict our movements. Meanwhile everyone was busy repairing gear, digging out stores from boxes repeatedly buried a metre deep, and preparing for our months of exploration. We were far too busy to suffer the frustration and boredom that I had feared in this mid-winter period.

The sea-ice had disappeared with the big westerly storms, but the changing winds filled first one bay then another with sluggish brash-ice, and lovely icebergs began to gather again in Dallman Bay.

Although we saw occasional Leopards, Crabeater Seals and Antarctic Petrels, we were clearly only on the fringe of the pack-ice fauna. Apart from one or two Gentoo Penguins there was rather a dull patch as far as bird life went. The Sheathbills and Shags were reduced in numbers, and the Snow Petrels temporarily vanished from the cliffs, though they were regular inshore. Occasional Cape Pigeons appeared, usually in the evening, but they did not seem to roost on Metchnikoff Point. Giant Petrels patrolled past as usual. The local Kelp Gulls stood about the brash-ice, or flew to and fro without apparent aim: only very seldom did I see them feeding (at a Crabeater carcass, attending Leopard Seals, or gathering to plunge-dive frenziedly among the skerries, together with Snow Petrels and Terns). The Antarctic Terns remained a constant joy, fishing among the loose ice in the sound, although now they roosted elsewhere. Once a flock of 60 rested head to wind on heaving brash-ice just off the granite outcrops of the colony: all were adults, only 2-3 still with the complete white foreheads of winter. Flying up in a calling mass, they suddenly splintered into pairs racing around the sound in noisy pair-flights.

Up to two dozen Fur Seals still remained. The Weddells dozed, half-covered in beds of drift-snow, but no longer performed their underwater dances. After a northerly blow an Elephant Seal appeared briefly. I was surprised to see the essentially sub-Antarctic Elephant and Fur Seals and the Gentoos remaining in winter, at the southern fringe of their summer ranges, and I began to wonder if a region of open water occurred here regularly. Satelite photographs might tell me the answer later. We were disappointed to see no more whales.

On 21st we celebrated Belgium's National Day with Francois. His father had presented a superb bronze plaque commemorating the landing on Brabant Island by the *Belgica* expedition. Above Buls Bay they had been the first expedition to sledge in Antarctica, and the first to camp in tents. Later they had overwintered in Antarctica, out in the Bellings-hausen pack, so altogether we felt many links with them. That day we formally placed the plaque on a big basalt boulder crowning the moraine above our base camp, and commanding wide outlooks southwest to Anvers Island and northwest over the Bellingshausen Sea.

After the July fluid-balance day Howard announced triumphantly that every one of us had now acclimatised. Later I again carried his chart recorder around in a rucksack for 24 hours, with nine thermistors taped to my body, and one unpleasant internal one. We each underwent this three times (in April, July and November), plus other days with 15 extra thermistors arranged through our clothing layers. The three main days were just to check that we were not spoiling the blood PCV results by contriving to keep ourselves warmer: the results confirmed that we were still receiving central cold stimulus. In fact, like the others, I was wearing little more in mid-winter than I had in summer. My basic clothes were two pairs of woollen stockings, cotton underpants, thermal longjohns and long-sleeved vest, helanca breeches (with braces to keep the waist loose), a woollen shirt, woollen sweater and a balaclava. Since autumn I had added an earband (round my neck) and woollen wristlets. I wore these basic clothes both day and night, changing pants and inner socks every three or four months, and thermal underwear and shirt less often. Outdoors I added two pairs of mittens, double boots plus snow-gaiters, and a zipped mountain jacket of Entrant. At night I slept in a single sleeping bag inside a Goretex bivouac bag, and since mid-winter I had taken to donning soft insulated bootees, wearing my inner mittens, and using a second Karrimat. When travelling I carried a sleeveless woollen pullover, a headover, second earband and spare mittens all inside my sleeping bag, plus waterproof overtrousers, goggles, more spare mittens and a Hot Mini hand-warmer in rucksack pockets, and an inner jacket rolled in a Karrimat outside my pack. I carried no dry change of clothes. Modern materials offer many great advantages — notably thermal under-wear for its dryness, Thinsulate insulation for its lightness, Holofil/superloft insulation for quick drying, Goretex/entrant for breath-able waterproof gear, plastic boots for easy unfreezing in the mornings, and zips for variable ventilation. However wool is still unbeatable for middle layers. The Eskimos showed Amundsen that their large loose clothes give the best combination of warmth when standing around and ventilation when moving, to prevent sweating. Unfortunately fashion now affects mountaineering gear and even the largest sizes are usually short and tight on me — good for posing in hotels, but bad on the hill.

On 25th we took advantage of a light wind to change tent partners again. I moved out of a cramped little box tent with Howard to join JB in the luxury of an Antarctic Pyramid with a central trench, the ultimate in base camp comfort. JB was a great tent-mate — completely relaxed and at home on the island, always busy, and cooking (in a flash) pizzas and other treats using the Breadmix which was still the taste sensation of the winter.

I spent several long evenings laboriously calculating hauling loads for one-man pulk sledges in various snow conditions. Then I analysed the results of a questionnaire everyone completed monthly, listing their top ten Pleasures, Miseries, Dreads and Cravings. The Pleasures and Miseries varied with recent happenings, but the Dreads and Cravings showed long-term trends. Fears of avalanche, injury and death had all steadily increased, but fear of someone(else) being killed was consistently the greatest Dread, and kept increasing: we each believed that it couldn't happen to ourselves but realised it could happen to others. Women came head, shoulders and body above all other Cravings: longings for female company, courtship, and making love had each steadily increased, but had all recently been overtaken by the want of family affection; only a craving for rich countryside occasionally challenged the girls' hegemony over our desires. (I didn't dream about the countryside so much either.)

In the last few days of July the numbers of Sheathbills and Blue-eyed Shags rose again. 35 Sheathbills gathered at another Crabeater carcass on the beach, with Giant Petrels and Kelp Gulls. In mid-afternoon on 31st, over 700 Shags flew up from Guyou Bay: straggling skeins passed low around the point, and neat Vs beat over the col; they then joined up beyond 'Easter Island' where they swung into wind, flying low in a long

Two Sheathbills.
(Tim Hall)

Man's inhumanity to seals:
Weddells doze
complacently on the beach
while team members
dissect a Crabeater
beyond.
(Jed Corbett)

ragged line-abreast. When some landed, the rest gathered in from each side: it was another example of the social techniques used by many Pelicaniformes to locate (or catch) shoaling fish, and explained these great winter concourses.

Despite being penned at base camp, the weeks seemed to be rushing by toward our planned move south. Now we skied everywhere for our daily business around camp and on the beach. Much time was absorbed each day digging out tents, digging into the hut and garage and fuel bunker, and digging down to locate boxes of food and general stores. The snow would continue to accumulate through August — the coldest month of the year. We hoped the pack-ice would at last arrive and stay, but I had virtually given up hope of being able to pulk around to 'Dayglo Point' over it.

August

Ice all over Dallman Bay. (Howard Oakley)

Jed digging out his pyramid, after the drift had corniced onto the apex. (Chris Furse)

August. The word brings to the mind's eye visions of hot summer fields and tanned bodies. On Brabant Island it was different — the equivalent of February on the Cairngorm Plateau, but darker and a little more remote.

Spindrift sifted against the tent walls when we woke on 1st. Unusually, it was worse once outside than it had sounded. All day a north-easterly blizzard obliterated base camp, and the bottom dropped out of the barometer.

Next day a dour calm had arrived. The pressure was 936 mB, and we were near the centre of a massive depression. The moraine drift had crept further across the camp, corniced above the apex of Jed and Howard's Pyramid tent like a Hokusai wave. Enormous breakers were thundering through the skerries, contemptuously riding over the lower ones, then building up to smash against the highest stacks, sending a wall of white bursting 50 metres up into the leaden sky before crashing down across the Shags' roosts. Down at the western point we watched a small berg 50 metres long (3000 tonnes?) trapped among the inshore stacks, heaving above us on the shore, then dropping far below the horizon, and turned like a toy by the seas. It was magnificent — from our safe stance ashore.

Then for five days, utter stillness came. The lonely silence of Antarctica is unique. People are shrunk to insignificance, infinitesimal organisms, witnesses to silent waiting rocks, water, snow, a world awaiting life's first start. Ripples gently washed the pebble beach. A few Weddells lay there, unable to surmount the storm-carved snow-cliffs above high tide. Fewer now came ashore: some dozed on pancake icefloes, others probably slept afloat. Two lonely Fur Seals stayed close together on the empty snow. One Shag fished close inshore, while lilypads of ice drifted serenely past. A Leopard Seal swam quietly, approaching. Suddenly the Shag sensed danger and scuttered noisily into flight. Offshore the evening sun broke through the layers of stratus cloud: a myriad of bergy bits peopled the horizon with blue mirages floating above the molten sea. Shouts from the butte-top echoed from the silent stacks. Occasional cries of Kelps and Terns disturbed the spell.

Ted and Jim found a lone Gentoo on the beach, and carried it up to camp for fun. Jed had been working solidly for two months on advertising photographs; immediately he seized the opportunity for Penguin Biscuits, and pilchards, which they tried to feed to the penguin.

In May JB had found some large (3-7 mm) mite-like creatures. Dr Bill Block of BAS radioed great interest, so JB dug down through the snow to collect two dozen more. Nestled in dry lumps of penguin feathers and debris under boulders, with clusters of eggs, they lay torpid, but near the warmth of a tilley lamp a few began to crawl. Howard examined them under the binocular microscope, and increasingly detailed descriptions were radioed back, to answer Bill Block's queries. Our excitement mounted as conviction grew that they were a new species — possibly the largest land animals in Antarctica. They appeared to be of the obscure family Opilioacaridae ('mites resembling harvestmen'), known only from Mauritius, the Seychelles, Ceylon, New Guinea, Australia and New Zealand. Their presence here could be very significant. They would probably resemble the Australasian species, transported by birds: however successful colonisation here would suggest ancient transport, when the climates were more similar. If they resembled the species from the western Indian Ocean, a two-stage bird transport via the sub-Antarctic Kerguelen or Crozet archipelagos was feasible. Either of these hypo-

Jed advertising sleeping bags with dozing Weddell. (Jim Lumsden)

theses would probably mean that Metchnikoff had been a snow-free refuge during recent ice-age maxima.

Arthropods moved on to the land late in the Palaeozoic Era, when Antarctica was joined with South America, South Africa, Australia and India to form Gondwanaland. I wondered whether these 'Metchnikoff Monster Mites' might have survived in a small locality from the early Mesozoic Era, when Antarctica began to separate from South Africa and Madagascar in the Triassic/Jurassic Perids. However the Antarctic Peninsula had been an odd separate piece of crust, joined with the Andes and probably not touching South Africa. The Peninsula (and the Scotia Arc around Drake Passage and the Scotia Sea) have a very complex tectonic history: they are the bits that do not quite fit the jigsaw. Even discounting my wild thoughts, the Monster Mites were very intriguing and the dull 'bugs' work was suddenly really exciting. It seemed a just reward for JB's year of careful preparations and for the painstaking fieldwork by him and Johnny Morris — both pressed men for the job.

The skies cleared on 4th, and next day Ted, JB, Jim and Nick left with three pulks, to reconnoitre the only possible skidoo route southward, up to the 2000 metre barrier of Harvey Heights. It was the first major journey building up to our breakout in spring. They planned to return in two or three weeks.

Three beautiful calm and sunlit days followed. Collecting rock samples above 'Cairn Point' on 8th, Peter, Francois and I looked down on seven-tenths pack-ice spread out from shore to the horizon. Hectares of ice had grown together, carpeted white with the falling snow, their junctions marked by sinuous dark lines in a repeated dovetail pattern, each tongue and groove shaped like a giant bracken leaf. Large pancakes collected in the interstices of the icefloe mosaic. Skiing back I fell stupidly on a gentle traverse and wrenched my knee (an old ligament injury): it was a timely warning before the spring pulking. We arrived back in thickening snowfall and Kim, Spotts and Mike returned soon afterwards from three glorious days climbing Mount Hunter's north-west ridge and ferrying stores by skidoo.

That night it blew another westerly gale and next day the sea-ice had disappeared, except for pack-ice trapped amongst our skerries and the lovely icebergs anchored in Dallman Bay.

The next two weeks were dull, pottering about Metchnikoff Point resting my knee, with dreary weather. We had heard little news from home. The first message for five weeks told us that six of our weekly bulletins had not reached our families or the second-summer party in England. Mark, the radio operator at Faraday, was very helpful, and found out that BAS Cambridge had been despatching our bulletins back to the Falklands! We felt somewhat unloved and forgotten. Then a second message came, telling us that all the first summer botanical and invertebrate specimens had been lost on the way back to Britain. I was glad that adrenalin was building up for the journey south, otherwise such negative news could easily have loomed very large in our thoughts.

Snow Petrels coasted westward almost every day, at rates of 100-200 per hour. Some foraged as they went, but most just sailed along the north shore, or took the short cut over the col, passing the garage at knee height into westerly winds. Odd Cape Pigeons sometimes flew by (usually in the evenings), but since mid-July we had seen no Fulmars, and very few Antarctic Petrels. Then, on 11th there was a big westward movement of Snow Petrels (1146 per hour) and Antarctic Petrels (522 per hour), with neither Cape Pigeons nor Fulmars. These occasional big movements were presumably related to weather systems out in the Bellingshausen Sea. I thought that the regular movements of Snow Petrels might be part of a great clockwise circulation around the Bellingshausen pack, but the movement dwindled with easterly winds in mid-August. Loose pack-ice returned again and Snow Petrels foraged close inshore, landing to sit on small lumps of brash then running to plunge their head and neck under water. This feeding behaviour explains why they stand and walk better than other small petrels.

On 15th a bad spell of warm weather began, with heavy wet snow and sometimes even rain. Kim, Peter and Mike returned from three days' geology at 'Pinnacles Spur' where they had found the slopes in dangerous avalanche condition, and crevasse-bridges treacherously weak. We all prayed that Ted's party was safe.

With all his kit prepared, and unable to get out on the skidoos, Spotts turned his energy to fishing at the entrance to the boat haven — belaying himself above a corniced cliff, and ledgering as if at Portland Bill. He quickly caught several 'Antarctic Cod' *Notothenia neglecta*. Kim, JB and Jed then caught more, and Jed nearly caught a Leopard Seal. The fish were in two age-classes: slim reddish ones about 21 cm long, and lumpy tapering older fish with darker barred sides and yellow bellies about 30 cm long. They were feeding on various small amphipods and other crustaceans, plus small fronds of seaweed, and took Crabeater-meat bait. After feeding inshore, at 4-5 years old they become pelagic and then start growing rapidly, reaching 90 cm and nearly 100 kg, and the Russians, Germans, Japanese and others are now fishing them commercially off South Georgia. Their white flesh had a pleasant, delicate salty flavour — but we were rather offput by the brown parasitic worms infesting their abdomens.

On 18th the wet snow and wind were so foul that Jed and I festered all day in our Pyramid — the first time for many months. Sodden snow drifted over the tunnel entrance and plastered the walls, unnoticed. Lack of ventilation and a temperamental stove gave Jed a splitting headache and just before supper he suddenly had to go out and vomit. It was carbon monoxide poisoning again. When ill, one feels like a little child, wanting comfort, love and cosy security. Here there was none. Squatting in the spindrift, vomiting, or lying in the dark as the wind howled mournfully outside the flapping tent, Jed must have felt miserable.

Next day the sea was again nine-tenths covered with loose pack. The wet snow had frozen to form a hard crust everywhere, including over the three skidoos, which Spotts took all day freeing. Wet snow fell yet again that night, and Jed and I decided that our basement flat was now really too compressed and deep. Getting out, we crawled up 60 cm, then stood up to peep out over the edge of the windscoop. It took us four hours to dig out the rock-anchored guys and free the valences from deep snow and slabs of ice and we finished just in time, as a north-easterly blizzard began at dusk. Inside the re-pitched tent, it felt like a new and spacious home. I had a complete change of socks, underwear and shirt, the first since March, and luxuriated in the dry warmth. Looking at my body while changing I was relieved to see that after seven months without washing it was (rather disgustingly) white. We didn't think we smelt at all.

On 22nd Francois and I skied together to the western point. On the snow there we found ten Weddells, the most for several weeks, and lying nearby was the sad corpse of a pup, born prematurely. It was 113 cm long, already covered with its thick woolly natal coat. (Weddells pup from mid-October to mid-November, and pups are about 150 cm at birth.) It was the first concrete sign of spring, but there were other signs appearing now. Kelp Gulls were beginning to form pairs, standing on the stacks, or flying together giving the long calls of summer, and their blood red bill-spots were noticeably brighter now. Over 500 Shags had recently returned to their roost-stacks and the caruncles at the base of their bills seemed to be larger and brighter yellow. The local Antarctic Terns broke off from fishing in twos and threes amongst the loose inshore pack-ice for courtship chases, and pairs now sometimes stood for an hour on lookout rocks in the drifted colony. Sheathbills more often visited the campsite, in ones and twos. With more sea-ice about, we surprisingly began to see limpets again, migrated nearly up to low-tide, and we also found several small pink starfish. Signy Island said that snow algae were now growing on their pack-ice, which would hasten the melt. However the wet snow stuck to the cliffs, with less exposed rocks and lichens now than ever before, and only a few Snow Petrels sailed around the butte occasionally.

Next morning Kim's shouts tumbled us out, to see little bursts of spray, brilliant white in sunshine against the inky sea two miles off among the pack-ice. Whales! A pair of Humpbacks swam slowly into the sound. We had seen whales only twice in the winter, in May and June (probably Killers) and the last Humpbacks had been seen last March. These were the first returning south from their tropical wintering grounds. One breached joyfully clear of the water, then they swam leisurely back out into the loose pack, as if they had just called to tell us spring would follow soon.

Within minutes Jed was shouting: 'The others are back!' We all rushed up past the garage on to the glacier. Ted's party were skiing down slowly with their orange pulks, while Spotts circled them driving Dutch Courage (his skidoo), like a frigate round a convoy. I think everyone was as relieved as me to see their cheerful faces. We put up two Super Nova tents for four of us base-campers; then Ted, JB, Jim and Nick each moved into one of the Antarctic Pyramids to relax, dry out, and swap news. That evening in the hut we celebrated their return, and Ted told the story of their 18 days together on the hill.

With the pulks dragging through soft snow, it had taken them four hard days to reach Lister Glacier. There they camped in cloud, unable to find the cache.

Next morning Ted went out first. Three metres outside the tent he suddenly dropped, through innocent snow, into the eerie blue gloom of a crevasse. He hit something soft — then closed his eyes, falling weightlessly, waiting for the awful thud, and end. Nothing happened. He wondered if this was what death felt like. Nervously, cautiously, he opened his eyes: he was lying on a soft snow-ledge just three metres below the patch of light where he had broken through. Below him the crevasse dropped into darkness. I would have lain there petrified: Ted clambered up the sloping ledge, bridged up the narrowing crevasse, broke out, found a safer site for his morning crap, and then went back to finish his breakfast. Later they found the cache (luckily the three-metre sledge upended to mark it in May was just showing), and dug out all the stores, lifting them up to the new surface.

On 10th they headed south up Lister Glacier, feeling their way for three days in cloud, very cold. They reached 'Paré Icefall' in clearer weather on 13th, camping below it at 1050 metres. That night it was cold to the bone. Next day they skied up the expected skidoo route, but had to traverse to and fro, up icy slopes of 50 degrees and steeper. The following day, while JB and Jim dug out and re-pitched the tents, Ted and Nick found a slightly more hopeful route up to the east, reaching 1500 metres; the skidoos would need winching for about 300 metres.

On 16th they skied west in freezing cloud, ice crackling off their clothes as they moved. They camped at 1200 metres on 'Rokki Plateau', where they were held up for five nights, by cloud and deep snowfalls. Snow like gravel buried the tents a metre deep: digging out was a losing battle, as the snow blew off the shovels. The stoves fumed with the bad ventilation, so they rigged pulks upside down as roofs for crawl-ways up from the tent doors to the surface, and connected the two tents by a rope, so they could find their way to dig each other out. Ted and JB went out in a brief clearance to check the skidoo route round the head of 'Precinct Glacier' toward 'Astrolabe Point', then raced back to beat returning cloud. They went on to half rations, which would last until 24th.

At last 22nd dawned sunlit and beautiful. They broke camp and raced north down the ridge, then descended an icefall in cloud on to Lister Glacier. JB and Jim fell behind on the 300-metre pull up to 'Noddies Col' feeling very weak — the old enemy of CO poisoning in buried tents. Nevertheless they came safely over 'Pinnacles Spur' and completed 15 km hard pulking in the day, before dusk and cloud overtook them just 5 km from base camp. Camped on the piedmont they listened to icefalls and avalanches off Mount Hunter: in the early hours Nick heard six falls.

After a leisurely start next day, they arrived back tired and happy from a successful winter journey. It had been Ted's first time leading a party here: he and all of them had overcome, and made light of, some really hard conditions, and completed the vital recconaissance. It had been Jim's first major mountain journey: he had thrived on the hard times as well as the easy, and was promoted to a Second.

There was now one week before our planned departure from Metchnikoff Point, with many final preparations still to complete. Ted's party had a meagre Sunday rest (on Friday 24th) which was spoilt by wind and spindrift. That day Mike received our first personal message from home, from his girlfriend Sally, delivered to his tent in an envelope by Kim, after a radio contact with Palmer.

The hut was now almost buried and we built an entrance tunnel roofed with cardboard boxes. Next day everyone turned-to for seven hours digging out all the stores boxes (buried a metre deep) and securing them for our absence, moving the remaining food to surround the buried hut, and getting out the last 45-gallon drum of kerosene which was under 4 metres of snow and had taken 8 man-days of searching. It was a grand day's work, and I for one was tired that evening. If spring was coming, the birth involved a heavy labour.

Early on 26th a big west wind got up. After a respite it rose again at breakfast gusting to about 100 knots with spindrift tearing off the crusty snow. A big gust broke a pole on Kim's and my Super Nova. Cramming the base-camp litter into our sleeping bags, we booted and spurred to go out and collapse the tent before it was completely wrecked. We emerged to find people busy under a howling blue sky. Three Pyramids were standing imperturbably, the fourth had disappeared. Nick and Francois had been lying in their bags when suddenly their tent had just blown away with a bang and vanished toward the sea. Gloves, gaiters, food, etc., whistled away in the storm. Miraculously Ted and JB recovered the tent lodged in rocks by the beach: it was completely undamaged, having blown away simply because the snow had been blasted off the valence. Poor Nick and Francois received more laughter than sympathy. Later in the day when the hooli eased, we all re-pitched their Pyramid and replaced our dome.

The storm blew for two days, although just 100 km south Palmer and Faraday were recording gentle 10–12-knot winds. The barometer wavered only a little, and Howard finally admitted that he really could not forecast next day's weather any better than the rest of us.

Howard had lent me his headphones, and each night I plugged into the spare socket of Kim's walkman tape player. It was lovely to hear music, to listen to the breathy song of women for the first time in eight months. I lay there, transported to company and comfort, forgetting the bucking flapping tent.

More wind followed, with wet heavy snow, and then rain. The pulks were lying outside each tent, being rigged and stowed for the move south; next morning they were filled with ice.

At last on 30th the wind eased. The sky was clear except for a streamer of high cloud trailing from the pallid silhouette of Smith Island lonely on our northern horizon. There have been very few landings there, and Tilman and the crew of *En Avant* vanished without trace on the way to explore it. Kim and I lay talking about plans for the future.

At the beginning of September we would head south. Most people were, like me, waiting until the last days to get all their gear ready. I was very glad that Spotts had been driving hard for three months to get our stores out on to the hill, ready to go. The next four months would be hectic, exciting, tiring and dangerous. The spring journeys were about to begin.

September

Camp near Roentgen Peak, 27 September. The rations are cached in the pulk marked by the ensign and skis, with the tents 10 metres downslope. (Jed Corbett)

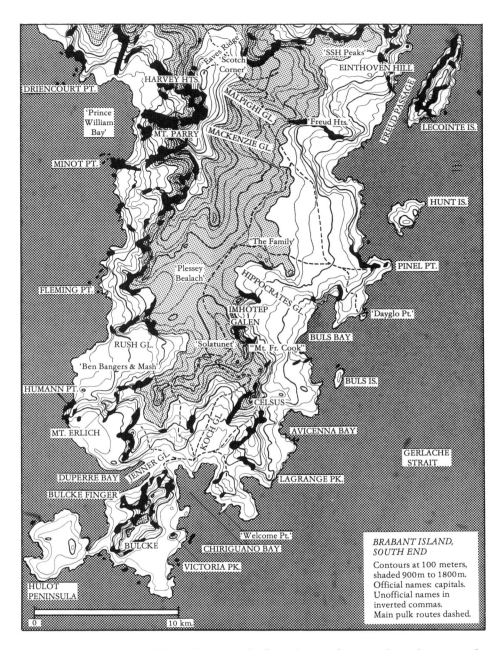

BRABANT ISLAND,
SOUTH END

Contours at 100 meters,
shaded 900m to 1800m.
Official names: capitals.
Unofficial names in
inverted commas.
Main pulk routes dashed.

September came in like a lion, with five days of westerly gales, mostly with foul wet snow, sometimes even rain. Each morning Kim and I looked out and decided not to leave that day. It was wearing for everybody, preparing each evening to go next morning, and then again frustration.

On 1st the whole ocean was entirely covered with ice. Smashed up lumps covered the surface like turgid white porridge and surged sluggishly inshore like cooling lava flows. Relentlessly the big seas tore the ice apart: dark lanes appeared first in the lee of Metchnikoff Point and then stretched away to Cape Roux. By 4th there was only about three-tenths ice; ribbons of white beyond the outer skerries marked the swells, 100 metres from crest to crest. The swell powered through the damping scum of miles of offshore ice to burst up skyward over the skerries. Occasionally a glimmer of sunlight backlit the white spray flung downwind by the gale.

We had seen no more Fur Seals since mid-August. Even Weddells seldom got ashore now. Jim watched one trying to come on to the beach; its head was caught with a sickening crunch as two growlers collided and the seal floated off, apparently dead. There were no stable floes to rest on, and over miles of ice we saw neither Crabeater nor Leopard Seals. Several remarkably low tides occurred at the beginning of the month, contrary to the predictions: we could walk across to islets we had never reached before, but were unable to fathom out why.

Because of the storms, my last few days watching the birds at Metchnikoff Point were probably unrepresentative. Under a hundred Shags now fought their way to and from the roosting stacks. The Kelp Gulls moved about, sometimes feeding offshore, sometimes in the icy wrack, sometimes standing in pairs on the skerries. The juveniles were becoming whiter below and darker brown above as feather-edges wore: later they would leave, possibly driven off by the territorial adults. Sometimes over 50 Terns foraged among the loose ice and pairs regularly visited the colony. Only 4 Sheathbills now frequented Metchnikoff Point, but they were scattered around the coast, investigating every possibility of food (even fallen skiers on the piedmont!). Francois threw some Crabeater meat outside the hut and within the day nine Sheathbills had arrived.

There were fewer Giant Petrels now; perhaps they were beginning to gather closer to their breeding colonies. On the radio we heard South Georgia reporting that their Giant Petrels were already 'staunchly defending their nest-sites'. At Bird Island the Wandering Albatross chicks were nearly ready to fledge after their long winter as nestlings: they would travel around the sub-Antarctic westerly windbelt — but perhaps some juveniles from McQuarrie Island would get blown south to visit us this spring?

Pipits were now singing in South Georgia. A year since hearing birdsong at home seemed a lonely time — now most of all in spring.

Snow Petrels were again often flighting and calling around the cliffs, and with the Kelps they were our most constant companions foraging inshore. During a big westward movement on 5th, one or two Antarctic Petrels and Antarctic Fulmars also passed. The one further concrete sign of Spring here was the return of a few Cape Pigeons fluttering briefly at the cliffs *en passant.*

In temperate zones, the seasons follow a fairly simple harmonic cycle. Due to the inertia of the environment, the seasons lag two or three months behind the cyclic driving force — heat input from the sun. (At Brabant Island, at mid-summer noon the sun is 50 degrees above the horizon: the maximum incident heat per unit area then is over 80 times that at mid-winter noon, with the sun at 5 degrees.) However in polar regions the spring rewarming is severely delayed by an additional inertia effect: most of the incident heat is wasted by reflection. The percentage of heat thus wasted is called 'Albedo'. Clean snow has an albedo of 90%, i.e. it absorbs only 10% of the available heat (farmland has an albedo of 20%, absorbing 80% of the sun's heat). Snow accumulates on land and pack-ice at sea over the winter months, reaching maxima in September. With their high albedo the frozen wastes of September are self-perpetuating. Now, waiting for spring, we cursed albedo.

Dirty snow has an albedo as low as 30%; it absorbs 7 times as much heat as clean snow. The droppings of penguins and other birds hasten the melt at their nest-sites. It is not only their early arrival in spring which achieves this: penguins and Cape Pigeons moulting at their nests in autumn, and Snow Petrels courting at their nests all winter, leave stains in the snow which locally accelerate the spring thaws. Colonial breeding helps this process, and for the same reason expansion of an existing colony is easier than establishing a new colony on clean pristine snow. The number of breeding species on any one suitable coastal point depends to some extent on the random chance of initial colonisations. Perhaps within a region there is some faint correlation between the total number of colonies and lengths of time exposed by glaciers — like that on British farmland between variety of bush species and hedgerow age.

Now we entered the buried hut down a tunnel of cardboard boxes. By our return in December the hut would be surrounded by scree and penguins: although excited by our coming journey south, we were sad to miss the spring return of the Chinstrap Penguins. The males would arrive in October and establish territorial rights, before the females arrived and pairing started. We had seen no Chinstraps for two months, but on 5th another lone Gentoo struggled ashore across the heaving porridge of ice — mostly tobagganning on its belly, occasionally standing up precariously as if walking on the water. Their staggered breeding begins before the Chinstraps; and now we begin to see small parties of Gentoos around the coast.

Everything was ready for the move south — except the weather. Ted had renewed scored piston rings on one skidoo, working inside a tent as protection from the gales. Soon after he had finished, his garage tent was wrecked by wind. The skidoo team would be the central thread of our splintered movements over the coming months.

Our plans were:

Chris, Jed, Mike, Francois and Nick — Pulk Party: north-east coast geology then 'Paré Icefall'.

Spotts, JB, Ted — Skidoo team: Ferry stores via Lister Glacier to 'Paré Icefall'.

Kim, Howard, Peter, Jim — Pulk Party: 'Astrolabe Point' via Lister Glacier, then join up at 'Paré Icefall'.

At last, 6th dawned sunlit and calm! Kim's party left with two pulks at midday. We followed later, joining them at 'Claire's Finger' cache as dusk fell (at 7.00 p.m.). We all had heavy packs with four months' gear. I was unfit now, and after five hours as horse on our one pulk I was knackered. Francois and I flopped into our tent at 9.00 p.m. and slept for ever. When we emerged on 7th, Kim's party had left. We dug out the cache, and that evening the skidoo party reached the cache. They had carefully cleared up base camp, our winter home, and did not expect to see it again.

Next day two of the skidoos were blown over working along the ridge in an easterly gale and freezing cold. We all retired to mend gloves and read. The easterly switched to a westerly gale and the day after the tents began drifting over. At midnight I only just managed to squeeze through the tent door and up through a metre of snow. Then I spent an elated hour digging out, with faint moonlight above the clouds and spindrift blasting through the beam of my torch planted in the snow. I was dry and felt warm: the temperature was −8°C. I got back inside with great blocks of ice in my beard, unnoticed until Francois laughed at me.

Howard's 600 hours of monitoring showed that our body temperatures were generally lower in August than they had been in May — yet we felt more comfortable, indicating psychological habituation as well as physiological. He had also accumulated 525 hours of temperature records in clothing and tents, etc. The inside of a tent with the stove on

Digging out tents at the 'Claire's Finger' cache. (Jed Corbett)

was 15-31°C warmer than the outside air; even a snowhole (at 7-12°C above ambient) was warmer than the hut (4-11°C). At night both tents and snowholes fell to 5°C above ambient so that our beards frosted in our sleeping breath. Howard had millions of bits of field data for computer analysis over several years. Right now he was probably analysing his aches after his first day as horse on a pulk.

We woke cold and clammy on 10th to find the tent walls bulging heavily on to us, only a narrow strip of daylight showing in the roof; we were buried in a gloomy sepulchre. Spotts helped us out by clearing the doorway: with each shovelful more sunlight shone through the tent walls. I could imagine how gothic stained glass windows burst through the gloom of medieval churches. (I had been reading Kristin Lavransdatter, only my fourth book in eight months!) The five of us broke camp and pulked across to Cape Roux. Halfway there the three skidoos passed us in convoy heading east; serpents of spindrift writhed past them in the westerly gale to smoke up off the ridge-crest into blue beyond.

After two days' geology we were held up at Cape Roux by three days of foul wet snow and rain. The Antarctic continent is often described as a cold desert, having very little precipitation. However Brabant Island is in the maritime Antarctic, and it has lots! The 16th was dryer, so we broke camp and left, putting our backs to the westerly wind. Jed led the five of us through cloud, roped in one long line with Nick in the middle horsing the heavy pulk: he had a long weary pull. At 400 metres we reached the top of the cloud layer. Our shadows played hide and seek in the drifting cloud wraiths, and beautiful gentle icefalls glittered above us in hazy sunshine. We pitched camp near the half-buried block of stores cached below 'Roentgen Ridge'. On one marker pole was a message from Spotts written five days before: one of the skidoo gearboxes had broken.

That open gentle slope was a burial ground, with spindrift or wet snow smothering the tents and the cache. On the afternoon of 18th a clearance allowed us a brief ski north to the coast, but otherwise we stayed in the tents for four days and five nights. At intervals we tunnelled our way out of the tent to dig out, but it was a long battle. Nick had developed a suspected duodenal ulcer a month before. (Howard advised exercise, without worry, and told me that if it burst, my only useful first aid was the Last Rites.) Now it was getting worse. Mike, Francois and I were sharing a compressed and gloomy tent, the three of us huddled inside — wet, uncomfortable and uneasy. It must have been much worse for Nick next door, though Jed was doing a marvellous job cheering him up. On 21st I woke cold and breathless: both doors were buried; a little patch of light showed in the apex of the tent and we could hear and see the spindrift there; the bulging sides creaked alarmingly and I felt very depressed. After getting booted up, it took me ten minutes to dig my way up through heavy damp snow. As I forced my head and shoulders to the surface, I met a wonderful surprise — the day was beautiful! Little clouds wafted about in the sunshine, and the spindrift was only ankle deep — just enough to smother the apex of our tent (and to go down my neck as I struggled out). It took us three hours to dig the tents out, then we moved them to new sites nearby. We laid out sleeping bags to dry — the first real drying day for many months. Jed suddenly started waving and dancing about, for over the ridge came the cavalry — two skidoos. Spotts and JB hopped off and we all gathered in the sun to swap ten days' news.

They had ferried this great block of stores over in the westerly gales of 10th and 11th, but then the gearbox seized solid on Dutch Courage. In flying spindrift they had another major operation loading the skidoo on to the big sledge and towing it back to 'Claire's Finger'. While Ted started stripping down the skidoo, Spotts and JB took the big sledge back to base loaded with pulks, for more food. The towing shackles had just been greased. Coming down to First Cache they suddenly saw the sledge overtaking the skidoos, disconnected. It accelerated gently into the cloud toward the crevasses and sea-cliffs on the right. They hurtled into the cloud trying to stop it, acutely aware of the shrouded cliffs beyond and below. Spotts just got in front of it and the sledge slammed into the tent on the back of his skidoo. It stopped! They recovered their breath — the sledge would only have been a material loss, but the pulks loaded on to it were vital for ferrying our stores southward. JB then went half into a crevasse and it took an hour to recover his skidoo. Conditions were really too bad for moving, but all three moved down to base later the same day in complete whiteout with JB's skidoo doing a nose-dive off a metre-high sastrugi. They spent three foul wet days at Metchnikoff Point while Ted made up pullers from ski bindings, etc, and removed the seized second gear from the gearbox layshaft. Coming back out on 17th in whiteout again they started pitching camp only to find the runaway sledge had broken all the tent poles, so they walked back into base for yet another night. For the last two days, while we were buried, Ted had been reassembling Dutch Courage, outside in the bitter ubiquitous spindrift. Spotts said that Ted's fingers were now really in a bad way, though not frostbitten black. Spotts had sent and received various radio messages through Faraday, but had heard nothing from Kim's party, who should come up as soon as they found the radio at 'Astrolabe Point'.

I decided that we must fetch Howard back to Metchnikoff Point, to tend Nick in case his ulcer deteriorated. The skidoos had one more trip, so this was the opportunity to get Nick back. Now Nick volunteered to stay

13 **March.** Claude Point from Metchnikoff Point (Chris Furse)

14

15

14 **March.** Dome tents in basecamp (Jed Corbett)
15 **April.** Camp halfway to Duclaux Point (Jed Corbett)
16 **April.** Camp and pulk on Roentgen Peak (John Spottiswood) Opposite

18

19

17 **April.** Reaching Duclaux Point (John Spottiswood) Opposite
18 **April.** Looking up out of Nick's crevasse (Ted Atkins)
19 **May.** Cape Pigeon (Peter Stuttard)

21

22

20 **May.** Antarctic Pyramids in basecamp (Mike Ringe) Opposite
21 **June.** Midwinter's Day in the hut (Jed Corbett)
22 **June.** Tents in base camp looking north (John Kimbrey)

23

24

23 **July.** Spindrift in basecamp and winter sun (John Kimbrey)
24 **July.** Weddell Seal asleep in the snow (John Kimbrey)

there by himself. I would not have asked anyone to do that, but his volunteering was a noble gesture, and too good to refuse — it would save Kim's party two or three weeks' ferrying Howard back.

The BAS ship RRS *John Biscoe* would shortly come down to Port Lockroy (to set up the staging landing strip for the Twin Otters flying down to Rothera), the first ship this season. Nick would radio to ask BAS if they could take him off from Metchnikoff as a precautionary measure.

Nick started packing his gear. We frantically thought what else he might need at base — our one radio, metatabs, a spare stove, etc. Nick shook hands all round, handing out chocolate, coffee bags, his Pieps transceiver. An hour after the decision it was suddenly farewell — unexpected and unprepared after six months together. Jed took photos. Nick took photos (to take home for our families). I tried to make a little formal speech of farewell. We all shook hands again, then the two skidoos left. Riding pillion, Nick waved once as they disappeared over the ridge.

After they had gone, we sorted ourselves out. Frank moved over with Jed, while Mike and I spread ourselves a bit. Two two-man tents was actually a more convenient party size. In the evening we hauled the pulk up to the edge of the plateau and skied up a little fin of snow and ice that blocked our view eastward from the Burial Ground to Cape Cockburn. The 21st (my 21st wedding anniversary) had been the third lovely day in September; only four other days had been reasonable for travel.

The equinox was another lost day of wind and wet snow, but 23rd began with broken stratus cloud and shallow spindrift. The four of us left the tents and skied eastward with light packs containing only bivouac gear (stoves, pots, two days' food and fuel, Karrimats, sleeping bags and bivouac bags, torches, snowshovels and snow-saws). We checked the cache on 'Roentgen Ridge': we had feared it might be buried and lost, so were very relieved to find the fuel and food sitting on top of the snow heavily crusted with ice, like an isolated sastrugi. Kim's party had located it and dug it out on 10th, their message said. By then we were basking in perfect weather — with Brabant's pool of sunshine surrounded by banks of cloud offshore. We skied down to Cape Cockburn, where five points rose from the glacier like the knuckles of a fist half-clenched upon the table of the sea. Mike was surprised to find that the massive planed brown cliffs, dropping 300 metres vertically below us, were graded conglomerates not granites. Parties of Snow Petrels drifted out of Bouquet Bay and winged westward past our shoulders, while a few flighted around a broken bit of cliff. Here at last was another sign of spring — Antarctic Fulmars were patrolling the cliffs and fluttering into the few possible nesting ledges. We got back to the Burial Ground at 7 p.m. A river of cloud was pouring down off Mount Hunter and billowing up as it reached the coast, to cloak the evening sun. Three cheerful figures waved marker flags as we approached through the cloud. The skidoo team had arrived with the last load of stores and pitched their tent. Nick was safely installed at Metchnikoff Point. It had been a truly satisfying day — joyful to ski in sunshine with light packs, grand to explore the first new area this spring, and good to feel tired after eight hours' moving.

As we breakfasted we heard the skidoos warming up, like racing cars in the pits. The three worked smoothly as an impressive and practised team. Spotts and JB ferried the first loads up on to 'Roentgen Ridge', while Ted prepared the next loads, syphoned fuel from drums to jerrycans, and serviced the third skidoo.

The four of us left at 11 a.m. in cloud, and snow began falling as Jed and Francois hauled our one pulk over the plateau. We reached the col by Roentgen Peak at 3 p.m. and pitched camp there, with snow falling heavily, and visibility down to 50 metres. I for one was exhausted from a pack weighing nearly 40 kg. Resting and eating supper the sound of snow on the tent was a muted background to my peaceful tiredness. I was content: we were now poised above Duclaux Point again, but this time (unlike in April) we had ample reserves of food and fuel, thanks to the skidoos. The winter party had been on the island for six months, and for Mike it was exactly the halfway stage. We felt that now at last we were truly started on the southward journey. Then we were held up again for five whole days.

A rising westerly storm battered the tents on 25th. It turned to freezing rain that evening, soaking Mike in three minutes, but coating the tents in a centimetre of icy armour plating. For two days the storm blew with hints of useless sun above the blasting spindrift. We lay in perfect comfort in the green daylight of the tent; it was a rigid ice pagoda which did not even flinch, while we listened to the roar of winds up to 80 knots or more, and the drenching sound of torrents of spindrift. On the fourth day the wind lessened, but veered north-easterly bringing raw cloud and wet snow: we re-stocked from the cache along the ridge, and started to reconnoitre the route down when the cloud thinned toward evening. The fifth day dawned clear as a bell, and at last we saw the marvellous panorama across Lister Glacier: a caul of cloud slid down from Mount Hunter, but Mount Parry jutted clear beyond Harvey Heights, and Morgagni led the eye around to the ice-free waters of Gerlache Strait and

The two Super Novas in spindrift near Roentgen Peak. (Jed Corbett)

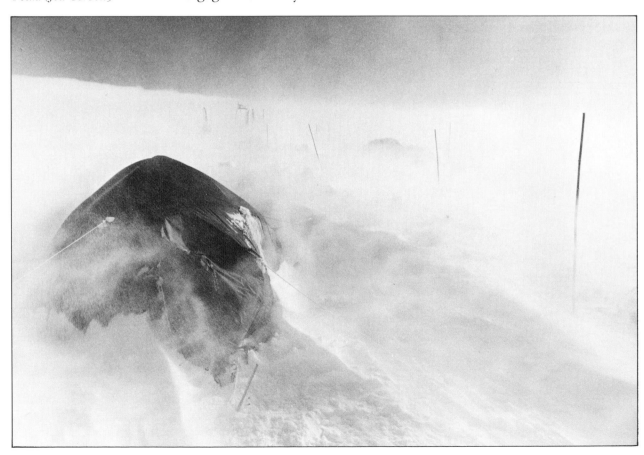

Bouquet Bay. Liege Island stretched northward, a varied ridge of snow and ice unattainable for us now, but inviting for the Second Summer Party. Then as we struck camp, the big winds off Mount Hunter hit us. Hastily we re-pitched the tents and clambered in again: now we felt the full force of the winds tearing and battering at the tent, no longer re-enforced by a rigid icy casing.

These big westerly winds with clear skies above had been a feature of the winter since July at least: they indicated depressions south of Brabant Island. In the first summer our big winds had been easterlies, indicating depressions north of us. The *Antarctic Pilot* (published by the Hydrographer of the Navy) states that depression tracks hereabouts tend more southerly in winter. We had been surprised how vague information was on weather patterns in the region, despite years of met. recording. Contradictory information had led me to hope that equinoctial gales would not be too prolonged and devastating. The mean depression tracks moving northward, and the sun moving southward, must produce general patterns of spring weather that vary up and down the Peninsula. One thing was certain: the days were getting longer, and there was now good daylight from 6 a.m. to after 8 p.m. Whatever our weather, spring was coming to the Antarctic, and the whole marine ecosystem was beginning to accelerate its activity.

As well as the wind-driven circumpolar surface-water currents, there are major north–south ocean currents. Cold Antarctic bottom water flows north to beyond the equator and this is replaced at middle depths by water-masses which carry nutrient salts into the Antarctic throughout the year. The microscopic plants of the oceans convert these nutrients into

Collecting rations from the pulk in a lull. (Jed Corbett)

organic material. To do so, they trap the sun's energy by photosynthesis, and therefore these phytoplankton are limited to the surface layers. They grow richly wherever upwelling water-masses bring nutrients to the surface. In the gloom below pack-ice there is reduced photosynthesis, so the phytoplankton also grow in concentrated bands around the edges of the sea-ice. Zooplankton gather to feed on these concentrations, and in turn provide a concentrated resource for higher predators.

Through the winter darkness the rate of primary production of phytoplankton is low. However the fringes of the sea-ice provide adequate densities of plankton to support pack-ice specialists like Antarctic Petrels and Snow Petrels. The icefloes themselves also provide safe resting places for other specialists like Crabeater and Ross Seals, and Adelie and Emperor Penguins.

As spring advances the pack-ice breaks up and melts. Vast tracts (about 16 million square kilometres) of waters with unused nutrients are exposed to the sun's increasing energy input and there is a great burst of phytoplankton growth as the sea-ice diminishes through the summer. Among the zooplankton adapted to exploit this annual boom, one organism dominates all others in quantity: *Euphausia Superba*, the 5-cm long shrimp-like crustacean called krill (with its relative *E. crystallorophias*) comprises half the total biomass of herbivorous zooplankton.

The life-cycle of krill involves a great circulation. The eggs sink and drift southward, then the young ascend to the surface layers, feed, and gradually work back northward as they mature. There appear to be several distinct populations of krill, where suitable patterns of ocean currents and pack-ice occur, and one of these populations is in the Bellingshausen sea. Swarms of krill sometimes tinge the waters pink, and they form the key middle layer in the very simple ecosystem of the Antarctic seas. Krill is the main food of the resident Minke Whales, and of the other baleen whales (Blue, Fin, Sei and Humpback) which come south in summer for this rich harvest. Krill is also the main food of Crabeater and Fur Seals, and of Adelie, Chinstrap and Macaroni Penguins, and it is an important dietary component for other seals, birds, fish and squid.

Some rough estimates are now available for the Antarctic, illustrating the narrowing triangle up through the food chain. The annual crop of phytoplankton is of the order of 20,000 million tonnes and, the annual production of herbivorous zooplankton is over 400 million tonnes, half of it krill. The herbivorous zooplankton in turn supports annual productions of about 40 million tonnes of carnivorous zooplankton, 18 million tonnes of squid, and 16 million tonnes of fish. It is easier to visualise the larger predators in terms of actual populations rather than annual production — the ecologists work out the relationships between these through their basic metabolic rates, varying from the low rates of the whales to the higher rates of birds. The total biomass of Seals is about 9 million tonnes (based on populations of 30 million Crabeaters, 1 million Weddells, 750,000 Furs, 600,000 Elephants, 500,000 Leopards and 200,000 Ross). The total biomass of whales is about 8 million tonnes (based on populations of 200,000 Minke, 84,000 Fin, 40,000 Sei, 10,000 Blue and 3,000 Humpback all feeding mainly on krill, plus 43,000 Sperm feeding on squid). For birds corresponding figures are even harder to estimate, but a total biomass of 1-2 million tonnes is probably of the right order, with over 95% comprised of penguins.

As on land, man can obtain greater quantities of food by harvesting low down the food-chain (e.g. growing wheat), but it is much less effort to let animals concentrate the food and then eat them. In the Antarctic mankind started typically by cropping the whales and seals, but without control, so that the whales and the colonial Elephant Seals and Fur Seals were taken to the verge of extinction. (The Crabeaters are safe, being dispersed and uneconomical to hunt.) Recently the Russians, Japanese, Germans, Poles and others have started to take fish also, mainly in the sub-Antarctic and temperate fringes around South Georgia and the Falklands.

Now man has also started to harvest krill directly with the Russians taking about 500,000 tonnes annually, mostly from around South Georgia. Krill offers the greatest untapped natural source of protein for mankind with a maximum sustainable yield of over 100 million tonnes per year. Much international scientific effort is now focussed on defining this figure more usefully for various krill populations, and on forecasting the effects of krill fisheries upon the populations of the natural predators.

I had planned our spring breakout for September, the traditional start of the Antarctic sledging season. Now we had spent 14 days holed up in tents since we left Metchnikoff Point on 6th. We had food and fuel on the hill with the skidoos to last us until mid-October, but time was slipping past, as two weeks was scant time to reach 'Dayglo Point'. I was also a little worried about Kim's party. I estimated they had enough food and fuel with them until 28 September, so I hoped they had got to 'Astrolabe' by now, and found the buried stores. Without radio we had no way of knowing.

On 30th we eventually got away. Moving in cloud and spindrift on an awkward mixture of soft drift and hard ice, we all fell a lot on the way down, so pitched camp at 350 metres on the glacier above Duclaux Point. The magnificent panorama of Bouquet Bay spread out before us — the colour of lead, varied through every tone from purest crystal-white to heaviest black where the sea reflected the basalt cliffs of Davis Island. As we pitched the tents, the westerly down-glacier wind rose, and one pole broke in the confusion. At midnight Mike and I went out to extend our snow-wall against the erratic gusts that were now coming up the glacier from the east.

Digging snow was a symbolic end to our September.

A breath of fresh air: Spotts leading the skidoo party. (Jed Corbett)

October

29 October. Looking back down from Mount Parry at the final ridge. Lines joining the marks intersect on Spotts and Chris going back. (Jed Corbett)

Frank and I lazed in the hot sun. (Francois had become so much one of us that now we all used the English name.) We were sitting on our climbing rope, in a little windscoop on the north slope of Duclaux Point. Below us, our ski tracks threaded through the icefall, mapping our way there. Behind us Mike attacked a mass of conglomerate rock, sintered black by the grey basalt lava flows. We luxuriated in the unaccustomed heat, Frank covering his face to avoid sunburn. October had begun auspiciously.

Later we clambered out along the sharp arête to the crown of the point. Each side the snow and ice fell away at 60 degrees, and I wore another hole in my breeches over the four pitches. Snow Petrels, Cape Pigeons and a few Antarctic Fulmars flighted past the sea-cliffs hidden below us — they had reoccupied their colonies, working up toward the breeding season.

Snow began to fall as we skied back up to our tents, perched on the glacier. Next morning spindrift blasted the tents, and katabatic winds accelerating down Lister Glacier drove a great white tongue of brash-ice out toward Hoseason Island. Then in the evening the wind died and the distant mountains of the Antarctic Peninsula were gilded by the sun. Lying in the tent before supper Mike said: 'Listen, the skidoos!' A faint droning drew nearer. Suddenly we realised it was above us, something quite alien. Rushing to open the zip, we saw a plane winging south, bright red in the sunset, perhaps a BAS Twin Otter heading for Adelaide Island to start the summer season. It was our first sight of outside humanity for over six months.

Next day in cloud and falling snow we hauled the pulk around to Lister Glacier. Jed found us the cache marked by an upended sledge, now nearly buried. Taped on to the sledge was a message from Kim.

Kim, Peter, Howard and Jim had got there on 12 September. In continued bad weather they had camped, until snow slumping off the icewall had flattened Kim and Jim's tent. Then they had dug a snowhole in the blizzard and all four moved in. They had been holed up for twelve

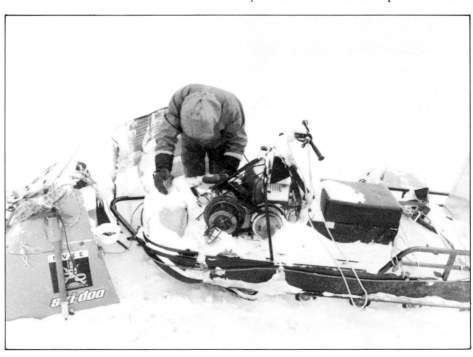

Ted servicing a skidoo. Behind him is a half-completed fuel drum sledge. (Jed Corbett)

nights, going on to reduced rations, while mending tents and keeping their spirits up. Finally they had got away on 24th, heading for 'Astrolabe Point'. That was just before our worst spell of weather, so I prayed they were alright.

After a quiet night we took the empty pulk back up the ridge in glorious cold sunshine to link up with the skidoo party, in case the deep powder-snow stopped them ferrying down the steep south side of 'Roentgen Ridge'. Halfway up we detoured to 'The Pepperpot', a cone of rock and snow close under Mount Hunter. Just as the four of us were climbing down off the summit, three black specks appeared around the next spur — the cavalry! As the skidoos passed our pulk, parked out on the sweeping snowfield, we could just make out one rider waving to us. They went on down to the cache, and then made two more trips. They moved into Kim's palatial snowhole, and after supper we all went in for a brew to swap news.

Since we left Spotts, JB and Ted ten days before at the 'Burial Ground' they had cheerfully endured appalling conditions — working in bitter cold and blinding spindrift, with the skidoos continually bogging in on the deep powder snow, and also suffering several mechanical defects.

They had managed to ferry stores (while we had festered for five days), moving in cloud, unable to see the snow surface, sometimes unable to tell whether they were moving forward or just skidding, with only their marker wands every 25 metres to guide them. Their hands had lost all feeling. Squinting against the winds howling down off Mount Hunter, their eyelids had frozen shut despite their face masks. Not only had they continued ferrying, but sliding behind one of the skidoos was a brand new steel sledge carrying a massive 300-kg load of jerrycans! Ted had made it out of an empty fuel drum, standing outside for three days, chiselling, sawing and hammering the steel. It was ideal for the skidoos — far better than the weak wooden pulks and the cumbersome steel

Ted, Spotts and JB sort out the stores they have brought by skidoo to the Lister Glacier cache. (Jed Corbett)

The Geology Pulk Party hauls up from 'The Precinct', the contorted ridge running down from the right hand side. (Jed Corbett)

sledges — and it freed a second pulk for us. For me this seemed the crowning glory to a winter of inventive work, by Ted, Spotts, JB, Peter and Kim in particular.

The 5th was another good day — overcast, but calm and clear with glaring light. Mike, Frank and I skied over to Virchow Hill. From its rounded snow top we had an all-round view of a vast amphitheatre of mountains across the wide sweeping glaciers, and of distant islands beyond the dark waters of Bouquet Bay. We skied on down the ridge (racing once to catch a runaway cooking pot rolling away to the sea-cliffs) and reached our goal — twin pinnacles of basalt bricks. Below the pinnacles a basalt feeder writhed up through a mass of sintered conglomerates, like a tree-trunk riven by lightning. At last Mike was getting days of geology, and these one-day explorations with light bivouac gear were a joy for all of us. As we started back, spindrift poured down over the rocks like a waterfall and clouds gathered threateningly. We were still unfit after the long winter and arriving back that evening to hear blows on a great gong (Ted cutting up another fuel drum sledge!), my feet hurt badly, after only 15 km. Tincture of benzoin would cure the blisters, and it was good to feel tired over supper.

Meanwhile the skidoos had brought down the rest of the stores. The two old machines had been unable to get up the drifted top ramp, so Spotts had made eight ferry journeys alone on Dutch Courage over that 2-km stretch, working like a demon to load a tonne of gear. Ted and JB had waited with the old skidoos at the foot of the ramp, below a hanging glacier — a nasty site, made more nerve-wracking by the deep rumble of an avalanche off Mount Hunter above them.

I woke before dawn, cold, with the stinging soreness of sand all over both eyeballs — snowblindness. Yesterday's flat light had deceived me into removing my sweaty goggles. There was nothing for it but to lie up all day, listening to the skidoos going off up Lister Glacier, and later returning in deteriorating weather. The September weather had delayed us badly, so we decided that our four-man pulk party would head on directly to 'Astrolabe', taking four mouths off the hill. However a gale of spindrift bringing deep drifts held us up another day.

The weather cleared that night and on 8th we plodded off up the monotonous bowl of Lister Glacier in hot sunshine. The skidoos were ferrying the last loads up to the head of the glacier, and towed our two pulks most of the way. Then we laboured 300 metres up toward 'Cushing Col', with the pulks ploughing a 15–20-cm-deep trough in the soft snow. Through the hot day, there were three avalanches off Mount Hunter, one big powder avalanche sending grey clouds billowing out across the glacier, backlit by the sun. Below our camp that evening lay the speck of the skidoo party's new cache camp and far back the miniscule ice-cliff marking Lister Glacier cache showed our progress south. Next day we suffered a typical bad day's pulking over the ridge in cloud — toiling upward in heavy snow, arguing about the invisible way down, then wrestling with capsizing pulks and heavy packs on traverses. However the rope brakes we had just started using worked superbly, and we dropped out of the cloud to camp at 600 metres on 'Terraces Piedmont'. Then we enjoyed two superb days of good pulking on firm hard snow in crisp fair weather. We relayed the loads through the fascinating icefall at 'The Precinct', down a gully between great icehouses into the deeply drifted high street, and then up out of another side alley on to the glacier. As we neared 'Astrolable Point' on 11th, anticipation built up, hoping to meet Kim's party. Skiing down the last 300 metres Jed spotted footprints, and soon we were coming down the last slope to two tents ensconced in huge snow-walls. A moment later the four of us were

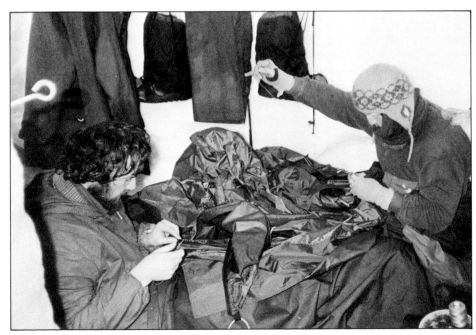

Jim and Kim mending their tent in the snowhole on Lister Glacier. (Howard Oakley)

shaking hands and exchanging salvos of questions with Kim, Peter, Howard and Jim.

Theirs had been quite an epic journey after leaving Lister Glacier cache on 24 September. They took six days progressing up to 900 metres above 'Cushing Col' toward 'Rokki Plateau'. As they reached steeper iceslopes on the shoulder of Rokkitanski a sudden blizzard had hit them, forcing them to dig an emergency snowhole. Wind, spindrift and enveloping cloud continued, but on 1 October they moved over the ridge to seek a way down on to the head of 'Precinct Glacier'. Starting down they were mazed among bewildering great crevasses, then the wind rose suddenly. As they pitched camp, three poles broke on Howard and Peter's tent. They sewed up the ripped outer, but, as they stumbled about in flying spindrift guying it over the snow-wall, Peter tripped over a side guy and the outer tore again. They were now too cold to make another repair, so they collapsed the tent and moved in with Kim and Jim. For three nights high winds and cloud held the four of them crammed into the one little dome tent, sitting up to support the poles, their clothes wet and cold, while they repaired the frozen flysheet. They had been on short rations at Lister Glacier cache, and since leaving it, and now their food was running out. Kim and Peter found a route down in a brief clearance one day. Finally, 4 October dawned calm. With three man-days rations left between them, they broke camp without having breakfast and felt their way down through the crevasses. They dropped out of the cloud at 900 metres and raced down toward 'Astrolabe', anticipating plentiful food and fuel, relaxation and comfort by the sea.

They found the food-cache, the radio and four jerrycans of paraffin — but only just: 4 cm of one marker cane was luckily protruding from the snow. Thankfully they pitched their tents and lay down to eat and eat.

In the previous 22 days they had eaten only 14 days' rations of 4,500 kcal per day. They were literally starving. The body has five main reserves of energy to make up calorie deficiencies, which are used roughly in sequence: (1) glycogen in the muscles; (2) glycogen from the liver; (3) subcutaneous fat; (4) muscle protein; (5) in extremis, fat protecting the main visceral organs. Howard believed that they had started to break down muscle protein for energy before using their subcutaneous fat, because of an independent physiological mechanism which reacts to cold by storing subcutaneous fat. Starvation weakens the body quicker in cold climates.

Next day they had started searching for the bulk fuel, general stores, and 100 man-days of missing rations which had been cached a little further down the slope. They found nothing. They dug for six days, first where Ted's sketch map showed the cache, then trenches across the area, then 'hunch digs' scattered about. Finally they started an open-cast snow mine across the whole area. Three days after we arrived they gave up, having shovelled over 500 cubic metres of snow (about 200 tonnes). We realised that the incredible had happened: the huge seas of early August must have overwhelmed the 5–10 metre basalt 'sea-wall' and then swept over 60 metres beyond it to reach the cache 15 metres above sea-level and carry off the fuel drums and other stores. Searching the now dry moat inside the sea-wall they had found a few fragments, plus one precious Bulldog snowshovel. Now we realised, too late, why the gravel of this campsite had been so clean and washed last March.

They were visibly thinner than before, and experiencing the physical effects of short rations, feeling exhausted after four or five hours' digging. Being less fit after so much time at base camp, Howard had found the journey hardest of all. Apart from physical fatigue he had been appalled by the savagery of the weather: he almost felt that the mountains and crevasses were actively hostile to men forced by starvation to move in bad conditions. The narrowness of their escape had made a deep gloomy impression on him: he was amazed that I still planned to go to 'Dayglo Point' when the cache there might have disappeared, and took me aside to warn me against going, requesting I leave written instructions about expedition jobs, like a will. Later I heard that he had also warned Frank and others that going south was too dangerous. Nor was Howard the only one: Peter definitely did not want to go south now, nor even Kim. It almost seemed to me that their party had been shell-shocked by the awful conditions they had endured. However the need to go south was now even greater. Among various radio messages Jim had received at 'Astrolabe' was a signal from HMS *Endurance* 'requesting' that we all be at Metchnikoff Point for changeover on 28/29 December. It was a service idiom, my senior officer's requirement, stated politely. So the second-summer party would be landed in the north, to explore the south. They needed to know whether they could rely on the cache at 'Dayglo Point'.

Jim also spoke daily by radio with Nick. After three weeks alone at Metchnikoff Point he seemed cheerful, and his ulcer was improving. He hoped to be picked up in November by the BAS supply ship, RRS *John Biscoe*.

On his second day alone (23 September), Nick had walked along the north shore toward the west end of Metchnikoff Point. He had been caught in a small slab avalanche and swept ten metres down on to the shore rocks. He was uninjured, but unable to move, lying with his buried legs awkwardly clamped in the snow. The waves breaking over him at first consolidated the snow like a vice. Alone on the point, there was no possibility of help. However after half an hour the waves began washing the snow away, and he was finally able to free himself, after a very frightening experience.

Nick had been recording the birds and seals at Metchnikoff Point, and now he had some company. One or two Chinstrap Penguins had started coming ashore regularly from 9 October as well as the odd itinerant Gentoos and Adelies, and single skuas had also passed by on 5th and 7th, the first this season. Nearly 500 Shags had roosted on the stacks recently: it seemed as if these great 'shaggregations' moved around nomadically, while smaller numbers formed stable populations scattered around the coast fishing inshore.

Nick also described a 'strange' bird that visited once at the beginning of October. It sounded very like a Light-mantled Sooty Albatross. These wedge-tailed birds are the greatest fliers of all the albatrosses. Nesting as far south as South Georgia, they regularly forage further south of the Antarctic Convergence, but so far I had only seen one myself, from *Endurance* last January, gliding carelessly through a gale 50 km west of Metchnikoff Point.

Up to two dozen Weddell Seals regularly hauled out at Metchnikoff Point now, but they were mostly smaller immatures, and surprisingly Nick had seen no sign of any pups. Two pairs of Crabeaters had just come ashore, each pair lying close together and not going into the water at all. The males were wounded as if they had been fighting. Crabeaters pup in September and these females without pups were probably two or three years old just coming up for their first mating; the males become very possessive at this time, protecting their chosen female in the weeks before mating in late October. Half a dozen Fur Seals had also briefly reappeared early in October, plus one Elephant Seal.

Frank remained keen to go to 'Dayglo' with me, because his grandfather had landed nearby at Buls Bay. However Jed had caught the pessimistic mood at 'Astrolabe Point', so I was greatly cheered when Jim came and said that he would like to go with us. Starting with little mountaineering experience, Jim was now enthusiastically volunteering for every long trip, staying cheerful and undaunted by any hardships. Mike also volunteered, but we agreed he should stay north for the geology. We had a group discussion about revised plans, but could not discuss them with the skidoo party as they had left their radio with Nick. So I decided that Frank, Jim and I would go up next day to meet the skidoos beyond Rokkitanski and continue to 'Dayglo Point'. Then, as Mike was cooking supper, there was a shout from the icefall above. Spotts, Ted and JB

Pare Glacier. Spotts on Dutch Courage with a loaded pulk sledge. (Jed Corbett)

tumbled down the slope on skis into the 'Astrolabe' camp like a breath of fresh air, cheerful, excited and optimistic. We clustered round in the evening sun to hear their story.

Soon after we left them at the head of Lister Glacier on 8th, a track drive halfshaft had sheared on one of the old ex-Transglobe skidoos. Characteristically, Ted had set to work at once on a complicated makeshift repair, pinning the shaft, stiffening it with angle bar, Araldite and steel swarf, and moving one caterpillar track bodily inward to match. It took him four days working outside at 'Pit Stop Cache', while Spotts and JB ferried gear on south over Virchow Ridge. As Ted tested his successful repair, JB returned with the other old skidoo limping along vibrating badly. Ted found two of the engine holding-down bolts sheared: without spares or any suitable bolts he made yet another major field repair by drilling and pinning.

On 13th, with all three skidoos working again, they moved the rest of the stores up to their final skidoo cache at 1,050 metres on Paré Glacier. Triumphantly they ranged two tonnes of fuel, food and other stores in a long rectangle on the piedmont, fenced by bamboo wands — the culmination of the winter's careful preparations and of 37 days' totally dedicated work, mostly in dreadful conditions. The same day they drove on up to 1,250 metres on 'Rokki Plateau'. They searched for a route down the icefall onto 'Precinct Glacier', but the cloud was too thick, so they pitched camp, having completed 25 km in one day.

On 14th they man-hauled two pulks laden with rock specimens and scientific equipment around the flank of Rokkitanski and 12 km down to 'Astrolabe'. Their journey was complete.

The spell of wonderful calm sunlit Peninsula weather that had started on 8th still continued — our first long good spell since May. Five green dome tents now clustered in a complex of snow-walls, like a white-washed kraal beside the abandoned open-cast snow mine. I could not help feeling that it would always be calm and sunny down there by the seaside, that the blizzards would only attack us in the hills, though I knew it was just wishful thinking.

Mike explored the point, finding the geology increasingly fascinating. The massive dark grey rocks with their big crystals were porphyritic basalts — but not lavas that had flowed freely over the country rock. These were gabbroic intrusives: the great columns with their varying orientation were the walls of a convoluted magma chamber that had cooled underground. The overlying older rocks and much of the intrusion itself, had been eroded away since. This was very different from the granites, conglomerates and basalt lavas that predominated at all the sites further north. Ted helped Mike to map the point in detail.

Peter was keenly planning botanical work at 'Astrolabe Point' over the spring growing-season. He marked up belt transects across both points, to study the various factors affecting the growth of the flowering plants, and the strange fact that here they both had many flowering heads, whilst there was only vegetative growth at Metchnikoff Point. Peter's die-tests had showed that the grass roots had died back over the winter, and now he would monitor their regeneration. In many places patches of dull yellowish-brown grass were already free of snow. Pearlwort no longer spangled the point with succulent green pincushions as in March; instead, wrinkled yellow plasters sat among the grass and along damp cracks in the rock. The bushy little *Usnea* lichens also looked shrivelled and wan, but bright orange, yellow and green crustose lichens provided splashes of colour. On slopes where melting ice glistened and moisture trickled downwards, rich lumps of mosses also burgeoned green and gold, as in the height of summer.

An iceberg grounded off the point had been worn to a U-shape by the waves. In any swell, spray burst up to 30 metres at one spot between the two towers, then showered down the inshore slope of the joining isthmus. Under the shower the surface of the berg was stained pink — snow algae thriving on the nutrients in the spray. A few days later the spray had washed away most of the pink skin, exposing bright turquoise ice below.

I enjoyed several hours' birdwatching in this seaside interlude. Cape

Pigeons now foraged inshore and a few fluttered about the colony, where inset ledges gave protection from overhanging ice above. Fulmars also passed by regularly; surprisingly most of them still retained the grey heads of winter plumage. I had hoped to find Snow Petrels nesting here, but only one pair flighted round the cliffs — though many passed by, or foraged in the brash. One Sheathbill visited our camp occasionally (finding no more food than we did in the diggings): since none nested here, it was presumably still foraging along its winter dispersal range of coast. A few Kelp Gulls hung about, including a teenage gang of 20 juveniles and now there were also some older sub-adults. The Wilson's Storm Petrels would not return until later, but I was disappointed that the skuas had not reappeared. Apart from the rather casual return of the Cape Pigeons and Fulmars, there seemed to be a hiatus in the spring awakening, as if the birds did not yet trust this lovely weather. There was one joyful exception: Howard had seen an excited gathering of eight tightly-bonded pairs of Antarctic Terns, and now three pairs occupied definite territories. Except for an hour or two during the day when fishing inshore, each pair stood on lookout rocks, displaying together on the ground occasionally, making frequent pair flights, and noisily protecting their territories against our intrusion. Their territories corresponded remarkably closely with last summer's skua territories: it would be fun to see how the Terns interacted with their major predator, and I asked Howard to plot territories over the next six weeks.

Peter did another round of interviews for the study of social structure of the team. Each person's replies were confidential, and the report would disguise names, but we all rather looked forward to putting names to the anonymous sociograms Johnny Morris would be producing. I would be very interested to see whether inter-relationships and structure changed much in these hectic last months, when we were splintered in several separate groups.

The skidoo team's embullient spirits had refreshed everyone, and the fine weather helped produce a more optimistic mood as the eleven of us recrystallised new plans. Peter and Howard would remain at 'Astrolabe' through November, doing botany, etc. The rest of us would first climb Mount Parry, with Kim leading a Himalayan style assault portering up a dwindling triangle of food and fuel. Then four of us would head for 'Dayglo Point' (Ted had opted to come with us as I had so much hoped), while the other five explored around Hill Bay if time and rations allowed. There was enough food in this belt of the island until the end of November; then people would have to return to Metchnikoff Point, where penguin eggs and a couple of seals could be taken to eke out the few remaining rations.

We had started backpacking rations up from 'Astrolabe Point' on 13th. It took us three days to get the 270 man-days of light dehydrated Arctic rations up to 300 metres, plus pulks, etc. It was a mindless sweating plod, up and down the same tracks, one team in crampons up the steep part, another on skis above. After a restful Sunday (on Tuesday 16th) we moved out next day, still in calm sunshine. We leap-frogged camps up the ridge toward Rokkitanski, ferrying rations in short stages, each carrying 10 man-days in our packs and another ten on a pulk. Despite the repetitive toil we enjoyed the glorious contrast with September weather, marred only by some cloud and one windy night.

Camped at 1,000 metres on 19th we watched the sun set behind Anvers Island at 9 p.m. A rich red afterglow rimmed Mount Francais and

the lovely ridges printed across the southern horizon. Anvers seemed to float above a band of obscuring cloud, without connection to the sea or to the little Melchior Islands sprinkled dimly below. Next morning a smooth blanket of white and grey cloud was spread all over the sea, inviting us to ski across its undulating surface. In crystal sunshine we found an easy route across the top bowl of 'Precinct Glacier' and sliding up a perfect ramp between two icefalls onto 'Rokki Plateau' at 1,300 metres.

Camp 2 above 'Astrolabe Point', with Mount Parry beyond, beckoning. (Jed Corbett)

On 21st, Howard and Peter sledged their last load up and turned back for 'Astrolabe' with two boxes of biscuits. Peter had made a hard decision, denying himself mountaineering adventure to do the more important botany. There was a reef of emotion just below the surface as we said farewells until December. 'Take care,' he said, and he meant it.

That day, six of us took three pulks up and over 'Rokki Plateau'. On that wide plateau the snow disappeared on all sides in cloud, while spindrift poured across from the south-west. Our little cavalcade reminded me of early black and white photos of sledging in the 'heroic' age of Antarctic expeditions. Our journeys were so much shorter, but we moved up and down steeper slopes, except on rare occasions like this. We passed Kim, Spotts and Jed's camp, where the three skidoos exemplified modern Antarctic travel. (BAS changed to skidoos some years ago, not because they could achieve more than dogs, but because of the problems of feeding dogs.) We traversed down and along the north-eastern flank of Rokkitanski. Ted leading, and Mike pulling the first pulk, had heavy work crossing the lines of hard drift snow. The sastrugi were about half a metre high, undercut at their windward ends to anvil shapes by the constant blast of spindrift sweeping along under the prevailing westerly winds. After travelling 15 km, the downslope wind suddenly rose above gale force, and we pitched camp in blinding spindrift. Dome tents are tricky to pitch and seven poles broke as we struggled with the flogging tents behind rushed snow-walls. One tent had to be collapsed and Jim moved in with Ted and Mike, while Frank joined JB and me. As we sat inside, brushing snow off confused heaps of sleeping bags, clothes and boots, and enjoyed the first brew of the evening, I realised how much we had learnt in the winter months. Now a blowout in the middle of nowhere was just an amusing nuisance, not really a danger.

I woke at 5 a.m., freezing cold despite sleeping in my duvet jacket. I shifted about, lying on my arms until they ached. Then I looked out. It was calm, and sunlight was already gilding Mount Morgagni. In hot sunshine we sledged on to pitch camp at 1,100 metres below 'Paré Icefall'. The skidoos arrived and we lazed around the camp in shirtsleeves, tired and happy to have got there in only five days, our faces covered with smiles and peeling sunburn.

Pastel blue and cream-coloured islands emerged from an endless carpet of grey cloud. Far to the north were the familiar serrations of Smith Island. Trinity Island hung poised exactly above the notch between Liege Island and Morgagni; from here it was clearly separate from the Peninsula mountains, which tapered away over the horizon beyond Morgagni Col. Hoseason Island was almost submerged in the cloud. Far beyond Hoseason another dramatic island showed faint but clear — it was Deception Island, 150 km distant. Springing from the spreading centre of Bransfield Strait, Deception's old volcanic caldera was used as a harbour by sealers and whalers, entering through one narrow gap in the crater rim, called Neptunes Bellows. In 1970 it erupted for the first time since its discovery. Visiting it in 1971 we had found steaming muddy flats, while the abandoned base huts stood like a wild-west ghost town, one swinging window shutter creaking eerily.

Above us, 'Paré Icefall' dropped from the ridge. Two black dots inching up past a slab-sided spire of ice were Ted and JB, wending their way up to 1,600 metres on skis to mark the route. Next day we toiled and sweated up and down the ice-fall with stores, moving from marker wand to marker wand in shifting mountain cloud.

Each evening Jim spent hours hand-charging the Clansman radio. That night from our high perch he made his first two-way contact with the Falklands. He passed a personal message from JB to his girlfriend: Sue must have been on duty at RAF Kinloss — two hours later Jim brought her reply, only the third personal message we had received in seven months! Time now seemed to be rushing headlong toward our departure, and we talked a lot about returning home, sometimes forgetting that Mike would stay behind after we left. Jim also got a message from Bill Block at BAS: Bill Hankinson had finally located the first-summer samples; the Metchnikoff Monster Mites were not an exciting new species, they were a circumpolar and bipolar tick *Ixodes uriae*, parasitic on various seabirds but also able to overwinter free-living. This news was a disappointment, but now we were too busy to mind.

The windless weather went on and on, though we were mostly in cloud as we plodded up and down the icefall. We moved camp to 1,450 metres above the steep lower section, and then to the top at 1,650 metres. As we arrived at the top camp on 26th one of my ski bindings broke. It was fair wear and tear, the first defect among ten pairs of these wonderful bindings in nine months' hard usage, but it was a set-back. I cursed myself for not changing it earlier, but without a murmur Kim and

Spotts went back down next day to collect the spare from the Skidoo Cache, far below in the sea of cloud which lapped halfway up the icefall. They returned early on 28th, emerging into sunlight from the cloud with heavy packs, as we were still breakfasting. The 30-metre-deep schrund halfway up the icefall had opened up two metres — still an easy jump downward, but an awkward climb up.

The mountain clouds had now evaporated, and we roasted in a glaring sun as we pulked the stores up along the broad whaleback ridge toward Harvey Heights. We pitched camp at 1,900 m that evening: the sun coppering the cloud carpet over the sea was still hot, and people stripped off to dig tent shelters. We were now sunburnt, particularly Kim and Frank, the redheads. What a contrast from September! I also recalled the contrast with the six of us camped there in March with twelve man-days rations between us. Now the nine of us were poised with 229 man-days rations. In eleven days we had travelled a total of only 25 km on the map, but Kim calculated we had each travelled about 138 km, with a total height gain of 7,000 metres carrying loads of 20-30 kg. I had been really enjoying being an unthinking beast of burden, leaving all the organisation, arithmetic and leadership in Kim's hands, but I also had to relearn the frustrations of a subordinate.

We slept early, ready for a 4 a.m. start on 29th. It was yet another calm and sunlit morning, hard and cold. Harvey Heights and Mount Parry cast long blue shadows out across the white clouds carpeting the sea. Breaking camp at 6 a.m. we set off across perfect hard snow, creaking in the cold, to make the first ascent of Mount Parry, 2,522 metres, the crown of Brabant Island. After three years dreaming of this, it was to prove a day of bitter personal disappointment to me.

Halfway up, Kim said we would pitch camp as soon as we reached the summit ridge of Harvey Heights. I had hauled a light pulk up, expecting to use it taking Camp 11 to the far end of Harvey Heights' gentle ridge. Now I foresaw an extra 3-4 km returning from the climb. It was the first time in nine months' grand companionship that I had felt the gap of years: at 49 my recovery rate from exhaustion was slower, so I had to pace myself to keep a reserve of energy to cover any eventuality. I worried miserably about that extra distance to follow the ascent.

Resting halfway up Harvey Heights. Mount Morgagni Liege Island and distant Trinity Island rise from a carpet of cloud below. (Jed Corbett)

We pitched the three tents on the bald snow pate of Harvey Heights' north summit — the furthest point we had reached in March. It was still only midday when we left with bivouac gear. As we skied along the gently rounded convolutions of the ridge, new views burst below us, first on one side then the other. On our right the ridges of Mount Parry dropped out of sight below the mushroomed ice-cliffs of the main ridge. Kim and Ted looked enviously at the north-west ridge, a classic snow and ice route soaring out of the cloud to blend into the summit block across a steep iceslope: its full 2,500 metres from the hidden sea below would be one of the longest ridge routes in the world. Lesser spurs projecting from the cliffs were festooned with mushrooms of snow, folded across them like gigantic white towels hung out to dry. On our left, the route to 'Dayglo Point' unfolded, down a ridge which waded far out into the clouds smothering Gerlache Strait, then down and along a broad piedmont highway to the south. Offshore the spine of Lecointe Island swam southward through the grey sea of cloud like a huge white Leopard Seal.

Changing to crampons we came over the last lump of Harvey Heights to overlook the more dramatic ridge that led across to Parry. It was a lovely winding mushroomed ridge, as if a giant had wildly squeezed out a 20-metre wide coil of toothpaste along the crest between the headwall of Mackenzie Glacier and the western precipices. Far beyond and far below the Solvay Mountains appeared at last, a galaxy of snow peaks, with black rock-faces frowning down around the clouds in Buls Bay.

After crossing the ridge we gathered for a final rest before the last 200-metre climb. It was 3 p.m. Now I felt that I would manage it, but I would be completely exhausted by the time we got back to our tents. Soon after we started upward again, Spotts shouted that he was stopping: two very

long days had knackered him. He was happy to wait for our return, but I changed ropes and went slowly back with Spotts. We watched the seven tiny figures gradually creep up, then stand at last upon the summit at 4.20 p.m. I imagined their elation, and should have felt pride and triumph for Kim and my whole grand team: instead I felt envy and unreasonable resentment. We chatted cheerfully, while inside I felt a bitter ache of broken dreams. We reached the tents at 7 p.m. and the others trickled back between 8 and 9 p.m. They were elated but exhausted after a very long day, covering 22 km; Ted and JB had even helped Mike collect a basalt sample from 2,200 metres, perhaps the highest sample from the whole Peninsula region. What really hurt most was that no one, except Ted, realised just how I felt. One day, when he was about 50 (I told Kim unkindly), a climber 20 years younger would overextend him on the hill, and then he would remember this day.

The First Ascent Party on the summit of Mount Parry. Standing l to r: JB, Mike, Jim and Ted. Kneeling: Kim and Frank. Taking the photograph Jed Corbett.

Ted and Jed generously offered to repeat the climb with me next day. I lay awake into the small hours, listening to rising wind and praying it would not stop us. When I woke, the sun was bright on the green tent walls. We skied off for Mount Parry from the sleeping camp. It seemed somehow fitting that we happened to be the three from the first-summer party. Yesterday's misery lifted away into a cloudless glorious day.

As we changed to crampons, a Snow Petrel drifted up from Malpighi Glacier, winged curiously past us and then soared along the 2,400-metre ridge on the cold west wind. The mountains here are beautiful, but utterly lonely; there are no eagles, no hares, no ptarmigan — no living thing to give surprise, variety and company. This lovely white petrel symbolised a very happy day — it had no reason to be here, no nearby nest, no possibility of food; it was up here simply for the joy of flight, like us for the joy of mountaineering.

We reached the little summit plateau, and walked up the final mush-

room jutting out beyond the western cliffs. The tops of many mountains are an anti-climax. Not so Mount Parry. From the airy sloping peak we looked down each side to stupefying ridges, dropping precipitously down and ever down into soft cloud far below us. At last I could turn all round without another peak to hide the distance. We looked down over all the island — north to Mount Hunter and familiar ridges, south to a whole new vista of peakier mountains, wide snow plateaux and the distant spire of Bulcke Finger. White cloud blanketed the seas, but far to the south beyond Anvers other blue islands stood out — the Argentine Islands 130 km away. The minute dot of our tent pricking the dome of Harvey Heights 5 km behind was the only indicator of the great scale of this mountain. We lingered an hour then headed back to laze happily drinking and eating before a dreamless sleep. Now it mattered not to me that I had missed the first ascent: I had seen my island from the top.

Opposite. Ted and Chris on Mount Parry. The cliffs beyond drop 2,400m to the sea. (Jed Corbett)

The First Ascent of Mount Parry, 29 October 1984. Kim reaches the summit. (Jed Corbett)

On the last day of October we dropped down in cloud to find the others camped at 2,100 metres on the great convex shoulder of Harvey Heights. A little below the tents the slope steepened and then dropped in frightening cliffs into 'No Go Corrie'. The cloud parted at last over Gerlache Strait, but cloud still filled the great void below where Hill Bay and 'No Go Corrie' cut deep across the island. We were perched on the bottleneck between the north and south which had restricted us so long: we called the spot 'Scotch Corner'. The others had brought up the food and fuel for the journey to 'Dayglo Point'. The four tents drifted up on 31st as I helped Ted prepare our three pulks ready for the morrow.

The *Antarctic Pilot* states that the worst weather of the year usually comes in October, but for us it had been the best month of all. For the last two weeks we had been burnt in almost constant sun, or calm mountain cloud, while far below us cloud had mantled the sea entirely to a depth of 300 metres. Despite satellite photography, the Antarctic's meteorological statistics are still built on records from the bases, all at low coastal sites. We thought that perhaps our October weather had been typical; the *Antarctic Pilot* might be wrong. Now we were full of optimism for November.

November

Howard and Peter's tent at 'Astrolabe Point'. Sunlight glints on the moat inside the seawall. Grass and Pearlwort were richest on the north side of this promontory. (Howard Oakley)

The 1st was glorious. The sun shone. Even the clouds below had cleared to show the blue waters of Gerlache Strait sprinkled with little icebergs. Ted, Jim, Frank and I broke camp and roped up, ranging our three heavy pulks in line. I did not believe our journey to 'Dayglo Point' was as dangerous as the majority had felt, nevertheless we were taking 100 man-days food and fuel to cover a retreat: we would leave caches on the way down, taking enough onward for a week's digging to find the food. I felt confident we would find the fuel drums and we could always spin out the food with penguins and seals.

The others came out to see us off. Next day, Kim, JB and Mike were leaving for a fortnight's geology down the ridge south of Hill Bay, and then they would rejoin Spotts and Jed at the Skidoo Cache, to climb elusive Mount Morgagni. We were taking the only radio with us, so we would not know each others' doings until they got back to Metchnikoff Point in December. Kim and Jed seemed a bit wistful — perhaps half wishing that they too had chosen to go south. Altogether it was another quite emotional farewell.

We all shook hands, then we were off. Soon their figures went back into the tents. A little later the tents themselves, now little dots, were hidden by the mountain slope.

All four of us were excited and in high spirits. At long last we were heading into new country, to the south. We traversed above the slopes steepening into 'No Go Corrie'. Alpine ridges dropped below us into clouds filling Hill Bay: we could make believe that down in the cloud was a friendly little alpine village with skilifts and restaurants, old men shovelling snow and girls on holiday laughing. In breezy sunshine, we went an easy pace and dropped down the ridge before Malpighi Glacier. We left our first cache (of 20 man-days) at 1,700 metres above a little icefall, and then pitched our two dome tents below, where the ridge levelled at 1,500 metres.

Now we were in a strange landscape, out of sight at last from any of the familiar northern landmarks, except one — above and behind us spindrift flared off the summit of Mount Parry. The sun slid behind the ridge, lighting the spindrift into orange flame against the blue. Here on the eastern slopes, sunset came three hours earlier, but it was still light enough to read at 10 p.m. The whole character of this eastern side differed completely from the north and west. Long ramp-like ridges ran down from Harvey Heights and Parry toward the sea, rock-faces along their flanks swept by falls from hanging glaciers above. Malpighi and Mackenzie Glaciers cut deep, classical U-shaped valleys far back into the island's spine; below us they debouched on to a broad piedmont before spilling together down a chaotic 700 metre icefall to the Gerlache Strait. Months ago studying the aerial photographs, we had seen only one possible way down to Malpighi Glacier, somewhere nearby. Making a quick recce in rising spindrift, we found the ramp; the best way over the top crevasse was just 50 metres from our tents!

We cooked and ate that evening in supreme content. Ted said that next time he completed my Likes/Dislikes questionnaire 'A small exploring group' would be his top pleasure. We all felt the same. Six or nine was cheerful and companionable, but four alone away in unknown places was real adventure and romance, the stuff of dreams.

The weather was lovely again as we descended next morning. The laden pulks rolled over time and again on the first steep slope. Without skis I found I could somersault sideways to untwist the flexible bamboo shafts, but after three or four such rolls, Frank had to come back to help unwrap our rope from the shafts. Ted experimented happily with a controllable rope brake as we crossed Malpighi Glacier to camp further down on Mackenzie Glacier. Yet another glorious day followed. We traversed gently down to turn the next ridge where it paused above the sea. There at 700 metres we left our second 20 man-day cache. The orange and green bags of rations sat like a beacon on a prow of snow, overlooking the final ruinous icefalls of the two big glaciers and the ribboned waters of Freud Passage leading northward. The coastal ramparts of the Peninsula were clear and sharp across the Gerlache Strait: it came as a shock to see on the map that here the strait was as wide as the English Channel. Those specks of sea-ice, brilliant white against the dark blue water, were really icebergs that would dwarf a ship. Opposite us, the waters of Charlotte Bay were mirror calm, reflecting the creamy tint of the snows behind. An old abandonned FIDS hut was marked on the map at Portal Point at the foot of a long ridge leading gently up to 2000 metres; elsewhere, rock-faces and steep icefalls hemmed the Peninsula, barring access to the sledging plateau above.

As we hauled the pulks south up over a gentle ridge I plodded in Ted's ski tracks, head down, my eyes on my ski-tips, avoiding stepping on the rope. The rope stopped. I looked up. Ted was leaning forward on his ski-sticks, looking ahead. We had turned the corner. Before us a great expanse of snow sloped gently up into the centre of the island, and there beyond stood the Solvay Mountains. Peak after unclimbed peak crowded our southern horizon as we sat on our pulks in the sun, eating chocolate and studying the map, trying to fit the familiar names to that tangle of mountains. It was a paradise for mountaineering — and the map was wrong!

The highest peak of all stood midway between Galen and Celsus Peaks, and without a name. But we could not look for ever, with another 11 km sledging to 'Dayglo Point'. We set off again, drawing the pulks easily across that open undulating plain of snow.

We stopped next overlooking Buls Bay which bit out a great chunk of water dominated by the rock-scarred faces of the Solvay Mountains. For Frank especially it was a poignant, long-awaited moment. There on the south shore of Buls Bay, his grandfather had made the first landing on

The Dayglo Party rests after arriving above Buls Bay, looking across to Celsus Peak and 'Mount Frederick Cook', in line above the two marks. (Chris Furse)

the island. With Amundsen, Cook, Arctowski and fated Danco he had struggled up to 300 metres, with three heavy sledges, the first sledges used in Antarctica, not unlike our own pulks. Near those striking nuna-taks of black rock that sprang from the piedmont they had pitched the first tent recorded in Antarctica — and no one else had camped on Brabant Island in 86 intervening years.

Gambling on finding the food at 'Dayglo Point' we cached the last 50 man-days stores from the pulks at 500 metres, taking just the two days' emergency in our packs. As Ted found a lovely ski ramp down the icefall we sighted the point. The lump on the map was a 70-metre hillock of snow; a hogsback of snow sloped down to its northern tip, where a little snow-covered rock-spit extended out. I searched the spit with binoculars, but could see no cache. It took another hour of rising anticipation to reach the point. Coming to the hogsback, Ted looked over the spine, and shouted: 'I can see some boxes!' Jim peered further over: 'There are marker canes on the snowslope above!' Five minutes later we were down on the low 50 × 15 metre spit, touching boxes and cartons exposed on the surface. We rushed about, laughing with glee and hugging each other in congratulation and relief.

Then, while Frank and I disturbed some Gentoo Penguins to erect the tents, Jim and Ted dug out the food cache. At intervals shouts reached us: 'Breadmix!', 'Custard!', 'Spare skis!', 'Araldite!'. We gathered outside the tents, greedily scoffing Mars Bars, projecting plans for the month now opening before us, and giggling about the imagined dangers of our journey south. Then we retired into our tents to enjoy the real danger — vast overeating. Tomorrow was definitely to be a Sunday, and the day after.

Our time at 'Dayglo Point' was like a seaside holiday. Even our weather luck continued. After two weeks' low cloud while we climbed Mount Parry in sunlight, then three completely cloudless days while we journeyed down, clouds now cloaked the hills above 500 metres, while we enjoyed sunny breaks beside the Gerlache Strait. We didn't even bother to build snow-walls until a windy day arose later. It was the first time we had camped right on the shore. Shattered icebergs, melting bergy bits and smaller brash were scattered over the strait, their reflec-tions lilac tinted in the evening light. Here the sea seemed almost like an inland lake, with mountainous coasts in all directions except far to the northeast where a small gap appeared between the Peninsula and Trinity Island. Growlers and old floes, grounded round the point, crunched and grumbled outside the tents, while small waves splashed quietly against our shores.

At high tide the waves washed up over the worn grey granite to nibble at the metre-deep cap of snow we camped on. The granite floor ran all along the neighbouring coasts as well, presumably an ancient intertidal platform. Now the glaciers flowed to the edge of the rock, where they fell off in 50–80-metre-high ice-cliffs. In the warm weather the ice-cliff facing us across the little bay shed pieces with a crack and rumble like nearby thunder. Even small falls made a thunderous noise, and occasionally larger falls sent waves rushing noisily across the bay, some casting lumps of brash-ice up on to the snow by the tent. Inevitably we called it 'Thunder Bay', perhaps misleadingly, because there are no thunder-storms in this region, where the troposphere has insufficient depth to develop so much convective turbulence.

At low tide a broad beach spit was exposed extending across 'Thunder

Bay'. It seemed to be an old moraine, with angular stones rather than rounded wave-worn pebbles. Some of the larger stones were beginning to gather close-packed in patches resembling the 'boulder pavements' which occur in the South Shetlands. Some larger boulders also sat on the beach, together with lumps of sea-ice as big as tents: a series of depressions running across the beach spit from the sea appeared to be associated with these, and the melting iceblocks often sat in gravelly hollows. It was impossible to distinguish cause and effect without a full year's detailed survey.

Sometimes we smelt a distinct organic seashore smell. Perhaps it occurred also at Metchnikoff Point, masked by the stench of penguins, but we guessed the sheltered waters of Gerlache Strait encouraged a richer growth of seaweed. In the clear shallow waters there were signs of advancing spring. Litte amphipods swam about like tiny fish. Jim saw one large pale pink jellyfish, and the limpets had now moved further up into intertidal rock pools.

A group of Kelp Gulls were based in the bay, sometimes foraging far out in the strait, but regularly gathering to feed in the shallows near the beach, swimming about and plunge diving. I identified limpets as their prey in the shallows but I never saw gulls feeding on those exposed at low tide. The adult gulls showed no territorial behaviour, and mingled with the sub-adults (second year?) which predominated. Two dozen Gentoos also foraged locally and came ashore to rest on the snow, braying mellowly beside the tents where they sheltered from the wind. Some had a powdering of white on their blue-grey chins and were probably first-year birds, not breeders.

Apart from the Kelps and Gentoos the spit was now merely a passing point for birds, but quite a busy one. A few Chinstrap Penguins sometimes came ashore on rough evenings, and buoyant Antarctic Terns overflow regularly. A Sheathbill visited the camp, looking remarkably clean and white: the winter hints of dark grey underdown had vanished with the spring moult, and the pink and yellow stains of summer had not yet appeared. Occasionally, passing Giant Petrels circled for a second inspection — perhaps our tents with rucksacks and ropes littered outside resembled dead whales with sundered entrails. Snow Petrels foraged inshore frequently, particularly on days when the south-west wind kicked up white horses in the strait, and drove the bergs and smaller ice through faster on their northward drifts. Those were also the days when we saw the other medium-sized petrels. Very few Cape Pigeons passed, but streams of Antarctic Fulmars headed south into the wind, a few still in winter plumage. Trying to photograph them with a 110 mm lens combination (standard 55 mm lens with a versatile 2 × converter) showed me how each species used a very specific flight-path: the Fulmars followed a band 50–100 metres off the point; the Snow Petrels meandered, investigating grounded icebergs, bits of brash-ice, the beach, and even the tents; a few south-going Antarctic Petrels swept along close over the shoreline.

A colony of Blue-eyed Shags in Buls Bay had been mentioned by the *Belgica* expedition. There was a constant traffic past 'Dayglo Point' to and from inshore fishing areas north to Pinel Point: apart from two flocks of 30–50, they flew singly or in parties of under five, and fishing parties were also of one to five birds. All this suggested a large colony nearby to southward. Frank and I skied 3 km to the tongue of snow projecting into Buls Bay, but the only possible colony site was a small islet off Buls

Island, still largely snow-covered. As many as 30% of these Shags were sub-adults without yellow caruncles on their beaks and with brown pale-tipped coverts, giving a distinct mottled appearance. I had looked in vain for such sub-adults among the great winter flocks at Metchnikoff Point — perhaps the juveniles fare north in winter, then return in spring.

We saw our first skua on 6th and thereafter their numbers grew gradually; most flew steadily southward, and none ever gave the bold postures and calls of territorial displays. A single Wilson's Storm Petrel flew past on 10th, our first of the year returned from the far north. The pace of spring was accelerating, but oh so slowly still!

Frank searched the fringe of shoreline rocks daily for seals. One or two Weddells hauled out, and twice he found pups. They were the first we had seen, now about a month old, with bands of yellow woolly natal coat remaining along their flanks. One was alone, but the other cuddled beside its mother, suckling greedily, although very fat and already three-quarters of her length. As the tide sloshed water at it, the pup baa-ed like a lost lamb, clambering heavily across the sleeping mother, until she led it off to swim around the beach. Single Crabeaters occasionally visited, inspecting the empty beach briefly then swimming off, their pale coats showing white under water (they are also called the 'White Seal'). On the evening we arrived, Frank had seen a whale blow far out in the strait, but that proved to be our only sighting: after the *Belgica* report of whales blowing all around, their scarcity had been a great disappointment.

We had decided to stay a week, digging out, mustering and re-stacking the cached stores, but events prolonged our stay. We found all the expected stores, with over 800 man-days of food and fuel for the second summer. On 8th we started backpacking more rations 500 metres up to the cache; high winds prevented ferrying next day, so on 10th (instead of moving out as planned) we carried up the second loads, eyes smarting in baths of sweat.

Returning to the camp, Frank suddenly spotted a ship out in the strait moving sedately past a little iceberg. A tubby, red-hulled ship with white superstructure and a little diesel funnel sticking up with an air of surprise, she looked very much at home. She was the first ship we had seen since *Endurance* left us in March. Aeroplanes had flown over occasionally as the brief summer season swung into action, but a ship was much more personal contact — through binoculars I could even seen people walking about. She was the BAS supply ship RRS *John Biscoe* — Nick might be on board! We felt slightly disappointed as she moved on northward. Then she swung back, and hove-to about 5 km off. Expectantly we watched and Ted put a big brew on, just in case. A dot emerged around her stern and came toward us, rapidly growing until we could see three orange-suited figures. The neat little inflatable nudged up against the rocks, and the four of us stood awkwardly welcoming two grinning Fids, and Nick. They could only stay briefly, but Nick managed to tell us his news.

At base camp the first dozen Chinstrap Penguins had started to walk up and inspect their snow-covered colonies on 24th October. By 27th total numbers had risen to about 100 and some had started gathering stones for their nests. Numbers had risen steadily to reach 1,300 by the end of October, when Nick had first seen a pair mating. In most penguin species the males arrive first and stake their claim to a nest before the females arrive, but this sounded as if Chinstrap females arrive with the males! There had been an influx of over 30 Gentoos recently: they breed earlier than the Chinstraps, so these were probably young non-breeders, rather than spring migrants heading further south.

All the other birds were also swinging into the breeding season. Single Cape Pigeons and pairs had visited their nest-sites regularly from 21 October when Nick had watched one shovelling snow out of a nest-ledge for over an hour. The Snow Petrels remained an enigma, with a few occasionally flighting around the butte, while large coasting movements headed west and south some days, as in winter. The first two Wilson's Storm Petrels had flitted around the cliffs on 28 October. He had seen one or two skuas daily from 20 October but most just flew past and the first sign of territorial occupation was one standing on the met. station rock on 31st. The Kelps had begun to frequent the colonial areas from mid-October. Sheathbill pairs had taken up territories and started their disjointed bowing displays from 20 October, and that was the last day he had seen a flock of them. Another big flock of up to 200 Shags had roosted on the skerries in late October.

Weddell Seal numbers at Metchnikoff Point had built up to three dozen by the beginning of November, but with no sign of any pups. The Crabeaters had left by the beginning of November, and no more Fur Seals had arrived.

John Biscoe had arrived off Metchnikoff Point on 3rd November to pick up Nick, and had also landed fuel and rations for the rest of us in December, which would be a relief for the local wildlife. Nick's ulcer had eased, and now standing in the boat smiling self-consciously he looked very healthy, as well as strangely clean.

Minutes later the boat sped away to the waiting ship. They had given us two cartons of food and a bag which made an encouraging clinking noise: 4 loaves of bread! Oranges! Apples! Onions! Turnips! Pussers Rum! Standing on the granite foreshore we bit into juicy fruit, a little bemused by the sudden visitation.

Next day Ted and Frank set off to take some final oddments up to the cache. Later, as I skied over the hogsback to visit the other end of the point, I saw them on our normal track, only it wasn't 'them'. It was one of them.

Through binoculars I saw one man digging (putting in a belay?), with just a rucksack showing, a rope's length below him. As I approached, I saw it was Frank on top. Ted had fallen seven metres down a very deep crevasse, but was alright, and Frank had been taking photographs, not digging. Frank came back to his iceaxe belay beside his rucksack, and soon Ted's head appeared over the snow. After hauling out his rucksack and skis, he walked down to us along the rope, blood on his face, and a nastily grazed thumb from the icy crevasse walls. Dragging on a cigarette, he told us that an innocent snow surface had dropped under him without warning. Frank had held him on the rope, and Ted had 'proved the system'. He had been held on his jumars, dropped his pack (already tied on to the end of the rope), tied his skis to the pack, banged in an ice-screw as extra protection, and then waited for Frank to come up along the rope on his jumar and confirm he was firmly belayed. Then he jumared up and out. He admitted the shakes would come later. How different was Frank's confident competence now from his inexperienced shock when Nick fell in April! We made him up to a Second straight away. We had all skied over that unsuspected crevasse many times, sometimes carelessly with slack ropes. The island was falling apart in the warm weather, and Ted's fall was a timely warning. He and Frank went on to complete their lift to the cache.

South-westerly winds channelling up Gerlache Strait next day swept spindrift across the slopes, and we delayed departure once more. That evening a tremendous bang sounded from the ice-cliff opposite, followed by a long roar. Ted happened to be outside and grabbed his camera as a whole section 30 metres long, 50 metres high, and about five metres back to the first crevasse (over 2000 tonnes) fell into the sea. He watched the baby berg wallowing, as the cloud of ice debris settled and the waves spread out. Suddenly he started to run, shouting to us to evacuate, as the waves were growing big enough to swamp the tents. We grabbed our boots and piled out, to see a series of waves racing toward our spit. In fact the first and largest wave just rode up on to the edge of our little snowflat. The roosting Gentoos had also fled in panic. Now we understood why penguins did not nest here!

We left at last next morning in glorious weather (I believed that 13th was a lucky date). At the 500-metre cache we loaded up the four pulks with food and fuel for 30 days: our packs weighed nearly 20 kg, and the loaded pulks about 70 kg. This would be the longest totally self-support-ing trip of the expedition, and the first time we had all had a pulk each.

This was perfect pulking terrain. We plodded off up gentle slopes on firm though rather sticky snow, and pitched camp that evening at 650 metres out on the spacious snowfield. We were still bathed in sunshine, but a heavy blanket of cloud was pouring over the spine of the island from the south-west, and great grey mushrooms boiled upward from the summit of Mount Parry through the blanket into blue above. A smooth, layered band of cloud hung on the wave over the whole length of the Peninsula. The Solvay Mountains had long been my personal holy grail, and now the whole south end of the island belonged to us four alone, for a month. It was good to be on the move again: but we did not know the frustrations that lay ahead of us.

After two days held up — by falling damp snow and our first blizzard in a month — we dug out from a metre of snow, and broke camp. Half a dozen Kelp Gulls stood on the snow nearby watching us: they seldom come this high, so I guessed they were passing on migration, but the two adults were performing muted mutual choking displays. We pulked steadily on, up undulations which were indistinguishable on the map, until at 900 metres we were stopped by snow sticking thickly to our ski-skins (2 kg of weight on your feet is equivalent to 15 kg on your back). We were now close under the three conical snowpeaks that we had dubbed 'The Family'. In the evening, after pitching camp, Frank and I skied over to a 1000-metre ring contour overlooking Buls Bay. As we reached the top, the cloud smothering us evaporated and we stood for half an hour watching errant patches of cloud wreathe first the black cliffs of Mount Imhotep, then the lovely parallel, curving patterns of crevasses below us on Hippocrates Glacier. Further south Celsus Peak jutted up like a stavechurch steeple: it looked about my climbing limit as a second, let alone leading.

Then for several days small depressions came through, with the barometer meandering slowly between 957 and 978 mB. For most of the time we were enveloped in calm cloud, with snow falling. The cloud was probably only a layer in some temperature inversion, but our camp was out on the featureless snowfields so we did not risk being unable to find it returning in cloud with our tracks filled in. Nor could we move camp

25 **July.** The cache near 'Claire's Finger' (John Kimbrey)
26 **August.** Ted's party arrives back at basecamp (Jed Corbett)
27 **August.** Chatting beside the hut (Jed Corbett) Overleaf

28 **August.** Ted preparing a skidoo in the garage porch (Jed Corbett)
29 **September.** Half drifted dome tents (Howard Oakley)
30 **September.** The Burial Ground — someone else's spindrift (Jed Corbett) Overleaf
31 **September.** Pulk and tents near Roentgen Peak (Jed Corbett) Overleaf

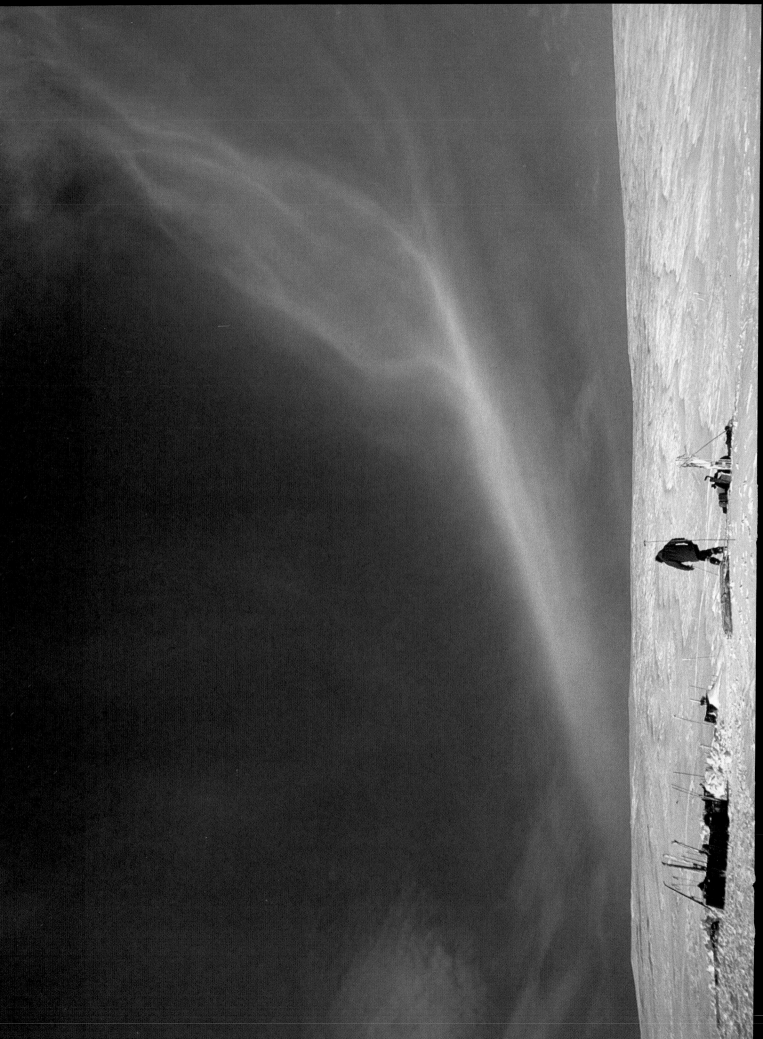

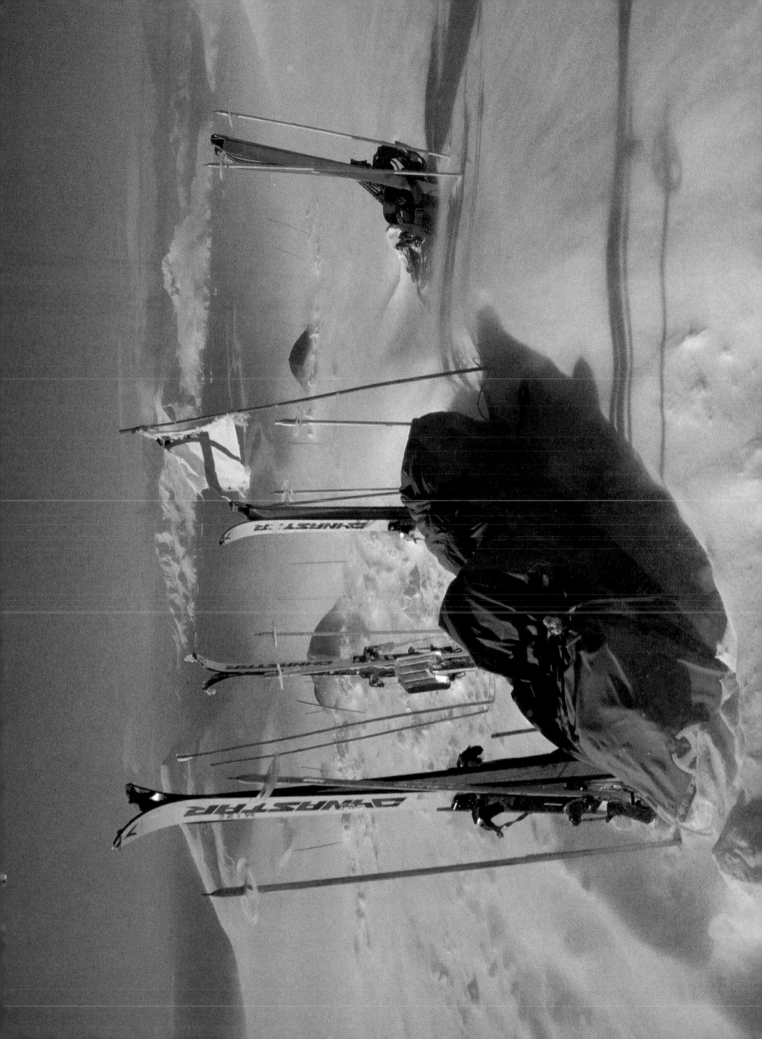

32

33

32 **October.** Snowhole on Lister Glacier — social evening (Jed Corbett)
33 **October.** Antarctic Tern (Jed Corbett)
34 **October.** Crossing 'Rokki Plateau' (Ted Atkins) Opposite
35 **October.** The summit of Mount Parry (Jed Corbett) Overleaf

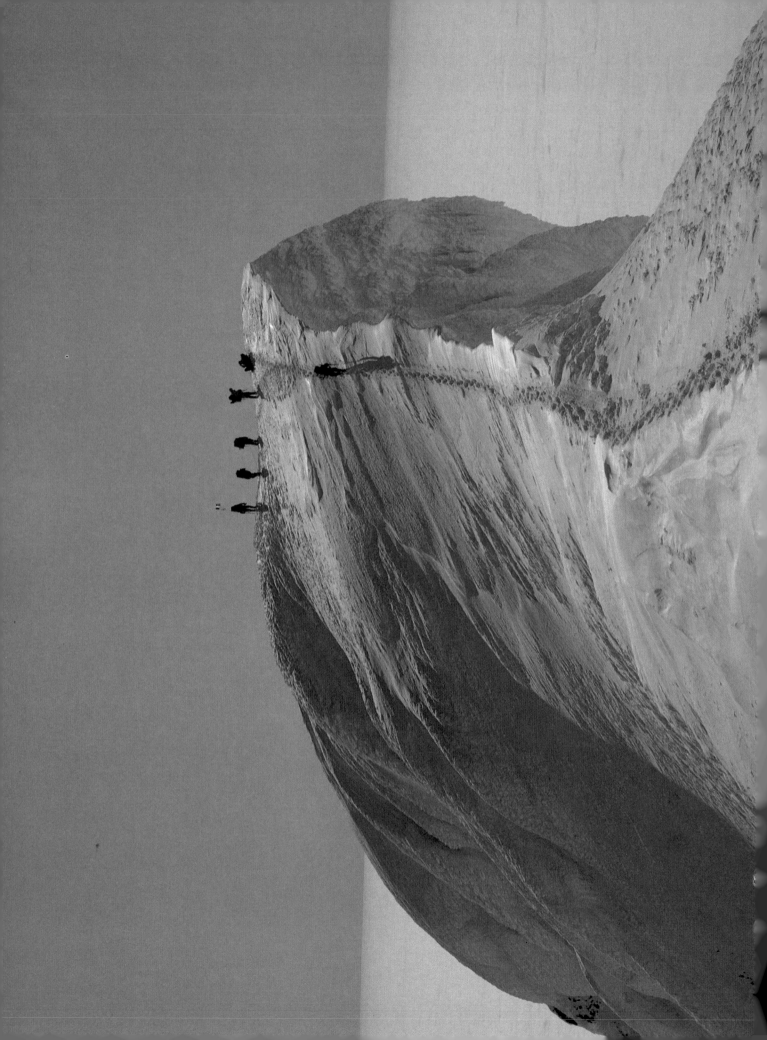

Camp below 'Mother Peak'.
(Chris Furse)

bodily because the deep soft snow was desperate for sledging. So for most of four days we lay up, passing round our last three books. Jim and Ted were running a chess championship. Sometimes Frank or I would go over to their tent for a game and other times one of them would come over to us. On 18th sunshine promised well and we backpacked loads up to 1,100 metres: then as we cached them, spindrift began to rip off the ridges, so we abandoned plans to climb 'The Family' peaks and hurried back while visibility lasted. A lone migrant skua flew south over the glaciers, heedless of us.

On the radio, Jim heard Bird Island reporting the first Fur Seal pups. If any did breed at Metchnikoff Point this season they would probably be a little later, the first bulls hauling out late in November, to establish territories by the time the cows arrived to pup early in December. We would hear when the other parties got there.

Although our radio received clearly, nobody responded to our transmissions. We seemed to be in a blind spot, but if it was an internal radio defect no one would hear from us until we arrived at base around Christmas Eve. Six weeks without word would be a nasty worry for our families.

Jim kept trying with the radio. He heard Faraday and Palmer bases discussing a Chinese expedition with two ships and 500 men, arriving soon in the Palmer Archipelago. China had evidently decided to join the rush into the Antarctic, which is building up as mineral and marine food resources are recognised, with nations jockeying for position as the Antarctic Treaty is renegotiated over the next six years. I was thankful that we were here on Brabant first, not following countless footsteps.

On 21st we planned an early start, but at 2 a.m. there was driving spindrift so we slept again. Waking to calm conditions at 6 a.m., we dug out and broke camp. The pulks were still heavy, despite the loads taken up earlier: they ploughed through the drifted snow and it was desperately hard work. We took turns trailbreaking, but the 2 km journey rising only 200 metres took us four hours. As we arrived on the flat col behind 'The Family', spindrift began to fly in a rising gale and we pitched tents hurriedly behind walls of 50-cm-thick snowblocks sawn out of the hard windslab. Diving inside was like entering a peaceful greenhouse, with the sun's warmth absorbed through the walls, though we could hear the moan of rising wind around the snow-wall.

Jim digging out a pulk on the frustrating col. (François de Gerlache)

As the evening wore on, the westerly wind steadily rose, pouring through the gap between Mount Parry and the Solvays, then concentrating again across our col. By 11 p.m., as I mended our stove, it had become the first serious wind over storm force 10 since September. We had almost forgotten the sensation of wind battering the tent, like a dog shaking a rat. That night the spindrift blasted away the bases of our walls like giant sastrugi. At 3 a.m. the storm reached a crescendo. Ted and Frank's wall was blown on to their tent. Ted went out and sorted things out in the hooligan: one pole appeared to have broken and the tent was deformed but still standing, firmly supported by the drift up its sides. It was probably the strongest continuous wind of the whole expedition. Through the next day it gradually eased, but spindrift driven at 80 knots blotted out the sun, which we could occasionally sense sailing above, perhaps in a clear blue sky. By early evening we were able to get out, and sawed out more big blocks to rebuild the walls.

Then the storm died away. At midnight we cautiously emerged and gathered outside the tents, now perched boot-high above the wind-blasted surface of the col. The world was calm and peaceful. Lingering clouds parted around the summit of Mount Parry, lit by the late sun. A last dark grey cloud poured silently up from the west, across the plateau and down into the shadows of Buls Bay. Playing football with a frozen man-pat, Ted and Frank soon had to stop, gasping painfully from the cold in their lungs: the air temperature was well below −10°C. In inner boots, without a rope, we walked over iron-hard windslab snow with harpoon-shaped sastrugi to collect the cached packloads. It was a grand feeling at last to be up on the high plateau, with 20 days' food and fuel, entirely self-contained and poised for the hills. We could afford to wait for this good weather, and we slept dreaming of a fine tomorrow.

We had longer to wait than we wanted, as two days of frustrating spring weather followed. Cold nights were followed by clear mornings and we set off on crampons to climb 'The Family'. Each day, warm air drifting south into Gerlache Strait formed clouds which enveloped us.

The first day we walked up 'Father Peak' and the next 'Mother Peak'. We knew their sharp icy summits offered superb climbing pictures with the marvellous backdrop of the Solvays, but each day we photographed only ghostly figures on the clouded summits, holding flags bedecked with ice crystals. Each day we returned along our trail of marker wands, to lie in the tents, cocooned in a white shroud.

At times like this, Frank and I wished we were down on the coast, able to study seals and birds despite the weather. I also felt guilty, spending this whole spring month mountaineering, remote from any breeding birds, and salved my conscience by geological and botanical reconnaissances. Patches of the underlying rock were exposed on the windward shoulders of 'The Family' peaks. Frost-shattered basalts just protruded through the snow, like flesh through grazed white skin. I hoped my amateur notes, and brick-sized samples, would help Mike decide which sites to visit during his brief summer in the south — it looked a rich area for geology. I found no lichens at any of these sites (between 970 and 1,180 metres high). These first macroscopic plant colonists occur in higher, colder and drier places elsewhere in Antarctica, so I wondered whether these rocks had only recently been exposed (or re-exposed) by glacial retreat.

Then came two days of north-easterly gales, with whirling spindrift forming long drifts behind the extra snow-walls we put up. After a winter of westerly storms with depressions arriving south of us, perhaps this marked the start of summer with most depressions north of us. It was now light enough to read my altimeter at 1 a.m. (the real midnight by the sun), but that was no help, as the barometric pressure hovered obstinately around 980 mB. We were still completely unable to forecast tomorrow's weather, nor even be confident of conditions four hours ahead.

We woke at all hours, ready to move whenever the break came. Throughout the year we had completed daily sleep charts, recording time of going to sleep, duration and quality of sleep, plus brief notes on external influences like weather. The 38,000 bits of data were for a psychologist, who planned to analyse the records to find out whether the circadian rhythms of the group and individuals were significantly affected by the long nights of winter and the long days of summer. I could not help thinking that the analysis would be fruitless — living in tents, our sleep patterns were always dominated by the weather, and disrupted by external requirements such as needing to travel. Only at base camp, in May and June, had any general trend appeared, of sleeping and waking late.

On the third and fourth days we woke at 3 a.m., 4 a.m., 6 a.m., 8 a.m., and then 12 a.m., but always the easterly wind drove cloud and spindrift over us, and the barometer hung steady. It was depressing and boring. We dozed, talked, cooked, ate and played chess. We had now read all four books. I counted peas (432 per packet — about 50,000 each over the year), and compiled expedition statistics (1,000 bars of chocolate and half a bar of soap each for the year; two torsos had been washed in eight man-years). With a pee bottle in the tent, we were only forced out once a day by nature — then we dug out the tent and pulks, collected rations and fuel from the pulks, and visited the other tent. In the 15 days since leaving 'Dayglo' we had sledged on only three days, and used another three half-days; nine days had been lost in total festers. I had abandoned my original plan to go down Rush Glacier and visit Humann Point; however, we were still in a good position for climbing in the Solvays, self-contained with stores for 15 more days, plus emergency extras.

At last we got away, on 29th, in thin cloud giving faint visibility at 100 metres. The fresh soft snow was desperate for sledging, the pulks ploughing a 10–15-cm deep trough. We took turns trailbreaking for an hour or two each, dragging the pulks about 8 km around an almost level traverse. We pitched camp on the wide undulating plateau northwest of Galen Peak. Then the clouds below began to evaporate. Gradually the cloudbase rose above us, until the pyramids of 'The Family' stood out in line, stark white against the leaden skies. Toward midnight patches of sunshine appeared across the Gerlache Strait: after so long enshrouded in clag and wind, hope rose slowly.

Reality exceeded hopes. On the last day of November bands of cloud obscured the sunrise, but had vanished by 8 a.m. In blazing sunshine we skied over to Mount Imhotep in shirtsleeves, without even bivouac gear in our packs. Frank led the short ascent, first zigzagging on skis up a 40-degree slope of deep heavy snow, then on crampons to the top. We felt sure that Imhotep was the mountain his grandfather had tried to reach in 1898, so Frank felt a special personal thrill when he stood on top. The pure white and pristine cobalt shadows of the nearby mountains contrasted with the distant snows of Anvers and the Peninsula, which had a distinct yellow cast. Far back on the snowfields our tents were a small black dot, hanging like a tiny trinket on the chain of our tracks of yesterday and today. We felt that we had earnt this good day, after two weeks.

December began with another superb day. We woke at 3 a.m., to avoid the awful heavy snow which had stuck to our ski-skins like anchors returning from Imhotep. We got away at 5.30 a.m., skiing up gentle slopes with the pulks sliding easily on cold firm snow. As we approached the faintly convex skirts of Galen Peak, the mushroomed tops of mountains one by one appeared around our arc of sight. We reached a flat snowfield, nestled at 1,250 metres in the heart of the Solvays. There we pitched our tents, with Galen and two other peaks above our back doors, and spread before us a ring of mountains, from the western Solvays and Anvers, to Parry's brooding mass and the eastern ridges. I called the snowflat 'Solatunet' (the sunny place) after the makers of our pulk sledges. It was only 8.30 a.m., so often breakfast time, and we had finished a days' uphill sledging. We slept for an hour or two in sun-warmed tents before skiing up to the nearest peak just south of us. From the top we caught our first overlook of the south end, with its dramatic rocky peaks and ridges. Far away to the south a little triangle of blue water showed over the long ridge of Anvers Island. It was the Neumayer Channel. This mountain top had been my first sight of Brabant Island, long ago in January.

Everything was great that day. In the evening, using a head-torch and a sailmakers needle, Ted found a discontinuity in the radio antenna cable and quickly fixed it. Jim's beaming delight was infectious as he enthusiastically talked to Faraday, Signy and Palmer Bases for the first time in four weeks.

Sunday 2 December really was a Sunday, as calm hill cloud enveloped us. We lazed about happily now — so different here in the heart of the hills from our fretting boredom of only four days back. The day ended on a high note as Jim got messages from Faraday about our second-summer party plans, and also at last with news of our first-summer photographs — Jed's pictures had won an Ilford Award and there had been an exhibition in Cologne. Jed would be over the moon when he heard. Anticipation of getting home was really building up: looking forward to seeing photographs of Brabant was strangely part of that anticipation.

Later that evening we suddenly heard on the radio: 'Faraday, Faraday, this is JSE Metchnikoff Point'. Jim leapt to answer them. It was Kim and Jed. Over the atmospheric crackle we heard their story of November above Hill Bay.

Kim, JB and Mike had dropped down the eastern slopes of Harvey Heights on 2 November, pitching their dome tent at 1,500 metres as a base for exploration down toward Freud Passage. Next day in glorious weather they had skied down the ridge above Malpighi Glacier to its seaward end, jutting out high between steep glaciers. While Mike collected basalts, JB had found some moss and lichens — at 810 metres by far the highest plants that we had found. The long ski back up to their camp was exhausting on clogging snow, and they arrived in whiteout. After a day's bad weather they had two days making four first ascents, first Einthoven Hill and then three peaks overlooking Hill Bay. One of Mike's skis came off and careered away downhill, stopping just two metres short of a huge crevasse. What luck we do have! Losing a ski so far from base could be really dangerous, as walking on this soft deep snow is desperate work. They returned, in whiteout yet again. After two more days bad weather their food was getting short, so on 9th they dragged the pulk back up, through heavy snow, to the cache at 1,900 metres.

They had a wonderful day on 10th, going out along the ridge toward Morgagni, collecting more rocks (inevitably basalts) and enjoying fantastic views down into Hill Bay and the chaos of its glaciers. It looked like an ice-bound version of Hades: Kim said that 'No Go Corrie' was one of the most frightening places he had seen.

Then foul November took them in its grip, exposed on the high whaleback ridge, obliterated by the racing cap of cloud. After two days festering they moved down to the head of 'Paré Icefall', but there another four days awful weather held them, a blizzard on 15th completely burying the tents. Finally they dropped down to the foot of the icefall on 18th, to find the three skidoos parked beside an empty tent.

Spotts and Jed had got back there on 2nd, and driven over to dig out the main Skidoo Cache on 3rd. Then they had stayed holed up in 13 days of wind and cloud, with snow building up to bury the tent occasionally. When the weather finally broke on 18th, they skied over toward 'Morgagni Col' and climbed the lovely 1,300-metre pyramid of snow and ice between the col and Harvey Heights.

Next day the five of them moved over to the main Skidoo Cache on Paré Glacier, aiming to climb Mount Morgagni, though food and time were running out for relief of the two at 'Astrolabe Point'. Morgagni had always been the peak that JB wanted most to 'bag', and Kim generously stood down to let him lead the climb. On 21st, Spotts and JB took two skidoos down to the col, driving an 80-cm deep trough through light powder snow by high speed 'barging' runs. Then they came back and picked up Jed and Mike.

From the col they skied up along the ridge through a contorted icefall, but when they reached the steep snowface that forms the main ridge of Morgagni, they found a deep covering of fresh snow. It was a classic avalanche slope: once again Morgagni had frustrated them, and it seemed likely that its 'lost world' snow plateau would remain unclimbed, a symbol of this unconquered island.

Driving back they were hit by a sudden blizzard, only 300 metres from the cache. The skidoos bogged in and visibility reduced to a few metres. Hastily they pitched their Super Nova and all four piled in. With hardly any snow-wall, the tent stood up to two days and nights of blizzard. Alone with two tents, just 300 metres from them, Kim was also on two-thirds rations.

In a short break on 23rd they joined Kim at the cache. Then for five days snow fell heavily and continuously totally burying the tents, the skidoos, the cache and even the three-metre sledge upended as a cache-marker. It was impossible to move: Kim took 20 minutes to walk 15 metres from one tent to another through chest-deep snow. Parties had met similar conditions before on Lister and Paré Glaciers: moist northerly airstreams must be trapped by the cirque of Morgagni — Harvey Heights — Rokkitanski — Mount Hunter to cause localised cloud and very high snowfalls. When the weather improved on 29th it took all day to dig out the skidoos and to move them and the cache two metres up to the new snow surface.

An iceberg batters the seawall at 'Astrolabe Point'. (Howard Oakley)

In fine weather on 30th, Spotts on Dutch Courage barged a track through awful snow up to 1,300 metres on 'Rokki Plateau', coming back to tow up the others (Mike and JB's old skidoos had left the track and vanished into soft snow, taking two hours to dig out). Then the three skidoos had headed on for 'Astrolabe Point', dropping off Kim and Jed.

At 5 p.m. Kim and Jed had set off down the ridge to 'Cushing Col', heading for base. At 'Noddies Col' their pulk had surprised them by tobogganning a kilometre down on its own to Lister Glacier, so after recovering it they camped nearby and reached Metchnikoff Point late on 1 December: their familiar winter home seemed very strange after three months' absence, empty with the ghosts of people gone, though now crowded with Chinstrap Penguins cackling incessantly on their eggs. It was good to be back, but somehow lonely, as they pitched their tent beside the hut, still deeply drifted with just the roof-ridge showing.

It was much later that I learnt from Howard how he and Peter had fared at 'Astrolabe' since 21 October. Working from their one tent, totally ignorant of what the rest of us were doing (or even where we were), they had lived exclusively on chicken-in-brown-sauce compo rations, and recorded the accelerating advance of spring throughout November, while the rest of us moved our tents around the snows. Peter had covered the botany, while Howard had collected terrestrial invertebrates, and found a new interest, making a typically thorough record of the birds for me.

Cloud had prevailed. Even our lovely carpet of low cloud in late

October had been a fog at sea-level. Rough seas in mid-November had again overwhelmed the sea-wall, and once two icebergs had crashed and battered at the wall, their towers as high as the cliffs. Their camp had been safe, although Peter had been swept into the moat for a swim while photographing the breakers.

Perhaps the spring melt was unusually late. In any case the snow had receded little by the end of November, even on the windswept north-facing terraces where the grass and pearlwort grew luxuriantly. Peter's transect work (and Howard's micrometerology), suggested that the main factors favouring the flowering plants were total radiant heat from the sun on the flat damp terraces on the northern point, with their rich organic substrate of limpet shells. Peter found that lingering snowdrifts often covered patches of mosses, whilst grass and pearlwort dominated all around: the length of season in the sun was vital to the flowering plants. Through November the pearlwort began to burgeon again,: perhaps this resulted from its deeper taproot compared to the grass, which was slower to recover from the winter. Why the two plants flowered here but not at Metchnikoff Point remained a mystery, but perhaps it was associated with the nutrients in the substrate. Mites and springtails were active under stones, but the midges had not yet emerged.

The first scattered collections of fresh black limpet shells late in October had shown when the Kelp Gulls started feeding on their main summer diet. Flocks of up to 50 early in November may have been migrants, but otherwise there was only a gradual change through the month, with the juveniles melting away. The local adults displayed no territorial or courtship behaviour and late each evening they usually departed north toward Claude Point. It seemed strange that none bred there, as the masses of decayed limpets underneath the grass indicated a large colony in former times.

By the end of October only one pair of Antarctic Terns still held a territory. They mated on 30 October and had laid two eggs by 9 November, an unusually early date this far south. The first skuas passed by on 27th October; soon three were patrolling the point quietly, and by 22 November eight pairs were established. The Terns maintained a noisy running battle with the skuas, sometimes continuing all night. The nesting pair and two non-breeding pairs kept up the attack, and others sometimes came and joined in. However it was a losing battle; the Tern's eggs disappeared on 18th, and although the pair remained throughout the month they did not lay again.

Among the staccato calls of furious Antarctic Terns were some distinctly softer calls; two Terns with white foreheads visited the point regularly early in November, and on 20th Howard saw a tern in juvenile plumage. These were all probably Arctic Terns, though very early.

November is the month when exceptional vagrants are most likely in the Antarctic — usually pelagic species such as Arctic Skuas, but occasionally unfortunate landbirds drastically overshooting their spring migration down South America. On 11th Howard found a strange petrel sheltering, and his description suggested a Soft-plumaged Petrel which roam south to the Antarctic Convergence in Drake Passage, in spring and autumn.

By mid-October some Cape Pigeons were occupying the south bay cliffs. Over the next two weeks many more arrived, and by 3 November pairs were at many nest-sites. Flocks of up to 300 fed inshore by day, and there were some massed flights around the cliffs at dusk. Some of the lower, wetter cliff sites elsewhere on the point were abandoned in the rough seas of mid-November. In the second half of November the Cape Pigeons settled to a routine: each morning flocks left the colonies empty, until they returned at 10 p.m. to roost in pairs at nests. No eggs had been found, but at the end of November the nests were occupied by day and the flock sizes were halved, as if incubation had begun. Small flocks of Fulmars foraged inshore and some fed amongst the Cape Pigons; at dusk small parties of Fulmars sometimes soared around the 'Astrolabe' cliffs before departing toward Claude Point.

The Snow Petrels' movements were enigmatic. At Metchnikoff Point all their big winter coasting movements had been to the west and south; Nick had noted similar movements on five days in early October before their numbers reduced, and Howard had also noted southerly movements of over 200 per hour early in October. Then over five days at the beginning of November a stream of Snow Petrels flew north over 'Astrolabe Point' at 120–600 per hour. Up to half a dozen pairs frequented the cliffs in the south bay, and after 16 November their paired flights ceased, as if they had started incubating under the overhanging cornices.

The Antarctic Petrels posed a surprise question. They first appeared on 5 November, trickling north over the sea by day and then flying south high over the glacier each evening in flocks of up to 50. These movements continued daily, some stopping to soar around the cliffs among the Cape Pigeons, and others feeding near Astrolabe Needle. There were still plenty around on 22nd, but then they disappeared. Possibly the pelagic winter populations were gathering in from the Bellingshausen Sea before moving south to breed, but the date seemed rather late.

The first Wilson's Storm Petrels arrived at the end of October, just two days after the first at Metchnikoff Point. Numbers increased steadily, and they were flitting everywhere by 18 November when Howard found some occupied nests. Toward the end of November, Black-bellied Storm Petrels started calling each night at about 11 p.m. and on 1 December one was seen flitting. Sad little pairs of legs from Wilson's Storm Petrels accumulated in skua territories from early November, and the lack of Black-bellied remains suggested that they had indeed arrived much later.

Over the latter half of November the skuas were forming pairs and establishing their jigsaw territories, with constant displays, and confrontations in flight and on the ground. By the end of the month their mossy nests were built and they were mating, but no eggs had yet been laid.

Blue-eyed Shags tore up lumps of moss at 'Astrolabe' in mid-November, but they flew off northward with it and none nested there. Early in the month a flock of 40 fished offshore, moving on from place to place in the manner of the winter flocks, and at the end of November 150 struggled in from Dallman Bay against a north-east gale, heading for Claude Point where there was a colony.

Out of radio contact for six weeks, Howard and Peter began to worry that something had happened to the rest of us. They were running short of food. On the last day of November, Peter had just started cooking their first penguin, when Spotts, JB and Mike came down the icefall.

Apart from its beginning and end, November had been a bad month for weather. Our several parties scattered about the island had all been hit by the same big westerlies, and later some north-easterly gales. However, in the gentler winds and warmer airstreams, cloud and snowfall had varied dramatically around the island. Now December had begun well.

December

Chinstraps coming up through the icy roadways at Metchnikoff Point. (Jed Corbett)

Mid-summers Day was only three weeks away. It was now as light as the long-ago January day when we arrived on the island. Lying in the green tent on 'Solatunet', I found myself still writing at midnight, in broad daylight. A big moon showed faintly in pale blue sky and Mount Parry below it was gilded by the evening sun. Next morning when we woke at 3 a.m. for an alpine start, it was still broad daylight: our flat snowfield was bitterly cold, shadowed by the Solvay mountains round it, but their mushroomed summits glittered from the rising sun beyond, while pale gold already spread down the eastern slopes of Parry.

In superb weather on 3rd and 4th, we made alpine starts and climbed Galen Peak and then 'Mount Frederick Cook' above our camp. They were each glorious mushroomed ridges, easy but interesting climbs. Drifting hill cloud on Galen Peak filtered the sunlight to make faint shadows: the twisting ridge melted into romantic distances, while glimpses of the crevasses far below on Hippocrates Glacier gave fleeting scale to the height. Hard sunlight the second day sharpened the crusted mushrooms of 'Mount Frederick Cook' with the sharp relief of cobalt shadows. The photographic images were fantastic, and I wished Jed had been with us. Only with the isolation of the camera's viewfinder did I notice how the sky graded imperceptibly around the horizon — in the north leached to palest duck-egg blue by the sun, then darkening round to the south, where the snow stood out stark white against an unbelievably rich deep royal blue. Each day we got back to the tents at midday and lazed around, stretched on our pulks and dozing in the hot sun.

The Directorate of Overseas Surveys had drawn the map of Brabant Island by photogrammetric techniques, using aerial strip photographs taken in 1956. Lagrange Peak and Hunt Island were the only ground control stations occupied, but hitherto we had found the map was remarkably accurate, although the scale (1:250,000) and the contour interval (100 metres) made it comparable to hill walking with a road map. Here in the Solvays we now found some major heighting errors: Galen Peak was 300 metres lower than the map showed, and was not the highest peak. So we recorded altimeter readings and barometric pressures everywhere, to compare with Howard's sea-level pressures. We called the highest peak 'Mount Frederick Cook', after the American doctor who landed with de Gerlache in 1898 (and later may have beaten Peary to the North Pole). Among the 63 medical landmark names spattered around Brabant Island, Cook was the only one who had been there.

The third fine day was a long one, skiing along the spine of the Solvays to the far south-west. Halfway there the cloudbed rose from the southern glacier basins to envelop us. We groped our way along in whiteout, feeling our way nervously down invisible slopes, which steepened into the unknown underneath my ski-tips. As Ted led up the ridge to the furthest peaks the clouds evaporated again and suddenly we were rewarded by gods-eye outlooks over an interleaved jigsaw of blue seas and white snow. Far away in the northern haze we could make out Astrolabe Needle and Claude Point, familiar places of long ago. The Melchiors lay scattered like a map in Dallman Bay. The southern end of Brabant was set out below us, differing dramatically from all that we had seen north of the Solvays. Corners of Duperré and Chiriguano Bays, and other bits of sea, intruded from right and left: the alternating sea and mountains showed up the vast scale, so often hard to comprehend on featureless snow. Underneath us, successive rock ridges and valley glaciers accentu-

Opposite. Jim and Ted between 'Ben Bangers' and 'Ben Mash', looking southeast over clouded Jenner and Koch Glaciers and Gerlache Strait to the Antarctic Peninsula, 15-30 kms distant. (Chris Furse)

ated the effect. Opposite stood Mount Bulcke's contorted summit ridge of snow, surrounded by rock towers like a crown of thorns. The Gerlache Strait led far into the south beyond. With binoculars I could just see several intertidal beaches, and imagined I could discern the dirty pink of little penguin colonies. Snow Petrels sailed over, gazing at us with their dark eyes and occasionally uttering their grating calls before swinging away beyond another mushroomed ridge: I hoped the second-summer team would find them nesting on these southern ridges. That day we made five first ascents along the ridge to 'Ben Bangers' and 'Ben Mash', and returned to 'Solatunet' exhausted, dehydrated and content, with aching feet.

On 6th, after yet another alpine start, we skied down across the head-wall of Koch Glacier to Celsus Peak — for a climber, the jewel of the Solvays. Ted led Jim on to an 80-degree iceface sweeping 200 metres up the prow of the northern ridge. Halfway up they escaped on to the side of the ridge. There Frank and I had found an easier way up through two bands of mushrooms: their 60-degree slopes were quite steep enough for us, with hard water-ice below a layer of snow. Ted led on up the northern ridge to where the summit mushrooms overflowed impossibly like snow-white Guinness froth 50 metres above us. We traversed around the west side underneath the penultimate mushroom, moving along the top of an airy 50-degree slope which dropped out of sight underneath us, to reappear 400 metres below as a tongue of avalanche debris across the glacier floor. The top layer of snow kept balling up on our crampons, needing a tap with the iceaxe every step or two. A hundred metres along, the mushroom ended, and a snowslope ran up into a snow-filled crevasse above the first mushroom. Just there the overhang of the top-most mushroom relented, to offer a vertical climb up a narrow gully (more like a chimney) between two ribs of rubbishy ice. Ted attacked the 20-metre pitch. At the top he met a rim of hard water-ice overhanging the rubbish he had chopped away, and had to inch his way out, hang back outward, reach over to get his icehammer in, and then mantleshelf up and over the crux. Frank and I decided that we had reached our limits, and started back down. We wished good luck to Jim, who was on the exposed slope below belaying Ted, and nervously waiting his turn. Ice-lumps showered down over him as Ted chopped away a good belay stance on top.

As we neared our skis 300 metres below, Frank spotted the two figures coming back down the top traverse. Ted shouted down that both of them had reached the summit. They had then abseiled off, leaving three icescrews (it was already 4 p.m., after a six-hour climb; it would be a hard ski back to our tents, and threatening cloud was now creeping up Koch Glacier). Their voices were clear in the silence. Ted came first down the 60-degree pitch through the upper band of mushrooms, and Frank and I turned to go on down to the skis.

The scream stopped us.

With a clutch in my stomach I looked up. Jim was hurtling down an icechute to the left of the pitch, tearing off a cloud of ice-chips. He fell free of the overhang, cartwheeling. Printed into my mind was the image of his body, legs upward like a ragdoll. The ragdoll crumpled on to the snow and ice-slope below, and was still.

The scream ended.

Silence. Only a heart-thump. Perhaps.

I have a shuddering horror of iceaxes flying around in a fall, waiting for the impact to embed themselves deep into your body. At the very least he must have broken bones — the fall had been a full rope's length, half of it falling free. We had worked out what to do if any of us were injured on Celsus. After getting him down to the col, one would stay with him while the other two left their packs and duvets for warmth and skied back to fetch tents, medical bag, radio, food and fuel, etc., and then returned. It would be very cold by the time we got back to him. Tomorrow we would take him on a pulk down to Buls Bay, the nearest place where a boat could land. Climbing accidents are notorious for happening in the anti-climax of descent, but it seemed somehow grossly unfair that this should have happened coming off our last peak, just before we headed north and homeward — and to Jim, the game newcomer to mountaineering, married two weeks before he left England. I felt sick.

Then the little heap on the slope moved. I held my breath, nauseated by hope and fear. A minute later Jim stood up! Then Ted shouted they were both OK! They walked down, and half an hour later we were all sitting by our skis drinking tea. Jim had been changing hands with his iceaxe and icehammer when his crampons had slipped; somehow he had fallen the 'wrong' side of a projecting mushroom halfway down the pitch; the rope had wrapped over this mushroom and the stretch in the rope must have absorbed a lot of the energy of his fall. As he fell he had seen just a whirling blue and white kaleidoscope; his only thoughts had been: 'Please no broken bones; please no crampon spikes in me'. He had landed on his back, knocking the wind out of him, but apart from an aching torso and bruises elsewhere he was completely uninjured, and remarkably perky despite the shock of terror. It seemed like a miracle to all of us.

Two hours later we relaxed in camp at 'Solatunet'. The 7th was a rest-day that we all needed. As if on cue, the weather deteriorated and we lay in our tents, listening to wind and spindrift, and the radio. Each evening Jim now spent an hour or two cranking the hand generator of the radio. Today Mike, the radio operator at Palmer, read us a message from President Reagan, marking the 25th anniversary of the Antarctic Treaty, signed in Washington on 1 December 1959. It was a standard pompous departmental draft, but the call for continued peaceful cooperation in the Treaty area did ring true. For once I envied the Americans a little: perhaps our people had more home affairs, or perhaps peace in Antarctica concerned them less.

Here in Antarctica people of all nations meet and work together and make friends. Jim talked with Wayne Trivelpiece, an American ornithologist working at Poland's Arctowski Base on King George Island. There he had ringed the Gentoos that visited Metchnikoff Point last autumn: he was surprised to hear of our recoveries, as he had thought 'their' Gentoos wintered in the Weddell Sea. He mentioned that all the birds there seemed to be 2 weeks ahead compared to last season (conversely we learnt that Fur Seals at South Georgia were pupping later this year).

Every evening we chatted with Kim and Jed at Metchnikoff Point. It was the first time that two parties had been able to do so, and somehow it made us feel much closer together, as well as the extra safety and being able to discuss changing plans. The two of them were still digging out the hut, stores, boats and garage, all buried under the heavy November snowfall. They gave me daily news of the wildlife.

Dozing Weddell Seals again littered the beaches at Metchnikoff Point, most of them large and fat in old yellow coats. Nick's seeing no pups around Metchnikoff Point in October had been very strange, with the local Weddell population of about six dozen: Jed saw one pup early in December, alone but still with some of its woolly natal coat, so perhaps they had pupped on shore-ice at nearby points? At the beginning of the month Jed had found a bull Elephant Seal, and one cow suckling a pup with some of its black woolly natal coat on its head. Jed thought they were a touching family group, but the bull would only be interested in the cow, and in fact was a bit of a failure for this polygamous species. The two adults left on 7th: pups are weaned at about 23 days, so this one had been borne about mid-November, two weeks later than those near Palmer Base, and over a month later than in their normal range much further north.

The Chinstrap Penguins were all sitting on full clutches. There was regular traffic to and fom the sea, with both adults roosting at most nests. In most penguin species, the females depart to sea for several days after laying to recover bodyweight; when they get back to take over brooding, the males in turn go to sea for some days feeding up, having been fasting ashore since they first took up territories four to five weeks before. Chinstraps seem to make more frequent (and thus more local) feeding trips throughout the breeding cycle.

The Cape Pigeons, Kelp Gulls and Terns had all laid when Jed checked nests on 5th, but a pair of skuas on the moraine had not yet laid, nor had they found any Sheathbill eggs yet. The enigma of the Snow Petrels deepened: they had seen only one pair briefly flying around, and there seemed to be none on the cliffs they had haunted through the long winter. Wilson's Storm Petrels were flitting all over the screes in the evenings, but most of their nest-crannies were still buried and they were unlikely to lay eggs yet awhile.

The wind worsened on 8th, with ominous sudden gusts. It took us two days to realise how lucky we were on 'Solatunet'. A big north-easterly wind was howling across the island, and in the lee of Galen Peak we seemed to get right and left hooks, coming first from the north and then down from the col to south-east of the tents. When the clouds cleared on 9th we could see spindrift blasting over each end of Galen's ridge, and whirling devils wandering round our flat snowfield. Sometimes we could see clouds of spindrift hurtling 50 metres over us from the north-east at the same moment as a full gale was tearing at our tent doors from the south-west. The Union Flag and Frank's Belgian flag wound themselves around their bamboo poles, and we built all-round snow-walls.

Jim started receiving weather forecasts from Rothera each evening. The base received facsimile copies from Cambridge of the weather satellite pictures, so they could see the weather systems moving in from the Bellingshausen Sea. On 9th they said: 'Things don't look too bright for you I'm afraid,' and somehow that warning was more foreboding than our usual guesswork. Kim and Jed were sitting through three days of rain and hail at Metchnikoff Point: a metre of snow simply disappeared. It was like 'the melt' that occurs each May in the Arctic, though this phenomenon is not emphasised in Antarctic literature.

At 9p.m. on 10th, Rothera gave us a better forecast, with cloud the main problem. Jim looked out and visibility was over 1 km, so he jokingly suggested we leave then. By 11p.m. we had broken camp. The skies were leaden with gusts still whirling about, and Ted and I exchanged

Elephant Seal cow and pup. (Jed Corbett)

glances wondering if we were crazy. Then we were off, over cold hard snow, with six days' food and fuel on the four pulks. By 8 a.m. we were 20 km away, breakfasting just south of Mackenzie Glacier, gleeful at our progress. After snoozing on our bags in sun-warmed tents we left again at midnight. The flat light obliterated the tell-tale shadows of crevasses, and we joined our two ropes together so there were three of us to hold a fall. Trailbreaking up through the minefields on Malpighi Glacier, Ted felt the crust dropping repeatedly under him with the heavy 'whump' of crevase-bridges going. It was nerve-wracking. By 8 a.m. the snow was softening as I took my turn trailbreaking on the steep pull up out of Malpighi. Thigh-deep in heavy snow, my skis slid on icy crust below; the pulks ploughed askant as we traversed up, and every few metres I had to stop, gasping for breath. Time and again the slab slumped under me, sounding and feeling as if a flock of birds took wing below my skis. The slope was only 150 metres high, but took us three hours. I was absolutely exhausted, and broke two poles as Frank and I put up our tent in hot noon sunshine. At 11.40 p.m. as we roped up, the sun dipped behind the Peninsula: in the stillness a lone Snow Petrel flapped high above the glacier trough, up toward Mount Parry. The southern sky stayed lemon-bright with scattered hunting clouds of pink, and the sun reappeared at 2.20 a.m. as we collected two days' rations from our 1,700-metre cache above. It was biting cold, and the snow was hard and good for sledging. Plodding up the shoulder of Harvey Heights, I stretched my arms out for the sun behind to warm my frozen thumbs: a gigantic blue shadow skied before me on the lilac snow, rolling from side to side like a grotesque, slow-motion, silhouetted langlauger. At 2,000 metres we traversed above the lip of 'No Go Corrie', catching our first sight of the gloomy waters of Hill Bay, far below in grey twilight shadow. Coming round the ridge we could not find the cache, and the ice-cliffs of 'The Eaves' had fallen on our old March campsite there, strewing huge blocks down the slope below. We raced north-west down the whaleback ridge. Unable to recognise the route down to 'Paré Icefall' where we had relayed up in cloud two months before, we put rope brakes on and slid down a soft blue glittering icebowl. It was only 9 a.m., but already the snow was knee-deep and soft as we pitched the tents at our old halfway porter's camp. We had made fantastic progress in three good nights, and now the long-familiar landmarks of the north were spread before us, reduced in scale by longer journeys. In a rising westerly wind we built snow-walls, before collapsing to sleep, in hot but flapping tents. The icefall dropped down a bulging spur, with our tents on a little sloping plateau halfway down.

That evening the downslope wind rose to a gale around the tents: a cap of cloud poured over the whaleback above us, then divided to hurtle down the corries on either side of our spur. We were camped as if on an island, while the föhn blizzard raged all around us and out across the piedmont down below. Waking at 7 a.m. to find the wind had dropped we were away by 9 a.m. We lowered the pulks over the schrund, skied down the lower icefall and traversed north to camp on the piedmont at midday, at 1,000 metres, only 25 km from base. That afternoon we sweated in the tents, lying stripped on our sleeping bags; however after supper the snow had hardened up enough for sledging. Avoiding the trap of Lister Glacier we pulked up to 1,300 metres. Ted found a new way down the north ridge of Rokkitanski with the rope brakes on, then we raced down to 'Cushing Col' and on down again to 700 metres. It was only 4.30 a.m. but already the snow was crystalline and slushy in the warmth. The sun shone through patches of mountain cloud, focussing a glorious creamy golden light on the mushrooms of 'Noddies Hat' above us. The south ridge of Mount Hunter ahead was a sharp blue-grey silhouette against the salmon and saffron of the eastern ridge, which melted into cloud above. On 'Noddies Col' we rested, watching an ice-cliff fall off Mount Hunter: blocks the size of cars bounced ponderously and rolled to a stop nearby. We could hear the muted roar of surf 900 metres below us in the cloud — we were nearing home! Finding ski tracks we followed them down into cloud, and rounding 'Wobbly Col' we came upon the snow-walls of an empty campsite. It was 8 a.m., so we stopped to light our stoves and cook breakfast sheltered in the walls. In the unforgiving plastic boots my feet hurt agonisingly, but now was not the time for stopping: we were only three long hours from Metchnikoff Point, or so we thought. Skiing down off 'Pinnacles Spur' the cloud engulfed us just as Ted found himself above an unexpected schrund. We belayed him down, then took an hour lowering the four pulks and sorting out the ropes again.

Then we found ourselves in a maze of big crevasses, treacherously bridged with rotten snow: we spent a tense hour in complete whiteout, skiing blindly on tight ropes, praying the snow would not drop below us, to dangle in darkness cumbered by our pulks. We cleared the minefield with relief, and plodded out on to 'Footsore Piedmont', tired and with aching feet. After a brief clear the cloud returned, and at midday we stopped to wait, frustrated but fearing crevasses in our exhaustion. After two hours we moved on, plodding on and on through cloud, until finally Frank in front stopped and raised his hand. We stopped too. Then we all heard it — the faint cackle of penguins through the cloud! At 4 p.m. we dropped down out of the cloud to see base camp below us. Long ago in September we had left it deep under snow; now the screes were bare and penguins crowded on the dirty slopes. We skied fast down from the skyline ridge and tumbled to a halt outside the garage, and there was Jed, leaping and capering about, laughing, chattering and shaking hands in between photographing three of us lying in heaps in the snow with pulks capsized around us. Our whole five-night journey (travelling 70 km, up 1,800 metres and down 3,000 metres) had been one long run of good luck, unbelieveably fast after all our earlier experiences. We had shown that one-man pulking was good for at least five weeks away.

The others had got back three days before from 'Astrolabe', and Mike and Spotts were now over at 'Cairn Point' surveying. Ted, Jim, Frank and I sank our first can of beer for a year, chatting with the others, then dropped our packs, ropes, harnesses and ironmongery. After that we went to say hello to the penguins, before finding our new tent-partners, taking our boots off, having a brew, and dropping into the sleep of the happy dead. It had been a long 26-hour night.

The 16th was a real Sunday. After a lazy breakfast of delicious compo sausages, I loafed about camp, enjoying the freedom of walking without a rope after five weeks, and pampering my blisters with inner boots only. That evening while Howard cooked he brought me up to date on their time at 'Astrolabe', and then their journey back.

On 30 November, coming down the final slope to 'Astrolabe Point', Spotts had dropped ten metres into a crevasse — 'fully prepared, in shirtsleeves, no gloves and loose harness' — but had climbed out within an hour. On 2 December the five of them (Peter, Howard, Spotts, JB and Mike) left 'Astrolabe' and spent two days at Claude Point.

Mike had worked along the clifftops above Guyou Bay, but they had been unable to get down below the lava cap above the point itself because treacherous ice still coated the gully down to the grassy terrace

Skua pair at basecamp, looking east. (Tim Hall)

and the pebble-banded sandstone. Howard had found Cape Pigeons incubating eggs, while Snow Petrels flew in and out of nest-crannies on the cliffs, and Fulmars sailed to and fro. Far below them some Shags were brooding beside the Chinstrap colony.

After pulking down and through 'The Precinct' they had been held up three days in foul weather, taking six days before reaching Metchnikoff Point on 12 December. That was standard time for 'the milk run', but no journey here was as easy as that implies.

Kim had set the boats to work. (Incredibly all five OMC outboards had started easily after their winter burial.) Hauling in a trammel net laid in the sound they caught three grotesque *Chaenocephalus aceratus*, white and grey Icefish with no red blood corpuscles, 60-cm long and shaped like a sea anchor behind their huge mouths. On 18th Kim and three others sped over in the boats to collect Mike and Spotts from 'Cairn Point' where they had established ground control for aerial photography. After metres of snowfall over the last three months, they had been amazed to find a ladder of iceblocks where our footsteps in July had compressed the snow five months before.

That evening we all gathered in the tiny hut for the first time since September. With just eleven days to go, all our thoughts were focussing on home, family, love, egg sandwiches, showers, brussel sprouts, sex, flowers, trees, armchairs, marmite on toast, and suchlike, but one more trip was planned — by boat to Claude Point, and hopefully beyond.

All around our tents the Chinstraps were incubating well-set eggs. On two expeditions I had been too late to eat a penguins's egg, but Kim had kept a couple on ice for me, so we made an omelette. It looked very ordinary yellow and white (I had been told the albumen remained disgustingly transparent jelly when cooked). Although very edible, it was bland and dull, and rather disappointing.

I spent the next few days around the point, catching up on the wildlife, after missing the whole great chunk of spring that I had stayed the winter through to see.

Weddells lazed on the beaces and two idly playing in a wave-swept channel were small enough to be this season's pups. Some were already moulting faded yellow pelts to grey. The Elephant pup was still on the beach. Unlike Weddells, the Elephant Seals are said to remain ashore throughout their moult (first the cows, later the younger bulls and last the harem masters), but adults occasionally coming ashore now were in moult. Our hopes of finding Fur Seals breeding had come to nought, but one female arrived, the vanguard of the summer influx. I also saw a Leopard Seal one evening, lazily patrolling to and fro in the surf line at the eastern beach, making unsuccessful dashes at returning penguins.

A mixed pair of skuas had laid two eggs on the moraine. A large flecked (female?) Brown Skua was mated with a smaller, neater, pinkish-brown South Polar Skua. The latter more southerly species has recently extended even further north to Signy Island, perhaps taking advantage of increased krill stocks, and the fish that prey on krill. In this region of overlap the two species sometimes interbreed, and usually the female is a Brown Skua, taking a second chance with a mate of the (later-nesting) South Polar species. The Terns were still incubating, but many of the Kelp Gull clutches of 1-3 had already hatched; we had to take great care that their cryptic downy chicks did not rush away from us and fall off the granite blocks on which they nested.

Wilson's Storm Petrels had started laying in the screes. One night, trying in vain to track down the little groups of Black-bellied Storm Petrels in the moraine, I saw a succession of Snow Petrels returning silently in pairs along the coast. There were few around the butte by day now, and I planned to top-rope down the rotten cliffs to determine whether or not they were breeding. Prospecting for the most promising niches, I scrambled along the top of the screes under the cliffs. Suddenly, as I eased around a corner, two big blocks of basalt came loose above my head. Trying to fend them off, I managed to push myself aside while tumbling down, then watched the boulders trundle on down to the beach 70 metres below. Limping back to camp I decided to leave the Snow Petrels in peace.

That evening I was enjoying a brew in Ted's tent, when Peter looked out through the door and said: 'There's a Rockhopper Penguin'. Disparagingly I assured him it must be a Macaroni, and explained that Rockhoppers are sub-Antarctic species, with only one aberrant breeding record in this region (at Clarence Island). The Macaronis on the other hand do breed in the Antarctic, though their southernmost known colony is at Deception Island, and we had only seen a few non-breeders. Then I looked out. It was indeed a perky little Rockhopper! It stayed for three days, looking rather disconsolate amongst the bullying Chinstraps.

Poor weather now prevailed, so the boats could not get away. Much of my time was spent in tedious administration, writing through the daylight nights. Gash (and some useful gear!) kept on surfacing as the snow thawed, and we spent a whole day clearing up the base camp area. I helped Ted tidy up the garage one last time, a sad task, splashing through meltwater and ice, remembering the busy place in winter. However the tiny creatures in the ground were enjoying the melt. Mites clustered on stones in the surface layer, and on warm afternoons a few midges could be found crawling on wet moss. Under the stones beside

The Winter Party (except Nick) back at basecamp. A motley crew, a grand bunch. (Jed Corbett)

the met. station the brown 'Metch Monster Mites' were crawling about, now like typical ticks with pea-sized grey abdominal sacks, but still apparently free-living in the detritus of penguins, rather than parasitic.

The skies cleared on 23rd, and on Christmas Eve, Kim and five others tried to go to Claude Point by boat. Once out of the sheltered sound they were drenched by the swell around the western skerries, so instead they ran a tripper service to 'Easter Island' off the point. Jumping off on to the rocks it was the first time we had been there. Ted played about in the sun climbing on lovely granite routes, while Mike and Peter explored beyond. The shelf at 70 metres proved to be a crumbled basalt platform, not the raised beach we had suspected, but there were wave-worn cobbles lower down, and also little patches of wet moss carpet, and the first standing puddle of water we had found outside a penguin colony. A pair of pink South Polar Skuas guarded two decorative greenish eggs, matching their skimpy nest of pale *Usnea* lichen, and nearby was the first 'club' of non-breeding skuas that I had seen.

Coming back to camp that evening I suddenly heard the plaintive peeping of a penguin chick. Within two days, eggs were hatching in all the higher colonies. This was nearly two weeks earlier than last season, rounding out the cycle of a whole year for me. We talked by radio again with Wayne Trivelpiece at Arctowski, and later with Dave Parmelee at Palmer: this breeding season was also early at both those stations, but there were interesting discrepancies. I wondered what were the relative differences between the resident and migrant species, the fish-eaters and krill-eaters, the primary foragers and the scavenger/predators. For example, why were the Sheathbills here still laying as late as this? I decided that afterwards I would correlate and compare dates, collecting data from as many other seasons as possible, from up and down the Peninsula and Scotia Arc, for all the breeding species, and then attempt to find patterns in the differences.

A little group was carol-singing with a tilley lamp around the tents that evening, and next day we had a short Christmas carol service, then a party, our last together here. Afterward I went up the butte lifting random penguins tails, recording eggs and chicks and looking ridiculous — I was still wearing a pink paper hat from a cracker.

Boxing Day was really filthy, with wind and rain. I was glad to have moved back up on to the glacier to share a Pyramid with Jed for the last few days, as we had promised each other long ago in March. We had a lot to do next day, preparing the 69 remaining stores boxes ready for *Endurance*. She was expected on 28th, but was not yet in radio contact. Finally she came up at 9 p.m. that evening, and we found we had an extra day.

We all had time for a last nostalgic walk around the point on 28th. There was a brisk westerly wind, but gradually the clouds cleared, with a movement of petrels to distract me from departure. Snow Petrels, Cape Pigeons and Fulmars were busily feeding along the outer skerries, and among those passing the western end were a few late Antarctic Petrels. Then in the evening a flock of 30 grey whalebirds weaved through the sound, the first I had seen here.

At midnight, JB, Mike and I found ourselves together in the hut, pottering, finding last little things to do. It had been a grand year, a time of companionship, of total reliance on each other, of hardship but also little comforts and much happiness. Now Mike would stay on another three months, while we journeyed home. Nothing needed to be said, we knew each other well enough. Of all the things we had discovered in this over-powering place, the greatest was comradeship.

At 3 a.m., as the light strengthened, I visited the top of the butte for a last count of Chinstrap eggs and chicks. Soon they would start the morning commuter rush, but now each pair was at the nest, one bird brooding, the other standing by sleeping. It was probably my last night ever in the Antarctic, and I wanted to store as many images as possible in my memory, but the expedition was so much a total impression, of place, of people, of wildlife and endeavour, that I could not grasp one isolated memory. Instead I walked back to the tent with just another question: do penguins sleep with their bill tucked behind their flipper because of inherited habit from their fluffy-feathered ancestors?

In the morning we stood about expectantly. Someone shouted that they could see *Endurance*. The tiny red speck grew out of the haze off-shore. Then came the whirring noise of a helicopter. I was to go first, and suddenly I was gone, to a hectic world of faces, places, timetables, machines, doors, corridors, plates, forks, showers, ties, and telephones — and home!

The changeover. Wasp bringing stores into Metchnikoff Point. (Tim Hall)

Second Summer Party

The Lifeguard under icecliffs near Duclaux Point in January. (Tim Hall)

After Clive Waghorn's seven-man Boat party had been landed at Metchnikoff Point on 29 December, the winter party luxuriated in warm comfort on board HMS *Endurance* as she moved round into Gerlache Strait. We scarcely noticed the wet snow blowing horizontally over the forecastle that night. Next day, as the two Wasps flew a cache of food and fuel into a low spit in Avicenna Bay, we heard that one of the boat party's dome tents had been wrecked in the gale (and they had arrived with few tents, expecting ours to be usable after a year). Mike Ringe said farewell to the rest of the winter party, then he was flown into 'Dayglo Point' in drifting cloud, with the rest of Steve Taylor's nine-man southern party and their base-camp stores.

On New Year's Eve, *Endurance* and her Wasps achieved a remarkable day's work in poor cloudy conditions. We recovered the stores from 'Astrolabe Point' but had no time to collect the skidoos from 300 metres above. After putting a cache of wornout tents and suchlike on top of Claude Point we worked down the west coast, reconnoitring cache sites, then landing two team members at each to receive food and fuel. We put in caches at Driencourt Point, Minot Point, Fleming Point, high on Humann Point, on the north coast of Hulot Peninsula, and finally in Chiriguano bay.

For the next two weeks *Endurance* was surveying, first north of Trinity Island, then south-west of Anvers Island, and sometimes we managed to talk with the parties on Brabant Island. *Endurance* then headed north for Port Stanley, where the winter party would disembark. Towards midnight on 15 January we passed 'Dayglo Point' 2 km off, able to see the party on the point and another party above, but unable to land.

The southern party spent the first ten days settling in at 'Dayglo Point', erecting their 2½-metre cube-shaped wooden hut, practising crevasse-rescue and sledging techniques on the piedmont behind, and putting out a cache at 500 metres. On 9th they set out to head south with a pulk each, but Graham developed terrible blisters, so they divided into three parties. Graham returned direct to 'Dayglo' with one party, while Mike, Stuart and Ronnie collected rocks on 'The Family' and above Pinel Point on the way back. Steve, Dave and Willie headed south, but high in the Solvays they were held up, first by gales, then by avalanche risk on the headwall of Koch Glacier. As they were running out of fuel they returned to join the others at 'Dayglo Point', skiing down from 500 metres as *Endurance* passed offshore on 15th.

Graham could not travel, with his feet reacting violently to the plastic boots, so Dave stayed with him at 'Dayglo Point' when the others set off again on 17th, pulking up behind 'The Family' and around to 'Solatunet' in the heart of the Solvays. Camped above Koch Glacier they were held by storm-force winds followed by cloud and heavy snow until 23rd; then they got partway down before being stopped by another three days' heavy cloud. Finally a day of beautiful sunshine allowed them to ski down Koch Glacier. On 29th they at last made contact by radio, and learnt that the boat party had arrived at 'Dayglo Point' to find Graham injured.

On 30th the boats brought Dave down to Chiriguano Bay. Three days later they brought more stores south, and ferried Paul and Simon to climb Victoria Peak, before landing them at 'Welcome Point', the larger of two low points projecting from the north shore of Chiriguano Bay. Paul and Simon spent ten days there making a geomorphological study of the intertidal beaches running like bars across the bays on each side of the point. Steve, Dave and Willie climbed the 900-metre ridge immediately south-east of Celsus Peak, and later the 900-metre peak at the far southern end of the main Solvays ridge. Mike, Stuart and Ronnie did scientific work on the northern flanks of Mount Bulcke and above Koch Glacier, before joining Paul and Simon at Welcome Point. The geology was very interesting for Mike, but Stuart was finding this part of the island remarkably barren of vegetation, and hence of invertebrates.

On 12 February all three parties rejoined above the cache site on the low point which had been named 'Kinloch Chiriguano', projecting into the head of the bay. They tried to arrange by radio for the boat party to fetch Stuart and Paul for work on the west coast, but breakdowns prevented it.

On 15th Mike and Willie left to climb Mount Bulcke. Next day they reached the northern peak to overlook the fantastic rock spires, and twisted arêtes of the ridge to southward. However, as they reached an awkward ice-step storm-force winds hit them, and they returned to join the others.

The party split into two groups from 18th. Steve, Paul, Ronnie and Stuart tried to get round to Hulot Peninsula, but were stopped by a nasty icefall on the north-east flank of Mount Bulcke. Then they took pulks up to 1,100 metres on the ridge east of 'Ben Bangers', aiming for Mount Erlich; however, after three days held up by cloud and wind on the ridge, and going on to half rations, they returned for a pre-arranged rendezvous. Meanwhile the other four spent useful time doing geology on the east side of Koch Glacier and then at 'Welcome Point' where they were treated to a magnificent display by some whales playing close inshore. The two groups rejoined once again above 'Kinloch Chiriguano' on 26th. At the end of February they worked on the northern flank of Mount Bulcke; and Steve, Simon and Willie had one fabulous day on Mount Bulcke, surmounting the ice-step and climbing two more summits before being stopped by a staggering vertical drop halfway along the ridge.

On 1 March they divided into two groups again to head back to 'Dayglo Point'. Mike, Paul and Stuart planned to return via Buls Bay but on reaching the 700-metre col south-east of Celsus Peak they found the icefall down toward Avicenna Bay dangerously unstable. So on 3rd they moved up to the head of Koch Glacier where very strong winds stopped them. Reaching the Solvays ridge at 1,300 metres next day they found the cached pulks with difficulty, in cloud; high winds knocked down their snow-wall on 5th, but the following day they went on to reach 'Dayglo Point'. Steve had led the other four on 1 March, spending a very hard day relaying two pulk loads up to 1,200 metres on the ridge east of 'Ben Bangers'. The following day they skied in cloud westward down the ridge toward Mount Erlich, but at 850 metres it became obvious they could not reach the peak from this side. In beautiful sunshine they traversed north-eastward into gale-force winds on 3rd, to camp north-west of Galen Peak. Next day Dave and Ronnie separated, and reached 'Dayglo Point' after a two-day journey. In the next few days, in fine spells between cloudy days, Steve, Simon and Willie climbed several peaks in the Solvays and then on 'Family Ridge'. Finally on the evening of 9 March they reached 'Dayglo Point' to find the rest of the party, and to learn of great events that had been happening elsewhere on the island, while they had been out of radio contact.

Victoria Peak and Mount Bulcke from the ice-worn beach at 'Welcome Point'. (Tim Hall)

The boat party had settled in quickly at Metchnikoff Point. By 31 December they had sorted out the stores, checked out the two Avon boats and commissioned the five-metre Lifeguard boat which they had brought south.

On 2 January the whole party went to Claude Point in two boats, landing in a cove near the penguin colony. Martin Hughes and the others explored the shore, finding a colony of Shags intermingled with the Chinstraps. Clive, Ali and Richard climbed up a rotten rock gully, trying to reach the tents cached on top above 200 metres, but they were stopped by dangerously loose rock at the western extremity of the terrace running underneath the black basalt cap.

The boats were launched into rising wind and waves bringing brash into the cove. The weather then deteriorated rapidly, and the passage across Guyou Bay was exiting into the teeth of a rising gale, with winds of over 60 knots tearing up drifts of spray as they came through the stacks into Metchnikoff Point. They found one canoe blown off the beach, and one dome-tent flattened on the glacier, and spent the next day mending tents in poor weather.

In bright weather on 4th they took the canoes around the local bays. Two days' bad weather then intervened, with a third tent wrecked, before Richard, Ali and Kerry were taken to 'Astrolabe Point' to fetch the tents from above Claude Point. The others returned via Claude Point, where they were swamped leaving the beach, before motoring close inshore all around Guyou Bay and back to base camp.

Richard, Ali, and Kerry reached Claude Point the same day, but their tent-poles were broken by a gale on 8th and they spent 24 hours sitting up propping the tent with their shoulders. Meanwhile at Metchnikoff the same gale had capsized an Avon moored in the boat haven: they righted it and recovered the two OMC engines; the following day they overhauled the engines successfully and righted the boat which had been capsized yet again. The three radioed that they had returned to 'Astrolabe Point' with heavy loads from Claude Point, and on 10th the boats went to pick them up. A swell was running on to the basalt sea-walls, and the first attempt at landing ended when the Avon was swamped by several breakers and driven on to the beach below the northern ice-cliffs: Tim managed to drive the boat off the beach despite a broken engine clamp, and the self-bailers worked successfully, to Tim and Clive's relief. They tried again on the rocky ramparts of the point, where Richard stood belayed, alternately chest-deep in water and two metres above the troughs, throwing kit into the two boats as they circled around judging the best time to approach. Once all the stores had been embarked they all returned quickly to base camp.

They took advantage of a brilliant day on 11th to take two boats around to Duclaux Point, where Tony Williams and Richard landed to collect rock samples. They returned to base the same day, with a tea-break at Cape Roux — how different from our two-week pulk trip to Duclaux Point in April!

The following day they reconnoitred by boat down to the cache on Driencourt Point. In just two weeks they had visited more snow-free areas than we had in the whole first-summer phase, dramatically showing off the value of boats. They had also progressed studies at Metchnikoff Point on botany, birds and seals, and Richard had caught and preserved several fish caught by trammel net. Now they prepared to circumnavigate

Basecamp at Metchnikoff Point, looking east past 'Cairn Point' to Cape Roux. (Tim Hall)

the island, realising that the days were already shortening in, and there was no time like the present in the short Antarctic summer season.

They set off southward on 16 January, another brilliant day, with four canoes supported by the Lifeguard and one Avon boat, all heavily loaded. The paddle across Guyou Bay in bright sunshine was spectacular and quick: the canoeists landed at Claude Point to eat and re-count the Chinstraps and Shags; then they paddled on south past Astrolabe Needle.

A series of rock-shelves and isolated stacks ran out from Driencourt Point. They found a gap in the reef, then turned in to land on a little crescent of shingle beach. After hauling the boats clear and securing them on the ice ramp above the beach they roped up to traverse the glacier to the cache, on a little granite platform, where they camped close by a colony of Kelp Gulls, with chicks still downy but highly mobile. The whole point was dominated by the cirque of cliffs and icefalls dropping over 1,500 metres from Rokkitanski, Harvey Heights and Mount Parry onto a glacier floor spread round the dark waters of 'Williams Bay', littered with bergs aflame in the evening sun. It was breathtaking, but very cold next morning shadowed by the cliffs above them. They spent the next day exploring the area, finding skuas and Terns as well as Kelp Gulls; canoeing out to the furthest stacks they also found a colony of Shags.

Clive and Martin Hughes in the Lifeguard below Astrolabe Needle. (Tim Hall)

On 18th, loading the boats took a long time as the tide was out, but then they paddled across to Minot Point. Landing on the best of the little rocky bays there was difficult, as the swell created large breaking waves that swept the inflatables backwards and forwards, periodically swamping them. They pitched camp on snow in the largest of the transverse gullies that were a feature of the point. A hot afternoon turned into a beautiful evening as the sun set behind Anvers Island.

Again they spent the next day exploring Minot Point, which sprouted from the roots of one of Mount Parry's tremendous ridges. Richard and Tim climbed the highest of its three rocky summits, at 450 metres. The northern cliffs had sloping terraces which were amazingly verdant, with rich depths of green and golden mosses, and both grass and pearlwort. South Polar Skuas nested all over the point, perhaps a hundred pairs filling the air with their piratical silhouettes and proud cries as they defended their eggs or young chicks. The shores were too steep for penguins to land, but the lack of Cape Pigeons was possibly due to the number of Skuas. They laid a trammel net inshore and Clive explored the largest of the little islets offshore, where rich moss also grew and Skuas nested. Tim, Richard and Kerry motored out toward a large iceberg drifting slowly north: as they approached within a kilometre it slowly heeled over and capsized, sending great waves out, drenching them as the boat plunged deeply.

The weather held, and next day they set off down the coast: Clive, Richard and Tony left first in three canoes while the others hauled gear over the rocky spurs into the inflatables. When the boats reached Fleming Point they searched in vain inshore before spotting a flare from the canoes, miniscule dots in scattered brash 3 km further out. Overcast weather and rising wind made paddling interesting through the brash off Rush Glacier, and reaching Humann Point they found brash pounding the only feasible landing on rocky boulders. Although the canoes could have landed, it would have been impossible to haul the inflatables up the steep ice above. As it was getting late they loaded the canoes onto the two boats and set off for the cache on Hulot Peninsula: they could not find a landing there, so they carried on through the Schollaert Channel. The swell in Dallman Bay was replaced by a choppy sea in Gerlache Strait where they headed into an easterly wind: progress was slow, wet and bitterly cold, and the conditions were very difficult for refuelling the engines. Altogether it was pretty miserable. However at last, late in the evening, they reached Chiriguano Bay and found a landing site on the north shore, which they called 'Welcome Point'. They warmed up hauling the boats out, and digging tent platforms into the icy slope behind.

They spent three days there, drying out, fishing and exploring round about. Richard and Ali climbed the 450-metre peak behind with Tim, who named it 'Mount Cherry' after his girlfriend. Clive and Kerry canoed all round Chiriguano Bay which was littered with ice driven in by the wind, and counted seals and birds. Using the inflatables Ali collected botanical samples from the low and virtually barren rocky islets in the bay, then they moved the cache of food and fuel to 'Kinloch Chiriguano'.

Three bad days of high winds followed, with heavy rain. Their three Wild Country dome tents stood precariously on pinnacles of ice with water running past around them, but they stood up well in the storm.

Finally the weather improved by midday on 27 January, so they broke camp and paddled out into Gerlache Strait. Visibility was low and paddling was interesting as they coasted northward under the ice-cliffs. They went into Avicenna Bay, landing on the spit to find the cache had been scattered by an icefall. There was another subtidal beach here and the canoeists paddled over to a hummocky islet to count the nesting Kelp Gulls and Shags. From there they laughed at the crews of the inflatables, as the waves from a big icefall washed them up on to the spit and then nearly swamped them.

After a picnic lunch they paddled on northward. Clive landed on the little islet off Buls Island to botanise, and found another colony of Shags. The southerly wind was now increasing to over force 4 and paddling was awkward: approaching the north end of Buls Bay the quartering swell was confused by reflected waves, with waves continually breaking over the decks as well as washing back as their bows speared through. Sea canoes have round bottoms, intentionally giving no inherent stability, so that they can ride the sides of big waves upright; but in these conditions balance is very difficult. Richard capsized, but screw-rolled upright at the first attempt, and they got through without further mishap.

They had been out of radio contact for two weeks, but as they approached 'Dayglo Point' in the evening they saw Dave Ball waving from outside the hut. Dave had been nursing Graham: two days before they had been securing stores in the storm when a full fuel drum had taken charge and smashed his right leg against a rock, fracturing it just below the knee. Tony quickly converted the hut into a hospital, and splinted his leg with plaster-of paris, reinforced with a GRP canoe repair kit.

At 9 p.m. they suddenly sighted a red ship passing through Gerlache Strait, the first they had seen. Clive, Tim and Martin Hughes leapt into the Avon and roared out to her, finally managing to attract attention by shouting as they travelled alongside at twelve knots. It was the MV *Polar Duke*, a Canadian icebreaker on charter through the US Coastguards to ITT Incorporated, the logistic operators for the US Antarctic Research Programme(!). She hove-to, and Clive clambered on board; they readily agreed to take Graham aboard in three days' time, when they were due to pass again, *en route* for Punta Arenas.

They re-visited Chiriguano Bay by boat next day, fruitlessly searching for Steve's party. However, later they managed to repair the radio antenna at last and contacted the others. On 30th they took Dave down the coast, both boats heavily loaded with food and stores for the others. The two parties met on the glacier above 'Kinloch Chiriguano after a month apart. Then the southern party picked their way carefully to the beach, while the boat party (in immersion suits) slid joyfully down on their backsides. Back at 'Dayglo Point' that evening they practised on Kerry, then strapped Graham into the stretcher: he had two hours to wait, but toward midnight *Polar Duke* finally appeared and he was taken out and safely embarked. The others stayed on board for a convivial two hours, then left at 2 a.m., steering an uncertain course through a snow-storm to 'Dayglo Point'.

At midday on the last day of January they took both inflatables north to look for a landing site on the next leg, and search for bird colonies. Speeding through Freud Passage past Leopard Seals asleep on old floes, they rounded Spallanzani Point and headed west. Through the narrows into Bouquet Bay they met a strong north-west wind and swell, but located a feasible landing beach under the frowning western cliffs of Davis Island, and on the way back found another possible place at the southern gates of Hill Bay. There were no other possible landing sites on Brabant Island north of Pinel Point, nor on either shore of Lecointe Island, a dramatic giant fin of rock and snow. However, at the end of an 80-km day, they found a jump-off rocky landing at the east end of Hunt Island below a Shag colony.

The first three days of February were busy ones, using the boats to explore from 'Dayglo Point'. On 1st, Ali and Tony visited Pinel Point to collect botanical and geological samples. On 2nd they all set off south at 6 a.m. taking more food to 'Kinloch Chiriguano', where they picked up Paul and Simon to climb Victoria Peak. Landing on the point below they split into two groups. Tim, Clive and Simon on one rope and Ali, Paul and Tony on another made the first ascent of the dramatic 490-metre peak straight up the snow ridge, to enjoy a superb panoramic view. Back in the boats they lay offshore, looking for Richard, Kerry and Martin Hughes, who were attempting a mixed rock and snow route around the northern face. Clive's heart stopped when he saw one figure searching a fan of avalanche debris. However they all returned safely; Richard had been searching for some gear knocked off his pack by a falling rock. They landed Paul and Simon at 'Welcome Point' before returning to 'Dayglo' after another long day. Next morning began badly, but the weather cleared soon, allowing Martin Hughes to ferry Richard, Tim and Kerry over to climb Hunt Island. After jumping off on to an impressive icy face they had a superb climb, with Kerry learning fast on exposed grade III-IV slopes. As Martin returned to 'Dayglo' alone, one of the Mariner outboards' shearbushes sheared as the propellor struck a lump of brash (as designed, to protect the gearbox). Two engines per boat gave a good safety margin, but two boats each with two engines was the normal oper-ation for all but such short 15 km return journeys. After replacing the shearbush the rest of the party all went over to Hunt Island to ologise, hauling the Lifeguard up the rocks with the Tirfor winch. The climbing party came down having climbed both the 470-metre main peak and the secondary peak. Martin had found a small group of Chinstraps among the nesting Shags — only the third penguin colony found around the whole coast of Brabant Island, due largely to the steepness of many coasts, and to the south-eastern spits being so low that they were sometimes swept by waves. The Lifeguard had been swamped by the tide rising, but they motored back in high spirits through bitterly cold wind and sea. After a late supper they demolished a bottle of Pussers Rum to celebrate a good few days of hectic work.

February 4th dawned fair, so they tidied up the campsite, packed kit into the boats, and set off at 4 p.m. on the second leg of the circumnavigation, the two boats following the four canoes through the slot of Freud Passage, dominated by great cliffs on either side. In two and a half hours they rounded Mitchell Point to reach the landing site they had sighted earlier. It was a tiny spit exposed in the middle of an umbilical cord of ice-arête linking an ice-covered peninsula to the glacier snout behind. Beaching the boats from each side with their bows meeting over the spit, they knocked a big lump of the arête down to form a bivouac bench above high tide, and hauled the canoes up on to the ice-ridge. There was no room for a tent, so two of them slept in the pulks, while the others lay like five sardines in their bivouac bags on the bench of ice.

Luckily the sea was quiet through a clear cold night. At 6 a.m. the sun woke the five bivouacing on the east side, while hoarfrost still thickly coated the two pulk-bunks on the west side of the arête. As they cooked breakfast, Martin sighted a cloud of Snow Petrels around yellow conglomerate pinnacles behind the point, the first strong indication of a breeding site since visiting Claude Point. However they could not risk another day there, so they left at 8 a.m., pausing to let Ali collect lichens off a small cliff before negotiating brash across the mouth of Hill Bay. At 11 a.m. they stopped for a rest and a brew on a little cobble beach under the nose of Davis Island. As they paddled out into Bouquet Bay, the largest of the grounded bergs before them capsized in an amazing display. Brash was pressed thickly in toward the coast of Brabant Island, so they headed straight across the bay toward Cape Cockburn, 12 km ahead. Clive, Richard, Kerry and Tony paddling were sweating in the broiling sunshine, and paused to rest while Tim took photographs in the brash. Leopard Seals rested on larger pieces, and Richard grew blasé, nudging his kayak up to one, until it raised its great reptilian head and gazed with cold eyes, measuring him. Approaching Cape Cockburn they met the long swell sweeping in from the Bellingshausen Sea, and soon they were battling into a force 4 wind and sea, with waves reflected from the cliffs soaring far above them. Head down, with spray washing the glacier cream off their faces, their four knot speed was much reduced. After 30 km Tony and Kerry clambered into the inflatables, exhausted. Slowly Cape Cockburn slipped astern and Cape Roux grew closer. Once there they entered the narrow eastern channel. One of the boats nudged the rocks to let Tony and Kerry put on warm clothes ashore, while the boat alternately floated and perched crazily at an angle of 40 degrees, as waves swept through. The boats would not fit through the narrows so went round outside, but Clive and Richard paddled through, knocking their paddles on the cliffs. It was not a place to capsize in the awkward crossing breakers. Fur Seals were gambolling in the surf and Richard watched one jump head-high, right over Clive's canoe. Beyond was an amazing scene of 'clapotis' (canoeists' slang for breaking cross-seas) and it took them half an hour to battle through 200 metres to rejoin the boats. Once clear, with Metchnikoff Point in sight, there was no stopping, and an hour later everyone was home, cold and exhausted, but elated. That day Clive and Richard had paddled 42 km, a nine-hour journey, the

Two kayaks approaching Buls Bay, with an inflatable beyond. (Clive Waghorn)

Breaking camp in morning sunlight at the bivouac point northwest of Mitchell Point — the only landing on Brabant Island between Pinel Point and Cape Cockburn. (Tim Hall)

last 27 km non-stop in awkward conditions. It was a weary but proud team who pitched tents that night.

They had completed the circumnavigation (a journey of about 160 km) in less than three weeks, plus much else besides. Clive and Richard had paddled for all but the 30 km around Hulot Peninsula, whilst Tony and Kerry had each paddled nearly 100 km, and Ali rather less. It was a tremendous achievement, the first real canoeing in Antarctica. They had finished just in time too, as bad weather set in for most of the next five days, while they rested, mended gear, collected plants on 'Easter Island', and prepared to put a scientific team into Minot Point.

Better weather arrived on 12 February and although the sea was still rough they went by boat to Minot Point. Next day Tim and Martin coxed the two boats, taking Clive, Richard and Kerry down to Humann Point. The landing was difficult, with a big swell flinging growlers and brash about, threatening the boats, while people and kit were landed on a rock-ledge. The threesome camped a little above on Rush Glacier, beside a rocky spur, preparing to visit Humann Point itself. However next morning Tim and Tony came back in the Avon to fetch them for help at Minot Point — huge breaking swells overnight had capsized the Lifeguard and damaged one engine on the Avon. After returning to Minot Point in the heavily-laden boat with only one engine into the teeth of a snowstorm they finally managed to overturn the Lifeguard, only to find one engine had been lost, sunk. While five stayed at Minot, Tim and Kerry in the Avon (with only one working engine) took the damaged OMC engine back to Metchnikoff Point to repair it or collect spare engines. Next day they returned with two working engines plus one for the Lifeguard. Leaving Ali and Tony at Minot Point, the other five returned to base camp with the two boats. There they repaired the swamped Mariner and damaged OMC. Little did they know another boat saga was to begin.

At midday on 15th, the five of them set off from Metchnikoff Point in two Avons with four OMC engines, heading for Humann Point once again. After stopping off Fleming Point to refuel, they suffered three gearbox failures in rapid succcession. It was a nerve-wracking situation as one boat, with one good engine, slowly towed the other 13 km back to Minot Point, to be met by a leering Leopard Seal. Ali and Tony joined them in a backbreaking operation emptying the boats, and getting everything up on to the rocks.

Next day Clive and Tim stripped the gearboxes, to find three identical ahead-clutch failures, preventing cannibalisation. As before with only one engine they limited the risk to two people, Clive and Tim, who set off at 11 a.m. and had a very rough passage in the Avon, particularly over the reefs at Claude Point, and through the skerries into Metchnikoff Point. Making up a second OMC engine out of various broken ones, and putting the Mariner on to the Avon they had a 'very exciting' ride back to Minot Point. Landing in the swell there was very difficult, and the Mariner's propeller was damaged hitting the rocks. The other Avon was launched and the second OMC engine transferred and both boats were loaded, with everyone getting soaked. Leaving Ali, Martin and Tony to ologise at Minot Point the other four headed back again. Off 'Astrolabe Point' Tim dallied to photograph two whales at close quarters, while out of sight ahead Clive wallowed off Claude Point with a broken drive shaft on his only engine. Luckily they sighted each other. When they finally reached Metchnikoff Point and hauled the boats out, the sun had long set. A tired and weary team fell into their tents. In 5 days Tim had boated over 300 km, to get back where he started from. It was still only 16 February.

They spent the next four days around base camp, doing various jobs and trying in vain to reconstruct a third usable engine from the four damaged ones. They abandoned plans to go to Humann Point by boat, and decided instead to go overland to 'Astrolabe Point' to lower the skidoos, before attempting the first ascent of Mount Morgagni.

On 21st, just before departing, Clive was badly bitten by a bull Fur Seal above the boat haven, a great slash deep into his left thigh. Richard gave first aid, while Tim and Kerry sped to Minot Point and fetched the doctor. Tony inserted 13 stitches, while Tim took photos, feeling rather sick.

Next day Tony stayed to tend Clive in base camp, while Richard, Tim and Kerry skied out with three pulks to put a cache of food and fuel up on 'Cushing Col'. They met bad weather, with a lot of cloud making route-finding difficult over the tortuous route, which they only knew by descriptions and the map. After four days they reached 'Cushing Col' and marked their cache. On the way back across 'Footsore Piedmont' Tim fell ten metres into a crevasse, but jumarred out, and they arrived back at base camp in the evening of 26th.

On 27 February Tim and Richard took Tony back by boat to Minot Point to do geology there, and help Ali and Martin with their botany and survey work. Then Tim and Richard returned to base camp rejoining Clive and Kerry. Between them, the three inflatable boats had covered over 1,700 km in two months, quite a remarkable achievement this far south, without any ship cover. Clive had skied halfway to 'Cairn Point' (alone and unroped) and decreed himself fit, so the four of them prepared to leave next day for 'Astrolabe Point'. It was to be an eventful journey, well publicised in the world press, and therefore I have covered it here in factual diary form.

28 February. Clive, Kerry, Richard and Tim left the radio at Metchnikoff Point and camped in gale-force winds on 'Footsore Piedmont' after a long day's pulking.

1 March. In cloud they relayed the pulks over 'Wobbly Col' and 'Noddies Col' and camped on the head of Lister Glacier.

2 March. Initially in good clear weather they hauled the pulks across the head of Lister Glacier. Cloud closed in, and they found the way down to the west off 'Cushing Col' barred by crevasses in 20 metres visibility. So they camped.

3 March. Starting in clear weather but high wind and spindrift they traversed south, rising toward 'Rokki Plateau' looking for the way west.

Richard and Tim with two pulks led on one rope, with Kerry leading Clive on the second. Traversing along a roadway between crevasses, the first rope moved up left across a fading crevasse line. Kerry followed their tracks. As Kerry crossed the crevasse, at about 10 a.m., Clive moved a metre left off the ski tracks. The roof of the crevasse fell under him, and Clive pendulumed to land 25 metres directly below Kerry on his back, partly jammed in the narrowing crevasse, and partly held by Kerry, who was straddled across the top of the crevasse. Blocks of snow and ice fell on Clive, and one broke his right thigh.

Richard and Tim came back immediately. They put in a deadman belay and secured Kerry, then put in another with a jumar on the live rope between Kerry and Clive, to protect Clive.

Kerry was shocked and bruised. Telling Kerry to dig a tent platform, Richard put another belay in for his rope and went down to Clive, who by then had freed his arms and released his rucksack. Richard helped Clive free himself, put the rucksack on a wedged snow block, saw that Clive's right leg was bent 'with two knees', and then jumared out. While Richard lowered a first-aid pack and a flask of hot chocolate to Clive, Tim rigged a 2 to 1 pulley system, with an alpine clutch.

Richard, Tim and Kerry then hauled Clive up, and through the crevasse lip, to lie in the blowing spindrift. It was half past eleven, just one and a half hours after the fall — good time in a real situation.

They dragged Clive into the Super Nova tent that Kerry had erected. The amount of blood suggested a compound fracture, but Richard found to his relief that this was due to Clive's use of the Omnipon pain-killing syrette. Richard straightened the break, and left Kerry to cut up a Willans sit harness and splint Clive's legs together.

Tim abseiled down the rope to get Clive's rucksack. Unable to find it, he jumared out, with some difficulty due to icing. Richard abseiled down: Clive's rucksack had gone, and the crevasse disappeared into blackness 60 metres below. Richard jumared out, once falling ten metres on iced-up jumars to be held on the figure-of-eight at the end of the rope. The temperature was about −10°C. With Clive's rucksack were lost his personal sleeping bag, etc., plus stove and tent flysheet.

At 5 p.m. Richard and Tim skied back up to the cache on 'Cushing Col'. Despite wind and spindrift they found the cache and returned at 8.30 p.m. with 14 man-days' Arctic rations, ten litres of kerosene and other necessities.

After deciding on the best course of action Kerry cooked an evening meal on the one stove. Richard and Tim then spent the night in the inner tent, while Kerry tended Clive in the complete tent, a Super Nova.

4 March. At first light, before 6 a.m., Richard and Tim said goodbye to Clive and Kerry and set off up over 'Cushing Col'. Conditions grew worse, with continuous cloud and strong winds making it impossible to stand upright. Finally, in the afternoon, they got down off 'Pinnacles Spur', where they dug a snowhole — but uncomfortable with no stove and only one sleeping bag between them. Later in the afternoon the wind eased to gale force and they pressed on, to reach Metchnikoff Point at 6.30 p.m. They had in one day of bad weather completed a journey which often took several days.

At 9 p.m. they contacted Faraday Base by radio, giving the details and the position of the tent near 'Cushing Col'. Faraday forwarded the message to Britain and to HMS *Endurance*. Rothera Base joined the conversation and offered help by Twin Otter.

Above 'Cushing Col', Clive and Kerry lay, talking, playing scrabble, and wondering whether Richard and Tim would get through. It was windy.

5 March. Endurance received the signal in the small hours in Port Stanley: her sailing date was immediately brought forward two days.

The Chileans at Rudolfo Marsh Base volunteered help; their Bell helicopters did not have the range for the return trip, but USARP offered refuelling facilities at Palmer Base. Since weather was bad on the Peninsula, these generous offers were declined for the time being.

At 5 a.m., *Endurance* signalled to Britain stating action in hand. (At home in Kent I received this at midday. Everything possible was being done, so I simply manned the phone while the story broke in the media.)

While preparing to leave Stanley, one of *Endurance*'s Wasps ditched with engine failure. The Senior Naval Officer in the Falkland Islands ordered RFA *Olna* to proceed south, embarking two anti-submarine Sea-

Kerry digging out the tent near 'Cushing Col'. (Tim Hall)

King helicopters of 826 Flight from RFA *Reliant*. Lieutenant Dave Issitt from *Endurance*'s Flight transferred to *Olna* to brief the Sea-King aircrews on Antarctic conditions, and about Brabant Island in particular.

Mr Ed Murton flew up from Rothera Base in the BAS Twin Otter that forenoon, in appalling weather conditions. He overflew 'Cushing Col', but saw nothing through the cloud.

At 'Cushing Col' the gale of wind continued. Clive was reasonably comfortable and the tent seemed secure. He and Kerry heard the Twin Otter in the cloud and hoped it meant that Richard and Tim had got through.

Richard and Tim had hoped to fetch the party from Minot Point to help, but the weather and sea were too rough, so they waited at Metchnikoff Point, talking by radio with Faraday and Minot Point (and with the Twin Otter).

6 March. RFA *Olna* was moving south across Drake Passage at nearly 20 knots, ahead of HMS *Endurance*, with Captain Pat McLaren of HMS *Endurance* in command of the two-ship task unit. (Captain McLaughlin of RFA *Olna* already knew the expedition, having taken the winter party south in RFA *Fort Austin* a year before.) Both ships met bad weather in Drake Passage.

Ed Murton flew up from Rothera again in the BAS Twin Otter. Again he met bad weather, but this time through a break in the cloud he spotted the tent on 'Cushing Col', with Kerry outside waving. The Twin Otter dropped a jerrycan of kerosene, but it disappeared.

Clive was in surprisingly little pain, but conditions in the tent were uncomfortable. The wind had dropped, allowing Kerry to go out, erect a good snow-wall and dig a snowhole in case the tent blew down. They saw the Twin Otter and knew that help was on the way. The jerrycan actually dropped within a rope's length and Kerry was able to recover it. Now they could afford to keep the stove burning for warmth.

Richard and Tim were still storm-bound at Metchnikoff Point. That evening they heard by radio that Olna with 2 Sea Kings might be in range next day.

7 March. At midday, *Olna* was 160 km north of Brabant. The two Sea Kings were launched. Cloud prevented their approaching 'Cushing Col', but they picked up Richard and Tim from Metchnikoff Point.

Clive off 'Emery Peak' approaching Cape Cockburn. 5 February. (Tim Hall)

The BAS Twin Otter once again flew up from Rothera, but could not sight the tent through the cloud.

The two Sea Kings attempted to fly into 'Cushing Col' again in the afternoon, but cloud cover continued, except for a momentary break at 5 p.m. when the tent was sighted. Tony was picked up from Minot Point, but then flying was discontinued at 9 p.m. in deteriorating conditions.

Clive was quite uncomfortable now. They heard helicopters, but after a brief glimpse of one nothing more was heard. Somewhat dispirited, he and Kerry settled into their fifth sleepless night.

Endurance was still coming south. On board were Ted Atkins of the winter party and Mac McLeod of the first-summer party, both now serving in her ship's company: they were busily making up deadmen and preparing to take a team of Royal Marines ashore to go up to 'Cushing Col' if the helicopters were still held up by cloud.

8 March. Cloud still smothered Brabant Island, and high seas made deck operation hazardous. However at 8 a.m. Richard, Tim and Tony were flown from *Olna* to *Endurance* to brief the Captain, the Flight and the Marine Detachment.

Low cloud prevented rescue, but the two Sea Kings flew round the south end of Brabant Island, picked up Mike Ringe and Stuart Martin from 'Dayglo Point', and then continued around the north end back to *Olna*. The Royal Marines in *Endurance*, with Ted, Tim and Mac, prepared to be landed behind Claude Point. Two five-man groups were lifted off *Endurance*, but the weather closed in so they were landed on *Olna* instead.

Clive and Richard paddling through brash, 5 February. (Tim Hall)

183

At 2 p.m. there was a break in cloud around *Endurance*. Lieutenant Commander John White took off in the one remaining Wasp (despite the ship rolling 20 degrees) and managed to sight the tent 'in a web of crevasses'. *Olna* was still in cloud, but the two Sea Kings were launched and flew in, to hover near the tent.

One Sea King winched Tony down to the tent, plus Richard and three Marines. Tony gave Clive painkillers and, with Kerry and the others, strapped him into the stretcher ready for winching out.

At 3 p.m. the Sea King lifted Clive out and flew him back to *Olna*. As the cloud closed in again, the others were winched out also.

Stuart and Dr Bill Bourne, *Olna*'s surgeon, treated Clive, who was remarkably perky. *Olna* set course back toward the Falklands.

Back in England the Picture Editor of the Mail on Sunday finished printing Jed Corbett's pictures and returned to London. The successful rescue, in only five days, had spoilt his story, but even he was glad, like all of us.

From beginning to end it had been a model major rescue, and had taken the remarkably short time of five days from the time of the accident to the moment when Clive was lifted onboard RFA *Olna*.

Kerry, Mike, Richard and Stuart stayed onboard *Olna*, going back to Port Stanley and Britain with Clive.

Tony was transferred to *Endurance*, joining Tim. On 9th the Wasp picked up Ali and Martin Hughes from Minot Point. The ship went round to 'Dayglo Point' that evening, and flew Tony ashore, but the other three had to stay on board.

Leopard Seal with Richard approaching, 5 February. (Clive Waghorn)

Endurance had brought the final recovery date forward to 15 March, leaving only six days for the seven men left at 'Dayglo Point'. So Dave, Paul, Ronnie, Simon, Steve, Tony and Willie could not risk any major exploration, and spent the week near 'Dayglo Point'.

Meanwhile Tim, Ali and Martin Hughes had sailed south to Rothera Base onboard *Endurance*, crossing the Antarctic Circle. While there, *Endurance* lost her second Wasp, luckily again without any injuries. On 15th the second summer team, with help from the Royal Marines of HMS *Endurance*, and Ted Atkins and Mac McLeod, managed to recover all the stores and scientific collections from Chiriguano Bay and 'Dayglo Point'. Next day, using two of the expedition's inflatables, they cleared Metchnikoff Point in a hectic five hours. However without a helicopter there was no chance then of recovering the three skidoos, lying at 300 metres on the ridge above 'Astrolabe Point'.

The expedition's time in Antarctica had ended. Now began the work of analysing scientific data, returning stores and tidying up.

Two kayaks in the Gerlache Strait. (Clive Waghorn)

Appendices

The Expedition

Team Members

First Summer Party

BILL Flight Lieutenant K.W. Hankinson RAF (31). (Deputy Leader, Botany, Meteorology, Psychology).
Navigator. RAF College Cranwell. Nomadic bachelor. Emigrant Ulsterman brought up in East Anglia, father RAF. The smallest team member, a chirpy, energetic, precise graduate in economics and politics. Ambitious career officer. Excellent organiser, forceful leader and thorough on sciences. Competent climber. One previous expedition to Ellesmere Island.

CHRIS Commander J.R.C. Furse RN (48). (Leader, Ornithology).
Dagger marine engineer, Fleet Maintenance Base, Chatham. Australian wife Faye, sons 17 and 19. Kentish, father artist/botanist/Admiral, mother farmer/artist/writer. Big, strong, ungainly, clever but silent. Dedicated Naval engineer. Good detail organiser, democratic leader. Mountaineer, not climber. Two previous expeditions to Elephant Island.

DICK Corporal R.J.C. Worrall RM (31). (Boats, Seals, Whales).
Coxswain, Royal Marines, Poole. Wife Sarah, daughter 1. From Dorset. Strong, fit, easy-going, steady, humorous storyteller. Ex-Naval stoker and policeman, promoted RM Sergeant April 1984. Prepared and ran boats with typical meticulous care. Competent climber. No previous major expeditions.

JED Leading Airman (Photographer) G.J. Corbett RN (24). (Still & Cine Photography).
Fleet Photographic Unit, Portsmouth. Virtually engaged. From Purbeck, father was Army. Lithe, charming, energetic, excitable, self-centred extrovert and chatterbox. Totally dedicated to photographic career. Enthusiastic, single-minded, thorough and artistic photographer. Inexperienced mountaineer. No previous expeditions.

JEFF Corporal J.D. Hill RM (27). (Radio, Assistant Meteorology, Fish).
Medical Assistant, Commando Logistic Regiment, Plymouth. Wife Julie, daughter 8 months. A Welsh-speaker from Neath. Short, strong, quick-witted, eager, intolerant and temperamental. A single-minded martial Royal Marine. Always seeking work, packed all expedition stores. Arctic-warfare trained but not a mountaineer. No previous expeditions.

Opposite. A pair of Blue-eyed Shags with young. (Tim Hall)

Bill

Chris

Dick

Jed

Jeff

Johnny

Kevin

Mac

Simon

JOHNNY   Doctor J. Morris (26). (Doctor, Terrestrial Invertebrates, Social Study).
Civilian, St Bartholemews Hospital, London. Fun-loving bachelor. Crazy Welsh medical family in Berkshire. Red-haired, strong, infectiously cheerful enthusiast, carefree but caring. Aiming to be a general practitioner or radiologist. He came for fun, tried everything and worked hard on sciences. No mountaineering or expedition experience.

KEVIN   Corporal K.W. de Silva (24). (Boat Driver, Maps, General Repairs).
Bricklayer, Royal Engineers, Maidstone and Camberley. Wife Carole. Father a Hertfordshire journalist. Big, strong, calm, gentle, humorous with questioning intelligence. Thinking out his future. Constantly mended and improved expedition equipment. Strong mountaineer & climber. Previous expeditions to Greenland and Nepal.

MAC   Marine D.J. McLeod RM (24). (Assistant Survey, Electrics).
Royal Marines, Poole. Family bachelor. Scot with homes in Angus and Surrey. Gangling, strong, quiet, thoughtful. Ex-Naval radio-electrical mechanic, undecided about future. Last-minute replacement, proved handy all-rounder. Climber. Mountaineering expedition to Mexico.

SIMON   Lieutenant S.P. Trathen RM (25). (Geology, Geomorphology).
Royal Marines, Arbroath. Eager bachelor. Ardent Cornishman from Redruth. Wiry, boyish enthusiast, tumbled speech, laborious fixing things, with contagious grin. Single-minded career Royal Marine. Geology graduate from Sheffield, but preferred physical action. Strong climber. No previous major expeditions.

TED   Corporal E.A. Atkins RAF (25). (Survey).
Vehicle technician, RAF Gutersloh. Lovable bachelor. Geordie born, father now Nottinghamshire miner and Parliamentary candidate. Small, jaunty, confident and unflappable with twinkling humour, getting and giving enjoyment in everything. Now aiming for a commission having been one of the lads. Marvellous inventive mechanic, practical surveyor and general fixer. Strong climber. Mountaineering expeditions to Rockies and Manaslu.

Winter Party

CHRIS (48), JED (25), and *TED (25).* Staying over, just a bit dirtier.

FRANÇOIS   Monsieur F. de Gerlache de Gomery (22). (Seals, Tent Repairs).
Recently Ardennes Chasseurs. Our youngest bachelor. Belgian from Zingem, grandfather discovered Brabant Island, father led Belgian Antarctic Expedition. Red-haired, pleasant, willing; youthful shyness fading with mastery of idiomatic English. Hoping to work in nature conservation. Dedicated work on tents though main interest seals. Good skier, not climber. One summer's archeology on Baffin Island.

HOWARD   Surgeon Lieutenant E.H.N. Oakley RN (29). (Deputy Party Leader, Equipment, Doctor, Physiology, Meteorology).
Physiologist, Institute of Naval Medicine, Alverstoke. Wife Do, daughter 1. Londoner, father ex-Army. Energetic, bespectacled, intensely

enthusiastic talker (always right), widely read and very clever. Physiology graduate from Oxford, research Cardiff and Copenhagen. Ambitious specialist in survival physiology. Very efficient, self-sufficient workaholic. Hillwalker and careful climber. No previous expeditions.

Ted

JB (Jon)   Corporal J.R. Beattie RAF (24). (Terrestrial Invertebrates).
Avionics Technician, RAF Kinloss. Retiring bachelor. Irish. Sturdy, bespectacled, quiet but humorous, pipe-smoking thinker & doer. Steady career aims. All-round practical supporter, thorough on sciences but mountains first interest. Skidoo cowboy. Mountain Rescue Party Leader, sound climber. No previous expeditions.

JIM   Corporal J.W. Lumsden 1QLR (26). (Radio, Assistant Meteorology).
Queens Lancashire Regiment. Married Christine on 4 February 84. Kirkcaldy family living in Burnley. Burly, easy-going, cheery, resilient jackdaw. Career infantryman. Conscientious on met. readings and excellent on radio. Occasional skidoo cowboy. Negligible mountaineering experience and no previous major expeditions.

François

KIM (John)   Sergeant J.M. Kimbrey RM (28). (Food, Fish, Boats).
Physical Training Instructor, Commando Training Centre, Lympestone, Devon. Wife Hazel, daughter 5 and son 8. From Oxford. Lean, tough, red-haired, energetic and playful humorist, strong leader with fixed opinions hard to cross. Tireless on stores and repairs, though his target was climbing. Skidoo cowboy. Mountaineering Instructor (Winter Certificate), our best climber. Previous expeditions to Mexico and Yosemite.

Howard

MIKE   Mr M. Ringe (22). (Geology).
Civilian, Nottingham University. Musical bachelor from Cambridge. Tall, lean, fit, practical, quiet, good-humoured, fitted in easily. First-class Geology graduate from Aston. Seeking career in geology after this 3-4 year Ph.D. research. All-round participator as well as gifted and dedicated geologist. Occasional skidoo cowboy. Natural mountaineer with no previous climbing experience, nor expeditions.

JB

NICK   Captain N.R.C. Evans PWO (32). (Geomorphology).
Prince of Wales Own Regiment of Yorkshire. Self-conscious bachelor from Somerset. Large, strong, clean-shaven, clumsy, determined public-school patriot. Very knowledgeable modern history graduate from Durham. Single-minded career infantry officer. Impractical, a dogged fieldworker though scientifically ill-prepared. Ski trooper with little mountaineering or camping experience, despite University and Sandhurst expeditions to Greenland.

PETER   Sergeant P.D. Stuttard REME (28). (Botany, Social Study).
Avionics technician, 3 Army Air Flight near York. Engaged to Julie December 83. A Blackpool man. Tall, quiet, strong, dependable, constructive. Two years of biology degree course at Manchester. Going for Warrant Officer Artificer, or commission. Practical all-round handyman, working thoroughly on sciences. Skidoo cowboy. Safe mountaineer. No previous expeditions.

Jim

Kim

Mike

Nick

Peter

Spotts

SPOTTS (John)   Lance Corporal J.K. Spottiswood RE (25). (Seals, Skidoos).
Signaller, 35 Engineer Regiment, Hameln. Piratical bachelor. A cockney from Chigwell. Enthusiastic, wiry, lively, cheerful, quick-witted extrovert with salesman's patter. Intelligent sapper, ambitious but with many competing interests. Always up and out early, busily fixing things. Skidoo trail boss. Strong mountaineer and climber, with Alpine experience but no major expeditions.

Second-summer Boat Party

ALI   Lieutenant A. Moffat RE (27). Botany.
Junior Leaders Regiment RE, Dover. Bachelor from Kent. Degree in agricultural botany at UCNW with postgraduate experience. Reasonable canoeist. Experienced climber with expedition experience in Alps and Himalayas.

CLIVE   Lieutenant Commander C. Waghorn RN (37). (Second-summer Leader).
Submarine Weapons Electrical Officer, Britannia Royal Naval College, Dartmouth. Mobile bachelor. Expert canoeist, with mountaineering experience. Leader of several white-water canoeing expeditions.

GARY   Lieutentant G. Lewis RN (27). (Ornithology, Equipment).
Supply Officer, HMS *Cochrane*. Bachelor from Devon. Keen bird-watcher, previous Supply Officer of HMS *Endurance* in 1980/81. Injured on journey south, did not reach Brabant.

KERRY   Lance Corporal K. Gill R.Sigs (22). (Radio).
4th Armoured Division HQ, W.Germany. Bachelor from Somerset and Buckinghamshire. Good skier and white-water canoeist.

MARTIN   Lance Bombardier M. Hughes RA (29). (Ornithology, Survey, Assistant Terrestrial Invertebrates).
Kiel Training Centre. Bachelor from Hertfordshire. Sailing instructor and skier with some climbing experience. Keen amateur naturalist.

RICHARD   Lieutenant R. Clements R.Anglian (25). (Fish, Seals, Stores).
Royal Anglian Regiment. Bachelor from Northumberland. Strong climber and canoeist, with experience in Tasmania, Mexico, USA, Canada and Europe.

TIM   Leading Airman (Photographer) T. Hall RN (27). (Photography).
HMS *Daedalus*. Bachelor from Kent. Mountaineering experience in Europe and Canada. Natural boat coxswain.

TONY   Captain R. Williams RAMC (25). (Doctor, Assistant Geology).
Royal Army Medical College. Bachelor from Surrey. Good canoeist and rock climber.

Second-summer Land Party

DAVE   Flight Lieutenant D. Ball RAF (33). (Travel and Administration).
Engineer, RAF Cottesmore. Wife Gerry, 2 children. From Hackney. Negligible mountaineering experience.

GRAHAM   Staff Sergeant G. Greenway REME (27). (Stores, Ornithology).
SEME Bordon. Wife Jenny. From Plymouth. Mountain and Arctic trained.

MIKE   Mr M. Ringe (23). (Geology).
Completing a year on the island. Now a mountaineering party Leader.

PAUL   Lieutenant P. Flint RN (27). (Geomorphology).
Supply Officer. HMS *Cochrane.* Bachelor from Cumbria. First-class graduate in geography from London, and postgraduate tutorial research studentship in geomorphology. Experienced hillwalker with some climbing around Europe.

RONNIE   Leading Airman (Photographer) A.M.R. Barker RN (24). (Still and Cine Photography).
HMS *Osprey.* Bachelor from Yorkshire. Some hill-walking & skiing experience, including the Alps.

SIMON   Second Lieutenant S. Allen 3RTR (22). (Radio).
3rd Royal Tank Regiment, Sennelager. Bachelor from Army family. Mountaineering experience in Scotland and Alps.

STEVE   Flight Lieutenant S. Taylor RAF (33). (Leader Southern Land Party, Meteorology).
Phantom pilot, RAF Leuchars. Wife Lynwen, 1½ children. From Gloucestershire. Mountaineer with Alpine experience.

STUART   Captain S. Martin RAMC (32). (Doctor, Invertebrates).
Royal Army Medical College. Engaged to Sarah December 84. From Home Counties. Degree in biological sciences and medicine at Leicester plus postgraduate work. Experienced ski-mountaineer.

WILLIE   Sergeant W. Lawrence RE (31).
74 Engineer Regiment, Ulster. Married. Strong climber with experience in Mexico, Rockies and Europe.

Equipment

Most basic equipment was drawn from Service sources, but many specialised items were obtained commercially. Some firms donated gear, others made valuable loans, and most offered good discounts. The list below covers only a selection of major items. Bound complete equipment lists, with detailed reports on many items, have been lodged with the Scott Polar Research Institute and the Royal Geographical Society.

Tents
1. Two-man Antarctic Pyramid tents from MFC Survival Ltd. Unbeatable base-camp tents, withstanding 100-knot winds and three-metre drifts, and needing no repairs over 15 months.
2. Super Nova dome tents from Wintergear/Wild Country. Very comfortable and popular mobile tents for two or three men. Modified with four storm guys and doubled poles ('Mountain' tents) they withstood winds of over 100 knots with snow-walls and also total burial. Dome tent poles troublesome especially in extreme cold.

Ali

Clive

Kerry

Martin

Richard

Tim

Tony

Dave

Graham

Paul

3. Snowline Conquest box tents from Touring Sport Ltd. Mobile tents withstanding 100-knot winds without snow-walls, but small for two men. Very helpful manufacturer is overcoming condensation problems.
4. Bombproof ridge tent from Nevisport. Good emergency skidoo tent for erection in storms. Small & heavy, condensation & drifting problems.
5. All other UK and several continental tent manufacturers canvassed. Eight other tents taken south, but none withstood winter conditions.

Clothing

1. Individuals varied in their selection of clothes. My own preferences are described on p. 96.
2. Many types of mittens were taken. None proved both good and durable.
3. Valluga ski-mountaineering boots. Double boots with soft inners and plastic outers are best for extreme cold, but Vallugas a bad choice.
4. Dolomite boots. Good boots, but single leather boots are bad in extreme cold.
5. Super Yeti gaiters. Marvellous.
6. Both visor goggles (against spindrift) and sunglasses (hot days) essential.
7. The best sleeping bags were various quick-drying Holofil bags.
8. Goretex bivouac bags from SCRDE. I will never camp without one. Tyvek paper bags were even better in winter.
9. 8-mm-thick closed-cell Karrimats. Most used two in winter. Wanted renewal after three months, but lasted a year.

Camping

1. Full-size Bulldog shovels were excellent. We had too few.
2. Spoon-bladed small Norwegian Army snowshovels. Take one each.
3. 40-cm-long icesaws. One per tent essential. Fit decent handles.
4. Optimus half-litre 111B paraffin stoves and 111T multifuel stoves ideal. The obsolete paraffin stoves were generally preferred.
5. Nester set of three pots per tent for cooking and eating ideal.
6. One dessert-spoon each for eating (handles filed as stove spanners).
7. Tilley stormlights marvellous in base. Service watertight right-angle torches and candles adequate. Good headlamps useful for digging out on bad nights.
8. Cleaning gear per tent: snowbrush, sponge, scotchbrite, J Cloths.
9. Cleaning gear per person: toothbrush, toothpaste.
10. Personal cassette players (from Sharp, Sony, Sanyo, Aiwa, Pioneer and Unisef) were the only complete respite from the environment.
11. Plastic screwtop pee bottles. Two litres in base, half for travel.
12. Lonza Metatabs for stove. Excellent. 20-40 tablets per tent per week.
13. Half-litre unbreakable Thermos flasks. Very worthwhile.
14. Dustbin liners and smaller polythene bags. Never enough.
15. Stuffsacks. Several each invaluable.
16. Paraffin. 1 litre per tent per day adequate even in winter.

Mountaineering

1. Dynastar Yeti 180-cm skis from Europasports. Outstanding.
2. Emery Altitude Plus ski-mountaineering bindings from Europasports. Outstanding and strongly recommended.

3. Pomoca Topfix adhesive skins. Permanently fitted to skis. Ideal.
4. Lowes Footfang crampons. Nothing else will do now.
5. Wooden pulk sledges from Solatun Sport. Essential for journeys of over a week. Great value with a few modifications.
6. Edelrid Everdri Kernmantel rope. Most 9 mm, some 11 mm. Good.
7. 5-mm Kernmantel for prussiks, etc. Never enough.
8. Troll 2.5-cm Superblue and 1.2-cm tubular tapes. Never enough.
9. Various harnesses from Troll. Mk 6 sit-harness with Europa chest-harness preferred for convenience on glaciers and pulking.
10. Ascendeurs. A pair of jumars worthwhile for crevasse falls.
11. Descendeurs. Italian hitches (or stitch plates) preferred.
12. Six snaplink and four screwgate karabiners each, plus spares.
13. Two or more icescrews each. One long one each for glaciers.
14. One Deadman each (Deadboys distrusted). Wings must point uphill.
15. One 70-cm Snowstake per party desirable for mushrooms.
16. Usual variety of iceaxes and icehammers. My preference was a 55-cm Stubai Manaslu axe and a Snowdon Mouldings Curver hammer.
17. One Silva 15 compass each. Excellent. Dip compensation desirable.
18. One Thommen altimeter each. Excellent. Invaluable for navigation.
19. One Pieps 11 avalanche transceiver each. Most failed. Something essential.
20. One whistle each. Essential (audible in crevasses, shouts inaudible).
21. Beanstick bamboo wands with motorway tape pennants. Invaluable for route marking and tent pegs. 750 not enough.
22. Cyalume lightsticks from Fonadek. Invaluable.
23. Hot Minis from CBE Associates (60-g sachets of metal filings). Gave 15 hours' warmth at 60 degrees, or several shorter periods. Good.
24. Berghaus Crusader rucksacks from SCRDE proved very good.

Tools and Repair Materials

1. One technician should make detailed checks before departure.
2. Individuals carried Swiss Army knife, pliers, screwdriver, spanner.
3. Repair kits made up for boats, canoes, skidoos, pulks, tents, skis.
4. Universal repair materials were Rotunda adhesive tapes, wrecked tents, parachute cord, Bostik 2402 adhesive, thread, sailmakers' palms, needles.
5. Don't forget the WD40.

Medical

1. Individuals carried first-aid kits in 'soap boxes', including morphine.
2. Small bags included in each pulk repair kit.
3. Two SAS sacks (30×25×20 cm) with skidoos for outlying caches.
4. Comprehensive base kit at Metchnikoff Point in four suitcases, plus Thomas splints. Second base kit highly desirable for south.

Electrical Equipment

1. Coordinator needed for preparations; make early choice of power source; prove charging arrangements; take adequate spare parts and multimeter. Capacitors failed in low temperatures.
2. Expendable dry batteries gave best overall reliability. 20 different sizes required. Duracell alkaline batteries dramatically superior.

Communications

1. Three Clansman PRC320 HF Transceiver sets lent by Plessey Military

Ronnie

Simon

Steve

Stuart

Willie

Communications. Outstanding. Utterly reliable except for accessories. Hand-charging useful.

2. Three PRM 4160T VHF 'Walkie Talkie' sets lent by Racal Telectronics.

Still Photography

1. Two Nikon FM2 and two Nikon F2A 35 mm cameras with 15 mm ultra-wide-angle, 16 mm fisheye, 20, 28 and 35 mm wide-angle, 50 mm standard, 55 mm macro, 135 and 300 mm telephoto lenses, plus 2× converters. The main quality camera outfits.
2. Four Rolleiflex twin-lens reflex 120 mm cameras.
3. Two Nikonos 35 mm underwater cameras lent by Pelling & Cross.
4. Seven Pentax SP1000 35 mm cameras with 35, 50 and 300 mm lenses, plus 2 × converters.
5. Four Olympus XA 35 mm compact cameras. Handy, beware exposures.
6. Two Polaroid SK70 cameras (for sciences and reconnaissances).
7. Two Fujica HDS waterproof 35 mm cameras. Excellent.
8. Pelling & Cross lent Second Summer two Hasselblad 120 mm cameras (CM500, 80 mm and 150 mm lenses, superwide 38 mm).
9. Benbo tripod from Kennett Engineering and a monopod from Gitzo.
10. Two Metz CT45 flashguns; Weston V and Lunasix lightmeters.
11. Total film exposed over the 15 months was:

35mm	510 rolls colour slides.
35mm	259 rolls black and white.
120mm	53 rolls colour negative.
120mm	119 rolls black and white.
120mm	48 rolls colour transparency.

12. Colour Processing Laboratories processed all colour film. Advertising material is available through them.
13. Topham Picture Library has a selection of pictures for sale.

Cine Photography

1. Two Beaulieu R16 battery-powered 16 mm cameras.
   One 10-150 mm Angenieux zoom, one 10 mm Angenieux fixed lens. Superb quality but charging problems.
2. Two winterised Bolex hand-crank 16 mm cameras with triple turret lenses. Reliable for bad conditions, but limited running time.
3. C-mount adaptors to utilise Nikon and Pentax camera lenses.
4. Two Uher 4000 Report tape recorders with Sennhauser microphones, 1 omni- 1 uni-directional. Restricted to base camp.
5. Bilora magnetic-head tripod.
6. Fuji Photofilm donated colour reversal film, requiring exact exposures. 60 rolls RT500 and 117 rolls RT125 used, each roll 30 metres. Recorded 38 Agfa 15-minute sound tapes.
7. Expedition film is being marketed by Pacesetter Enterprises Ltd.

Boats

1. Two Avon five-metre inflatable boats. Excellent seaboats, durable.
2. One 510 inflatable boat from Lifeguards. Even better seakeeping and larger capacity, but very difficult to haul out.
3. Five OMC 35-HP outboard motors. Very good until gearbox defects.
4. Two Mariner 40-HP outboards from E.P. Barrus. Reliable, but heavy.
5. Drysuits from Multifab Ltd for coxswains. Good.
   Aircrew immersion suits rather more durable.

6. Tirfor Junior winch. Invaluable for hauling out (plus L-floats).
7. Four Nordkapp sea kayaks from Valley Canoe Products with rafting brackets, deck compasses, watertight compartments and pumps. Could carry 30 days' gear, ex-mountaineering. Nordkapps are best.
8. Lendal Pacemaster paddle blades with fibreglass shafts. Excellent.
9. Canoeists wore thermal underwear, aircrew fibrepile 'bunny' suits, cagoules and buoyancy aids from NWWC, Goretex overtrousers, Splashsport fibrepile paddle mitts or Suzy mitts.
10. Gear in canoes was stowed in modified Coleman Dry Sacks, Valley Canoe Products Aquasacks, and BDM containers.
11. Safety equipment for each canoe comprised, a LOCAT beacon, a white parachute flare, a day/night flare, a seawater-activated light, a safety/rescue line, and a spare paddle.

Skidoos

1. One new Alpine 503 donated by Saccone and Speed and Courage. Modified by MVEE, Chertsey, as recommended by BAS and the Transglobe Expedition.
2. Two secondhand Alpine 640s, serviced and modified by MVEE.
3. Two BSC steel Dilly sledges. Too heavy; Nansens more suitable.
4. Two sledges made by Ted Atkins from fuel drums. Excellent.
5. Dead Giants (70×80 cm Deadmen) used as winch anchors.
6. Tirfor Junior Winch. Essential for crevasse recoveries.
7. 2.5-cm diameter towropes, improved by bungee shorteners.
8. Methanol excellent for starting, and as antifreeze additive in fuel.

Scientific Instruments

1. Porton Anemometer (lent by Victor Instruments Ltd) in base camp.

Spotts with rucksack contents in August. (Jed Corbett)

Hand anemometers out of base. 65-knot scales inadequate.
2. Golf 11 Laser Rangefinder system lent by Oilfield Measuring Devices Ltd and Lasergage Ltd. Tripod mounted 9-km range. Tremendous potential for single plane-table mapping.
3. Invertebrate funnel extractors from York University mounted by Peter Stuttard in primitive dalek for icebucket/Tilley Lamp operation.
4. Fully waterproof compact monocular or binoculars essential.
5. Binocular microscope very useful.
6. Grant Instruments 9-channel chart recorder. Very reliable, checkable.
7. Grant Instruments 45-channel data logger. Reliable but no check.
8. Beckman digital multimeter used with thermistors, humidity sensors.
9. Aga Thermopoint 80 infra-red 'gun' for remote surface temperatures.
10. Yacht Echosounder (never actually used).
11. Schmidt hammer for rock hardness/weathering.
12. PC XT microcomputer donated by IBM, with 'Smart' software donated by Paradigm: invaluable for post-expedition analysis.

Containers

1. Most stores were packed in collapsible plywood cases.
2. Triwall cardboard boxes proved useful shelters in winter.
3. Watertight barrels from Bowater International, and smaller Schermully flare bottles were both invaluable.
4. Standard strong wooden boxes about 60×40×40 cm were wanted. These would have been ideal for building a shelter.

Food

Two basic types of standard Service rations were provided, plus a range of bulk extras intended to make up the basic rations to 5,000 kcal per man-day.

A total of 1,800 man-days Compo rations and 2,300 man-days Arctic rations were landed on the island for 1984, but about 700 man-days remained at 'Dayglo Point' when the winter party left. Through 1984 the expedition spent 4,049 man-days on the island, and in that time 3,400 man-days basic rations were consumed. John Kimbrey made up most of the bulk extras into 'Kimpo' base camp rations and 'Kimpack' travelling rations, to stretch the food in the north over the winter. The actual average intake per man per day was thus about 4,000 kcal, including 120 g protein, 152 g fat, 560 g carbohydrates and 13 g salt. We felt quite hungry.

The three tables in this appendix list all the items of food. While returning on board HMS *Endurance,* the winter party met and voted by a show of hands on the quality and quantity of each item. Our net votes are shown in these tables.

Arctic Rations (dehydrated)

In 1 man-day packs weighing 1.5 kg, 4,500 kcal per man-day.

ARCTIC RATIONS	MENU ABCD	QUALITY VOTES + Excellent : Satisfactory − Poor	QUANTITY per 1−Man-day pack	QUANTITY VOTES + More needed : Adequate − Too much
Breakfast				
Porridge	ABCD	5+	100 g	2+
Apple flakes	A C	8+	30 g	7+
Apple & apricot flakes	B D	10+	30 g	7+
Drinking chocolate	ABCD	8+	70 g	4+
Snack-pack				
Biscuits AB plain	ABCD	3+	85 g	2+
Meat paste: beef	A	2+	30 g	3+
chicken	B	2+	30 g	3+
chicken & bacon	C	5+	30 g	3+
ham	D	4+	30 g	3+
Biscuits, squashed-fly	ABCD	6+	85 g	2+
Chocolate: Rolos	ABCD	8+	105 g	−3
milk chocolate	A C	3+	55 g	−1
biscuit & fruit	B D	7+	55 g	3+
Nuts & raisins mixed	ABCD	5+	45 g	:
Dextrose tablets	ABCD	2+	30 g	−2
Drinks				
Instant tea	ABCD	4+	2 sachets	5+
Instant coffee	ABCD	9+	2 sachets	8+
Beef stock	ABCD	1+	1 sachet	:
Sugar	ABCD	−4	30 g	7+
Powdered skimmed milk	ABCD	8+	15 g	3+
Main meal				
Soup: chicken	A	2+	30 g	−1
vegetable	B D	6+	30 g	2+
Oxtail	C	−9	30 g	−7
Meat granules: beef	A	4+	60 g	5+
curried beef	B	10+	60 g	5+
mutton	C	−4	60 g	−2
chicken	D	6+	60 g	1+
Mashed potato powder	A C	−2	60 g	5+
Pre-cooked rice	B D	10+	85 g	2+
Freeze-dried peas	ABCD	6+	45 g	−5
From Bulk. Vitamin tablets	ABCD	:	one	:
Sundries				
Salt	ABCD	1+	1.25 g	−7
Booklet of matches	ABCD	−5	1 booklet	1+
Handy-Andy paper tissues	ABCD	9+	1 packet of 6	:
Toilet paper	ABCD	−7	10 sheets	:
Wooden spatula	ABCD	:	one	−2

Compo Rations (tinned)

In 4-man-day packs weighing 10 kg, 3,900 kcals per man-day

COMPO RATIONS	MENU ABCDEFG	QUALITY VOTES	QUANTITY 4—Man-day pack	QUANTITY VOTES
Breakfast				
Baked beans, tomato sauce	ABCDEFG	10+	454 g (1 tin)	9+
Sausages	A C E G	9+	454 g (1 tin)	9+
Bacon-grill	B F	2+	454 g (1 tin)	4+
Baconburgers	D	2+	425 g (1 tin)	6+
Beefburgers	EF	2+	425 g (1 tin)	:
Luncheon-meat	A D	7+	454 g (1 tin)	4+
Drinks				
Teabags	ABCDEFG	5+	4 × 15 g	6+
Instant coffee	ABCDEFG	4+	4 sachets	8+
Sugar	ABCDEFG	2+	395 g (1 tin)	6+
Instant powdered milk	ABCDEFG	2+	45 g (2 tins)	5+
Supper				
Powdered soups: mushroom	A	4+	85 g (1 pkt)	−1
mulligatawny	B	−3	85 g (1 pkt)	−2
chicken	C	2+	85 g (1 pkt)	−2
oxtail	D F	−10	85 g (1 pkt)	−9
green pea	E	3+	85 g (1 pkt)	−1
vegetable	G	5+	85 g (1 pkt)	1+
Meats: Goulash	A	:	910 g (2 tins)	−1
corned beef	B	9+	682 g (2 tins)	3+
steak & onion casserole	C	9+	910 g (2 tins)	:
chicken curry	D	1+	910 g (2 tins)	:
steak & kidney pudding	E	4+	910 g (2 tins)	−2
chicken in brown sauce	F	−4	910 g (2 tins)	−3
stewed steak	G	:	910 g (2 tins)	
Vegetables: carrots	A D G	5+	283 g (1 tin)	1+
mixed vegetables	B	3+	283 g (1 tin)	4+
processed peas	C EF	−5	283 g (1 tin)	2+
mashed potato powder	ABC E G	−5	170 g (1 pkt)	−1
pre-cooked rice	D F	8+	283 g (2 tins)	2+
Puddings: apple	A	−1	682 g (2 tins)	−3
rice	B E	−1	682 g (2 tins)	:
mixed fruit	C G	5+	682 g (2 tins)	2+
fruit salad	D	9+	682 g (2 tins)	8+
pears	F	7+	682 g (2 tins)	6+
peaches	F	9+	682 g (2 tins)	6+
apricots	F	4+	682 g (2 tins)	3+
Snacks and Miscellaneous				
Chocolate: milk	A C E G	5+	4 × 60 g	5+
biscuit & fruit	B D F	:	4 × 60 g	5+
Boiled sweets	ABCDEFG	:	113 g	−7
Oatmeal blocks (tin of 5)	A C E G	8+	5 × 30 g	5+
Rich cake	B	10+	340 g (1 tin)	8+
Margarine	ABCDEFG	5+	227 g (1 tin)	
Processed cheese	ABCDEFG	7+	227 g (1 tin)	6+
Pilchards & tomato sauce	C G	−2	425 g (1 tin)	−8
Jam: strawberry	B	9+	255 g (1 tin)	:
marmalade	A	5+	255 g (1 tin)	1+
raspberry	C	7+	255 g (1 tin)	:
blackcurrant	D G	9+	255 g (1 tin)	2+
apricot	EF	5+	255 g (1 tin)	:
Vitamin tablets	ABCDEFG	:	1 tablet	:
Biscuits AB plain	ABCDEFG	7+	170 g (12)	4+
Salt	ABCDEFG	1+	30 g	−9
Mustard	ABCDEFG	2+	8 g	2+
Jiffy tin-opener	ABCDEFG	9+	1	:
Plastic reclosure tin-lids	ABCDEFG	9+	2	:
Matches (book, in sweet-tin)	ABCDEFG	−4	1 booklet	4+
Toilet paper	ABCDEFG	−8	24 sheets	4+

Bulk Extra Rations

Except where stated all these rations were provided by the RN Victualling Depot at Botley, Hampshire.

BULK RATIONS	SOURCE	QUALITY VOTES	TOTAL QUANTITY for 12 months	QUANTITY VOTES
Cornflakes		−1	600 × 21 g	−3
Rolled oats		4+	71 kg	−4
Frosties	Nabisco	3+	?	:
Jordans Crunchy	Jordans	7+	?	5+
Milk chocolate	Nestlé	10+	425 × 60 g	9+
Plain chocolate	Nestlé	6+	425 × 60 g	5+
Yorkie bars	Rowntree	9+	?	8+
Mixed chocolates	Rowntree	5+	4 large tins	4+
Mars bars		4+	144 bars	10+
McDougalls Breadmix		9+	61 kg	6+
Plain flour		:	50 kg	−4
Egg powder		0		9+
Spaghetti, pastas, pizzas		0		10+
Margarine		1+	18 kg	−3
Sardines		7+	200 tins	4+
Stewed steak (in tins)		:	65 kg	:
Boil-in-a-bag meals	Heinz	8+	30 × 2-man	6+
Pickled onions		10+	24 bottles	5+
Sweet pickles		5+	24 bottles	2+
Chutney		10+	24 jars	5+
Tomato sauce		6+	24 bottles	2+
Brown sauce		4+	24 bottles	−1
Instant soups (= sauces)	Heinz	8+	212 tubs	2+
Instant sauces: onion, etc.	Colmans	8+	400 packets	5+
Currants		6+	48 kg	:
Sultanas		7+	48 kg	2+
Herbs and spices		8+	individual	10+
Tinned potatoes		8+	87 kg	5+
Tinned beans, tomato sauce		7+	43 kg	6+
Tinned tomatoes		8+	87 kg	:
Dried onions etc.		0		9+
Tinned apples		3+	87 kg	:
Tinned pears		7+	43 kg	:
Tinned pineapples		10+	87 kg	3+
Dried apricots, etc.		0		8+
Jelly cubes		6+	434 packets	−7
Instant custard (Batchelors)		9+	400 packets	8+
Evaporated milk in tins		8+	288 tins	:
Condensed milk in tubes	Nestlé	10+	?	9+
Large teabags		2+	150 × 10	−4
Instant coffee		5+	50 packets	4+
Real coffee bags	Kenco	10+	?	8+
Rise & Shine fruitdrink		9+	50 packets	8+
Whisky (some were gizzits)	Various	8+	60 bottles	:
Pussers Rum	Int.Dist.	8+	24 bottles	:
Newcastle Brown Ale	J. Biscoe	10+	36 cans	6+
Limpets (boil, add pepper, etc.)	Local	2+		
Antarctic cod (fry or boil)	Local	2+		
Chinstrap breast (marinate, fry)	Local	3+		
Chinstrap egg (fry, omelette)	Local	6+		
Crabeater steak (fry, stew, raw)	Local	7+		

Medical and Physiological Aspects   by Howard Oakley

The potential problems of living and working in the cold included hypothermia, local cold injuries and other environmental diseases, but injuries and conventional medical, surgical and dental problems could not be neglected. Our mobility and living in tents increased both the risks and the difficulty of treatment.

Hypothermia occurs when the rectal temperature falls to 35°C or below, but in the field the key to diagnosis is suspicion and watching for initial subtle behavioural changes. Prevention relied on selection of clothing and maintenance of shelter; immersion accidents while boating were minimised by using effective drysuits and lifejackets/buoyancy aids. In spite of dampness, and windchill effective temperatures down to -60°C or lower, no serious case of hypothermia occurred. In contrast, peripheral cold injury was almost universal: all cases were mild frostbite, resulting from only brief superficial freezing but with long-lasting numbness from the resultant nerve damage. All the winter team had at least two frostbitten fingers and several had frostbitten big toes, but the only serious consequence was residual sensitivity to cold for a few weeks.

Dehydration is a common problem when exercising in the cold. Fluid is lost by sweating while travelling, when it is difficult to replace; in the evenings the cold produces diuresis, with large volumes of urine passed overnight nullifying the brews drunk after pitching camp. Dehydration did not produce constipation on the island, but it increased the viscosity of blood, predisposing to frostbite. The main focus of the physiological research was on this phenomenon: blood samples and 24-hour fluid balance records were used to assess whether dehydration was abolished by acclimatisation. Almost all of the winter team did show a great reduction in dehydration (i.e. they did acclimatise) after about three months on the island. 24-hour monitoring of skin and rectal temperatures (and other environmental measurements) were undertaken to ascertain whether this resulted from adequate cold stimulus. Much analysis remains to be done, but it already appears that dehydration occurred as a result of initial cold exposure, and was abolished later by acclimatisation to continuing cold. In contrast, the morphometric results from periodic weighing and skinfold-thickness measurements in winter have raised very difficult questions. There was a significant weight loss early in the expedition, a month before the maximum dehydration of the blood. This overall weight loss included a substantial loss of lean body mass as well as of fat from the body (but not from the limbs). Thereafter there was a sustained increase of lean body mass and fat on the body through the winter. This does not appear to have been due to fitness changes. The changes in lean body mass are unlikely to have been changes in the dry mass of body cells and were more probably due to substantial shifts in fluid levels. Much more analysis of the data, especially blood and urine samples, will be required to examine this phenomenon.

Fumes from stoves in buried tents can lead to carbon monoxide poisoning. If initial headaches and nausea are ignored this can build up insidiously in the blood stream to dangerous levels, putting the heart and nervous system at risk for several weeks. The first attempt on Mount Parry failed due to CO poisoning, and all but one (the heaviest smoker) of the winter party suffered the early symptons at least once.

The only potentially serious illnesses were Simon Trathen's bronchitis in March 1985, and Nick Evans' duodenal ulcer in July-October 1984.

Frequent and troublesome dental problems had been anticipated.

Although the oldest team member lost a dozen fillings there were few pain cases, no extractions, and only a few fillings needed over the winter. Coltosol or Cavit fillings usually lasted 5-8 weeks.

Valluga boots caused many severe blisters. Most were treated successfully with tincture of benzoin, but Mike Ringe and Graham Greenway were each totally incapacited for a period, and John Kimbrey developed a deep infection requiring a long course of Erythromycin.

In the first two phases traumatic injuries were remarkably few, with no fractures, and sutures only required three times (Bill Hankinson needed nine in his scalp when nearly killed by a falling craneload in Valparaiso; Bill again, and John Kimbrey, three each after cutting themselves). The second-summer party was less fortunate. Gary Lewis developed a trapped sciatic nerve/slipped intervertebral disc on the journey south and never reached the island. Graham Greenway fractured his tibia during a storm at 'Dayglo Point' and was evacuated. Clive Waghorn needed 13 stitches in his left thigh after a nasty Fur Seal bite in February 1985. A week later, Clive broke his right femur cleanly 10 cm above the knee in a 25-metre crevasse fall, and was evacuated.

Medical preparations and preventive work were essential. A doctor was in each team, with two in the second-summer party. All team members were screened beforehand (with blood tests in case cross-matching was necessary), and all were instructed in first aid. The general strategy was to bring any casualty back by pulk to base camp, where a comprehensive medical and surgical kit was held.

Psychology and Group Social Studies

The circumstances of the isolated expedition living in tents seemed to offer interesting prospects for studies. No interest was elicited within the Services, but projects on circadian rhythms and the effects of cold stress, were arranged with university researchers. Johnny Morris also set up a study on group social interactions which Peter Stuttard undertook during the winter, and the data will be analysed under supervision of the Consultant Psychologist at St Bartholemew's Hospital.

I put together a questionnaire which was completed by all the winter party on the journey south, and then every month or so through the expedition. Given lists of suggested items, and encouraged to add their own, they ranked their top ten Cravings, Pleasures, Miseries and Dreads from 10 points down to 1. Scores for each item were calculated on each occasion from 0 to 100% (multiplying the percentage of maximum possible points by the percentage of team members including that item in their top ten). I hope to get professional help to analyse the results and to determine significant variations over the duration of the expedition and between different categories of team members (e.g. married/unmarried). Listed below are the top few items, ranked in order of their mean score over the whole time in the field; the overall mean scores are shown after each item, with (in brackets) the score anticipated on the journey south.

Cravings
1. Female company 51% (35%). Consistent, maximum in August.
2. Family affection 48% (17%). Consistent, maximum in July.
3. Making love 45% (32%). Consistent, maximum in October.
4. Countryside 22% (33%). Almost constant.
5. Friends at home 20% (13%). Consistent, maximum in July.

6. Courting, dancing 15% (9%). Fairly constant.
7. Driving a car 10% (18%). Consistent, maximum in November.
8. Bath or shower 8% (27%). Highest at beginning and end.
9. Comfortable bed 3% (21%). Always low down the list in the field.
10. Clean clothes 3% (12%). Only featured at beginning and end.
11. Films and theatre 2% (15%). Only ranked by a few individuals.

Pleasures

1. Warm night in dry bag 34% (80%). Consistent, maximum in July.
2. Listening to music 26% (not anticipated). Almost constant.
3. Inside a secure tent 21% (12%). Fairly constant.
4. Small exploring groups 21% (10%). Maxima when it was happening.
5. Good meal or brew 19% (21%). Almost constant.
6. Calm sunny day outside 19% (57%). Consistent, maximum in August.
7. Warm hands and feet 17% (6%). Maximum in mid-winter.
8. Good travelling snow 15% (not anticipated). Varied with activity.
9. Dry boots and clothes 13% (37%). Consistent, maximum in July.
10. Reading 11% (7%). Consistent, maximum in August.
11. First ascents 11% (47%). Maxima when it was happening.
12. News from home 8% (21%). Maxima at beginning and end.
13. Unexpected discoveries 8% (45%). Tailed off after June.
14. Good snowhole 7% (8%). Peaks each time snowholes were used.

Miseries

1. Cold damp night 42% (24%). Consistent, maximum in mid-winter.
2. Wet boots or clothes 30% (37%). Consistent, maximum in July.
3. Tent insecure 29% (23%). Consistent except peak in August.
4. Bad travelling snow 26% (not anticipated). Fairly constant.
5. Cold hands, feet or face 22% (40%). Consistent, maximum in July.
6. Frustrated plans. 19% (20%). Consistent, maxima when travelling.
7. Bad pulking 17% (not anticipated). Maxima when it was happening.
8. Blisters or toothache 7% (50%). Low except in first month.
9. Poor equipment 5% (27%). Low apart from a peak in June.

Dreads

1. Someone else killed 70% (45%). Consistent, reaching 86% in August.
2. Being avalanched 56% (37%). Maximum 76% in November.
3. Being injured 34% (52%). Low after arrival, over 40% from June.
4. Another party missing 33% (46%). Fairly constant, reflecting events.
5. Losing results 17% (7%). Rose to 32% August to October, then fell.
6. Tent wrecked 17% (9%). Consistent, maximum in November.
7. Being killed 17% (18%). Low after arrival, then fairly constant.
8. No food or fuel 16% (14%). Peak of 48% in October.
9. Crevasse fall 15% (9%). Peaks of 29% in April and November.
10. Frostbite 12% (not anticipated). Dropped off after July.
11. Bad news from home 11% (1%). Peaks 20% in June and November.
12. Operating on someone 7% (23%). Dwindled after July.
13. Expedition not successful 6% (15%). Fairly constant, zero August.

Acknowledgements

Expeditions are only possible because there is so much goodwill among people at home. Many people think that Service expeditions are different, but they are not. A Joint Services Expedition has a status in the Services akin to a needy artist who is a cousin of a large family. Most of the family are pre-disposed to help him, but none of them have any obligation to do so, and all have their own homes and families to look after. Their response to him depends upon his personality and approach, and upon their personal opinions of art in general and of his paintings in particular.

This expedition received marvellous help from hundreds of organisations and thousands of individuals. Without their help we would never have explored Brabant Island. The list below includes financial and equipment sponsors, as well as many who helped us by advice or influence, though to save space I have omitted many firms who also helped considerably by selling us good equipment at commercial rates, some at good discount. Space has also prevented me naming individuals within organisations who assisted us — to name all those in HMS *Endurance*, the British Antarctic Survey and the Tri-Service Stores organisations would need over eight close-packed pages.

We thank all those who helped us.

AB Biscuits Ltd. Addis Ltd. Aeromedical Evacuation Section HQ1 Group RAF. Albert Reckitt Charitable Trust. Allied Lyons Ltd. Mr & Mrs Ansell. Army Birdwatching Society. Army Canoe Union. Army Mountaineering Association. Army Staff College, Camberley. Asst Chief Defence Staff (P and L).

Professor Peter Baker. E.P. Barrus Ltd. Jem and Marie Baylis. Berghaus Ltd. Bowater International of Stockport. Tony Bray (Bradford Stamp Centre). BRNC Dartmouth. British American Tobacco Co. British Antarctic Survey. British Canoe Union. British Embassy, Santiago. British Kiel Yacht Club. BOBC Norway. Amanda Broughton. Mr Dave Burkitt. Cdr and Mrs Malcolm Burley. Mr and Mrs I.M. Burlingham.

E.A. Carey (Europe) Ltd. Catterick Garrison. CBE Associates. COD Bicester. COD Donnington. Charles Turner Ltd. Colmans Ltd. Colour Processing Laboratories Ltd. Comacchio Company RM. Comité Antarctique Belge. Commandant General Royal Marines. Commander British Forces Falkland Islands. Commander-in-Chief Fleet. CinC Naval Home Command Benevolent Fund. Commando Training Centre RM. Commando Logistic Regiment RM. Corah Ltd, Leicester. Cotswold Covers Ltd. Major David Counsell RA. Courage Breweries Ltd. Croom Helm Publishers Ltd.

Surgeon Captain David Dalgliesh RN. Dr Herbert Dartnall. Davie Mason & Co. Defence Medical Equipment Depot, Ludgershall. D. Director Training (PE) RAF. Mr J.E. Dickens. DG Aircraft (Navy). DG Army Medical Services. DG Naval Personal Services. DG Stores and Transport (Navy), several sections. Director of Infantry. Director Movements (Army). Director Movements (RAF). Director Naval Education Services. Director Naval Officer Appointments. Director Naval Operations and Trade. Director Naval PT and Sport. Director of Overseas Surveys. Director of Public Relations (Navy). RRS Discovery. Duracell Ltd.

Edinburgh Trust. Emtrad Ltd. Engineer in Chief of the Army. Europasports Ltd. Captain Everett RN.

Falkland Islands Logistic Battalion. Faraday Base (BAS). Mrs Betty Feltham. Miss Laurie Feltham. Professor O. Gonzales Ferran, Santiago University. H. Fine & Sons Ltd. Fisons Pharmaceuticals. Flag Officer Medway. Flag Officer Portsmouth. Flag Officer Scotland and Northern Ireland. Fleet Amenities Fund. Fleet Maintenance Group Chatham. Fleet Photographic Unit. Mr and Mrs J. Flint.

Fonadek International Ltd. Foreign and Commonwealth Office. Mr Robert Fox. Sir Vivian Fuchs. Fuji Photo Film Ltd. Rear Admiral and Mrs. J.P.W. Furse. Mrs Faye Furse. Furse House.

Baron Gaston de Gerlache de Gomery. Gitzo et Cie. Mathew Gloag & Son Ltd. Professor Rainer Goldsmith. Dr John Gordon.

Mr and Mrs Nick Hadden. Dr Jim Hansom. Mrs Maureen Hardy. Surgeon Vice Admiral Sir John Harrison. Dr Geoffrey Hattersley-Smith. Hawker Siddeley RAF 50th Anniversary Awards. Hawkins and Manwaring Ltd. H.J. Heinz Co Ltd. Hellma (England) Ltd. HMS *Bar Protector*. HMS *Caledonia*. HMS *Centurion*. HMS *Cochrane*. HMS *Cochrane* Wardroom. HMS *Daedalus*. HMS *Dryad*. HMS *Endurance*. HMS *Nelson*. HMS *Osprey*. HMS *Pembroke*. His Royal Highness The Prince of Wales. T.B. and Mrs D. Hood. Sir Rex and Lady Mavis Hunt. Hydrographer of the Navy Department.

IBM United Kingdom Ltd. Ilford Ltd. Inspector Physical & Adventure Training (Army). Institute of Naval Medicine. Institute of Terrestrial Ecology. International Distillers and Vintners (UK). Rear Admiral Sir Edmund Irving. ITT Antarctic Service Inc.

Mr A.G.E. Jones. Joint Air Reconnaissance Centre. Joint School Photographic Interpretation. Joint Services Expedition Trust. Joint Services Mountain Training Centre (Scotland). W. Jordans Ltd. Junior Leaders Regiment RE, Dover.

Karrimor Weathertite Products Ltd. Kenco Coffee Co. Ltd. Kennett Engineering Ltd. Kiel Training Centre.

Lasergage Ltd. Leroca Ltd. Mr. Michael Lethbridge. Admiral of the Fleet Lord Lewin of Greenwich. Lifeguard Equipment Ltd. Lofthouses of Fleetwood Ltd. Logistic Executive Army. Long John Ltd.

Mrs G.A. McCory. McMurdo Ltd. Malvernian Society. Marine Biology Laboratory, Plymouth. Measurement Devices Ltd. Medical Directorate General (Navy). Meteorological Office. Military Vehicles and Engineering Establishment. Corporal N. Moffet RE. Morris, Nicholson and Cartwright. Mount Everest Foundation. Mukluks Ltd. Multifabs Ltd. Mr Ed Murton.

Nabisco Ltd. Natural Environmental Research Council. Naval Party 8901, Falkland Islands. Nestlé Co. Ltd. Nikon UK Ltd. Nikwax Ltd. Nuffield Trust for the Forces of the Crown.

Mr H. Oliver.

Pacesetter Enterprises Ltd. Palmer Station (USARP). Paradigm (UK) Ltd. Midshipman K. Park RN. Pelling and Cross Ltd. Personnel Management Centre RAF. Petroleum Centre RAOC. Philatelic Bureau, Stanley. Pilkington PE Ltd. Plessey Electronic Systems Ltd. MV *Polar Duke* (icebreaker). Polar Postal History Society of Great Britain. Polysox Ltd. Commander J.E. Porter RN. Prince of Wales Own Regiment of Yorkshire. Principal Supply & Transport Officer (Navy) Devonport. Principal Supply & Transport Officer (Navy) Portsmouth. Procter and Gamble Ltd. Professional Dental Care Services Ltd. Professor Geoffrey Pugh. Mr & Mrs Paul Purkiss.

Queen Elizabeth Military Hospital, Woolwich. Queens Lancashire Regiment.

Racal Telectronics Ltd. Rank Film Laboratories Ltd. Regional Ordnance Depot, Thatcham (AT Store). Mrs Barbara Ringe. Miss E.J. Robertson. Rodolfo Marsh Base (Chile). Rolex Enterprise Awards. Rolex (UK) Ltd. Rothera Base. Rowntree Mackintosh. RAF Brize Norton & VC10 Squadrons. RAF Cottesmore. RAF College Cranwell. RAF Germany. RAF Gutersloh. RAF Kinloss. RAF Leuchars. RAF Leuchars Officers Mess. RAF Lyneham & Hercules Squadrons. RAF Mountaineering Association. RAF Ornithological Society. RAF Outdoor Activities Centre, Llanrwst. RAF Strike Command. RAF Support Command. Royal Anglian Regiment. Royal Army Medical College. RAMC HQ Mess Fund. Royal Botanic Gardens Edinburgh. RE Chattenden. REME Adventurous & Enterprising Activities Committee. RFA *Fort*

Austin. RFA *Olna.* Royal Geographical Society. Royal Marines Association branches: Australia, Bletchley, Canterbury, Deal, Eastbourne, Glamorgan, Gosport, Kidderminster, Merseyside, New South Wales, North Devon, Stoke on Trent, Newcastle on Trent. RM Eastney. RM Poole. RM Poole Corporals Club. RM Poole Sergeants Mess. RM Sports Association. RM Stonehouse. Royal Military College of Science, Shrivenham. Royal Naval Engineering College, Plymouth. RN Hospital, Haslar. RN Kayak Association. RN & RM Mountaineering Association. RN Sailing Association, Medway Branch. RN Stores Depot, Copenacre. RN Stores Depot, Llangennech. RN Victualling Depot, Botley. RRS *Bransfield.* RRS *John Biscoe.* Royal Scottish Geographical Society. Royal Scottish Museum.

Saccone and Speed Ltd. Sailors Fund. St Bartholomews Hospital. Sir Samuel Scott of Yews Trust. School of Military Survey, Hermitage. School of Electrical and Mechanical Engineering, Bordon. Mrs M.G. Scott-Easton. Scott Polar Research Institute. Senior Naval Officer Falkland Islands. Services Sound and Vision Corporation. Shaftesbury Marketing Ltd. Shakespeare Ltd. Mr Oliver Shepard. Signy Island Base (BAS). Smiths Co. Ltd. Snakpak Food Products Ltd. Society Expeditions. Society Professional Civil Engineers (N. Ireland). J.W. Spears & Sons Ltd. Special Air Service. John Spencer Associates. Mrs E. Spottiswood. Dr Bernard Stonehouse. Stores and Clothing R & D Establishment. Strand Insurance Brokers. Mr & Mrs Donald Strang. Survival Aids Ltd. Swix Sport AS. Syndicated Features Ltd.

Taylors Eye Witness Ltd. Teachers Whisky Ltd. Technique Hair Studio, Sevenoaks (G. and D. Mills). Telegraph Sunday Magazine. Tirfor Ltd. Topham Picture Library, Edenbridge. Touring Sports Ltd. TransAntarctic Association. Transglobe Expedition. Trenchard Memorial Awards Scheme. Tri-Wall Containers Ltd.

United Biscuits Ltd. US Antarctic Research Programme. US Coastguard Service. Dr Michael Usher.

Valley Canoe Products Ltd. Dr Bill Vaughan. Vector Instruments Ltd.

Waddingtons Games Ltd. J. Walter Thompson Ltd. Warner Lambert Ltd. Gino Watkins Memorial Fund. WEXAS. Wilkinson Sword Ltd. Mr & Mrs Ken Wilson. Wilson Marshall Ltd. Wintergear Ltd. Williams and Glyn's Bank Ltd. Chief Petty Officer Steve Williams RN. Wimpey Homes Ltd. World Discoverer. Wrigleys Ltd. Wyeth Ltd.

Yachtspeed Industrial Services Ltd.

1st Battalion Queens Lancashire Regiment. 1 Training Regiment RE. 3 Flight Army Air Corps. 3 Royal Tank Regiment. 3M UK plc. 4 Armoured Division, HQ Signals. 35 Engineer Regiment. 36 Engineer Regiment. 45 Commando Group. 74 Locating Regiment RA. 826 Squadron (Sea King helicopters).

The royalties from sales of this book are being used by the expedition to defray costs.

Brabant Island

History

On 19 February 1819 the South Shetlands were discovered by the storm-driven brig *Williams*, and her Captain, William Smith, returned to land there in October 1819. Edward Bransfield surveyed Bransfield Strait in the *Williams* in January 1820 and while doing so he sighted Trinity Island. Sealers working the South Shetlands began to use Deception Island as a secure harbour the following season. In February 1821 Thaddeus von Bellingshausen's Imperial Russian Expedition (completing an unheralded circumnavigation of Antarctica), discovered Alexander Island: he then sailed north in a blizzard, passing, but not sighting, the Palmer Archipelago. In fog near Deception Island, Bellingshausen's two ships encountered the sealer *Hero*: Captain Nathanial B. Palmer of the *Hero* was one of the first to sight the Antarctic Peninsula, but he did not venture toward Brabant Island.

In February 1821 John Davis, Captain of the sealing brig *Cecilia*, found more sealers than seals in the South Shetlands. After visiting Low Island he sailed south-east, reaching 64°S near the Peninsula: he was possibly the first to sight Brabant Island. Eleven men in the sealer *Lord Melville* from London wintered in Esther Harbour, King George Island, in 1821; they were probably the first men to winter in Antarctica. In 1824 James Hoseason, mate of the brig *Sprightly*, charted Hughes Bay around Hoseason and Intercurrence Islands, possibly going as far south as Two Hummock Island. Hoseason and other sealers almost certainly sighted Brabant Island during the 1820s and some may even have landed there, but they were generally secretive, and few records remain. By 1824, sealers from Britain and New England had virtually stripped the South Shetlands beaches, and in 1829 Webster reported finding not a single seal there.

In February 1829 Henry Foster, commanding HM Sloop *Chanticleer*, landed on Hoseason Island, and named the highest mountain to southward Mount Parry in honour of the Hydrographer of the Navy and former Arctic explorer.

As the seals dwindled, the Enderby Brothers, oil merchants of London, sponsored further explorations. In 1832 John Biscoe in the brig *Tula*, with the cutter *Lively*, made the first recorded landing on the Palmer Archipelago, on the west coast of Anvers Island. Not realising it was several islands he named the area Graham Land after the First Lord of the Admiralty.

Each of the three major national Antarctic expeditions in the 1840s (d'Urville, Wilkes and James Clarke Ross) approached the South Shetlands, but none of them closed Brabant Island. American sealers continued to visit the region sporadically and in small numbers through the 19th century, particularly in the periods 1843 to 1854 and 1871 to 1880. Brian Roberts' chronological list mentions a few American voyages before 1873, and 15 in the next 20 years, but without details of where they went. Robert Headland of the Scott Polar Research Institute is updating that list: he has so far found no records relevant to Brabant Island, although it is known that some sealers landed south of Anvers Island. At some time in this period Anvers and Brabant Islands collectively became known as Palmer Land.

In 1873 the steam whaler *Gronnland*, under Captain Edouard Dallman, sailed from Hamburg to explore the region on behalf of the German Society for Polar Navigation. In November 1873 he reached the South Shetlands, meeting a little fleet of sealing schooners from Stonnington, Connecticutt. He approached Cape Cockburn, but did not land: clearly this was already a well-known named feature, though inaccurately charted. He also discovered Dallman Bay but believed, understandably, that Brabant and Anvers were joined parts of Palmer Land. South of Anvers Island he discovered and named Bismark Strait, which he believed led ENE and probably broke right through the Peninsula.

Adrien de Gerlache, a young Lieutenant in the Belgian Navy, personally initiated, organised and led the expedition which inaugurated the 'heroic age' of Antarctic exploration in 1898. He bought the Norwegian sealer *Patria*, which he refitted, and renamed *Belgica*. One of his several aims was to discover the strait which was supposed to lead east from Hughes Bay right through the Peninsula. After proving that no such strait existed, he pushed southward into the unknown Gerlache Strait and on 30 January 1898 de Gerlache and Danco (Belgian), Roald Amundsen (Norwegian), Dr Frederick Cook (American) and Henryck Arctowski (Polish) made the first recorded landing on Brabant Island, at Cap d'Ursel on the south shore of Buls Bay. With one tent, one stove, two small Nansen sledges and ten metres of silk rope they spent five days and nights on the piedmont; protecting their tent with snow-walls they reached about 500 metres, but were unable to get up the icefalls above. It was the first time on record that anyone had used tents or sledges in Antarctica, and was also Amundsen's first stay ashore there. Many of the names around the Gerlache Strait derive from the *Belgica* expedition. de Gerlache discovered the Schollaert Channel separating Brabant and Anvers Islands and then sailed south through the Gerlache and Bismark Straits into the Bellingshausen Sea. There the *Belgica* was beset, and the expedition wintered in the pack. They were probably the third party to winter in Antartica (in 1877 a gang of sealers from New London had wintered under an upturned boat on King George Island, where all but one died). In 1903-5 Jean Baptiste Charcot passed Brabant Island in the *Pourquoi Pas?* and named Pointe Metchnikoff, Cap E.Roux, Claude Point, Astrolabe Needle (in honour of d'Urville's vessel) and Duperré Bay.

In 1913 an expedition in SS *Hanke*, sponsored by Christian Salvesens the whaling company, visited the South Shetlands and the Palmer Archipelago. They visited Duperré Bay, which they named 'Shackleton Bay', and their geologist David Ferguson collected samples there, plus a smaller collection in Buls Bay.

Since 1906 whalers had been working from harbours in the South Shetlands and Deception Island but from 1931 the industry became entirely pelagic and Brabant Island was probably a familiar sight to the whalers. The *Discovery* Expeditions were primarily concerned with whales and whaling, but between 1930 and 1937 *Discovery II* completed a running survey of the South Shetlands: no landings appear to have been made on Brabant Island, but Hill Bay is named after Lt Cdr Charles Hill RNR who served in and commanded *Discovery II* over an eight-year period. Very few other expeditions worked in the Peninsula region between the wars, but John Rymill's extraordinarily successful, though little publicised British Grahamland Expedition of 1934-7 certainly sighted Brabant Island on passages in *Penola* to and from their bases further south.

Despite the increasing scientific activity by many nations since 1943,

de Gerlache, Amundsen, Danco, Cook, Arctowski and one other with two sledges above Buls Bay in 1898. (Courtesy of Baron Gaston de Gerlache de Gomery)

we have found records of only four subsequent landings. Parts of the east coast were surveyed for the Falkland Islands Dependancies Survey in 1952 and 1955 but no landings were recorded. Two bases were established within sight of Brabant Island (the British hut at Portal Point on the Peninsula and the Argentine station in the Melchior Islands), but both were abandoned before 1980. A dilapidated beacon found on Minot Point, and a square of turf cut out nearby, are evidence of an unrecorded landing, possibly from the Melchior Islands' supply ship.

In 1956, Hunting Aerosurveys overflew Brabant Island at 3,900 metres, taking aerial photographs for FIDS. Helicopters landed survey parties on the summits of Lagrange Peak and Hunt Island to establish ground control, but neither party moved far, nor do they appear to have stayed for more than a day. When the Directorate of Overseas Survey map was being produced in 1959, Brian Roberts at the Foreign Office gave names to many unnamed features: 33 of the official names (all medical landmarks) derive from that paper exercise.

In 1964 a FIDS geologist, Dr Roger Bayly, landed by boat briefly somewhere on Brabant Island. BAS have been unable to find records describing that landing.

In 1975 Chilean geologists made a rapid three-day reconnaissance of the region using helicopters from MV *Piloto Pardo*. In the course of one day they visited a number of sites around Brabant Island.

The fourth recorded landing since the Second World War was just two weeks before we landed. The American research vessel *Hero* circumnavigated the island after Christmas 1983, landing an ornithologist briefly at 'Astrolabe' and Metchnikoff Points, and recording bird colonies elsewhere. We were rather surprised to find this quick visit published in the BAS Bulletin, the first work on Brabant Island with which BAS had been concerned after 20 years of neglect. However this followed an established pattern, as the first post-war scientific visits to Elephant Island and Gibbs Island each occurred when plans for Joint Services Expeditions to those islands were already well advanced and published.

With nine nations now operating bases in the Peninsula region,

36

37

36 **November.** Pulking back above 'No-Go Corrie' (John Kimbrey)
37 **December.** Halfway up 'Mount Frederick Cook' (Ted Atkins)
38 **December.** On Celsus Peak looking toward Anvers Island (François de Gerlache) Overleaf
39 **December.** Ted on the summit mushroom of Celsus Peak (Jim Lumsden) Overleaf

40 **December.** Looking back south to the Solvays (Chris Furse) Opposite
41 **December.** Pulk party approaching 'Noddies Hat' at sunrise (Chris Furse)
42 **Second Summer.** Southern Party Mountain dome in the Solvays (Steve Taylor)

43 **Second Summer.** Chris paddling off Metchnikoff Point (Tim Hall)
44 **Second Summer.** 'Dayglo Point' from the boats (Tim Hall)
45 **Second Summer.** Boat party in the Gerlache Strait (Tim Hall) Opposite

46

47

48

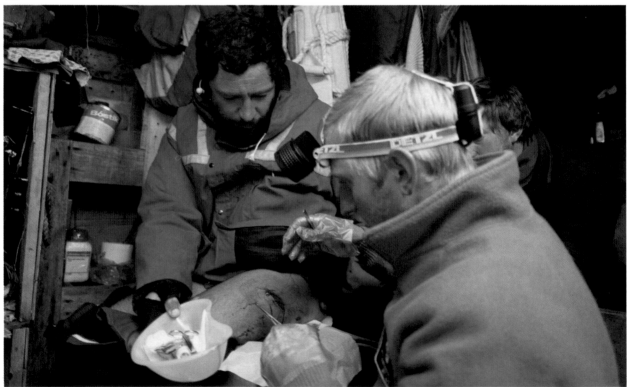

46 **Second Summer.** Richard paddling past icebergs in Bouquet Bay (Tim Hall)
47 **Second Summer.** Avon crossing a wave-worn iceberg (Richard Clements)
48 **Second Summer.** Tony stitching Clive's Fur Seal bite (Tim Hall)

increasing political and commercial interest in Antarctica, and tourism increasing (the Chileans have recently built a hotel and all-year airfield on King George Island), it seems likely that more-frequent visits to Brabant Island will occur in future. However we believe that it will remain unspoilt, protected by its violent terrain.

Geology   by Mike Ringe

The only published description seen before the expedition went into the field was by Araya and Hervé. On a one-day helicopter reconnaissance in 1975 the Chileans flew around Brabant Island, inferring faulting from the topography and collecting samples from several coastal sites. They described various formations, notably the lavas in the north, suggesting these had spread from feeders at Duclaux Point and Davis Island. They also described a magnetite found on Guyou Bay, resembling the richest ores in the Andes, but possibly an erratic at this site. Since returning, I have also unearthed another paper, by Ferguson, describing collections made in Duperré and Buls Bay in 1913.

My own fieldwork covered most of the north down to Virchow Hill and 'Astrolabe Point', and the south all around Koch Glacier, plus various outcrops on the main ridge and the east side, from Paré Glacier to 'Dayglo Point' and the Solvay Mountains. The brief preliminary outline below is based on my field observations, plus preliminary laboratory analysis of Simon Trathen's collections around the north.

Brabant Island's geological setting is at the apex of the spreading back-arc basin of the Bransfield Strait. Early geochemical analysis has shown affinities with both the South Shetland Islands and the James Ross Island group.

Exposures appear in general to become progressively younger from south to north. Tuffs and conglomerates on Mount Bulcke were the oldest rocks found (probably Cretaceous, under 140 million years old), and volcanics from 'Cairn Point' have been potassium-argon dated at under one million years old.

Large-scale intrusives, probably of Andean age (Cretaceous, perhaps about 96 million years old), were found both in the north-west (from Metchnikoff Point to Cape Roux, and inland to 'Claire's Finger') and in the south-east (at 'Dayglo' and Pinel Points). These are xenolithic quartz diorites, although compositional variation is common; in places they show metallic sulphide mineralisation. (The Andean intrusive suite forms a large proportion of the Antarctic Peninsula.)

There appear to have been two main phases of faulting. Large-scale NE-SW faulting cuts the island, but is very difficult to define because of the almost complete glaciation. Coastal NNW-SSE faulting is apparent in the north-west as distinct parallel-sided bays, where preferential erosion has occurred along fault-lines.

On the northern slopes of Mount Bulcke, Cretaceous (?) conglomerates include excellent examples of large, rounded water-eroded clasts, and are interlayered with 1–2 metre-thick bands of tuff, indicating a contemporaneous phase of explosive volcanic activity. Samples from the north-east shore of Chiriguano Bay should provide details of its subsequent history, involving at least three later phases of basaltic intrusives.

The mid-section of the island is composed of great thicknesses of coarse tuffs and conglomerates, interlayered with basaltic lavas and sills (these overlie the conglomerates, although the true relationships are unclear as yet). Sampling in this area was limited on both coasts, and will provide only a general outline of this phase.

At 'Astrolabe Point', a fresh high-level basaltic intrusive exhibits excellent cooling columns and possible in-chamber crystal separation. It probably relates to the young lavas further north.

At Metchnikoff Point, the Andean(?) intrusive exhibits an eroded upper surface, overlain by a coarse basaltic-rich Hyaloclastite about 35 metres thick. There these agglomerates show no depositional structures but at 'Cairn Point', and elsewhere around the north and north-west coast, cross-bedding and grading are a common feature. The agglomerate thickens considerably toward the east, and at Cape Cockburn it reaches at least 330 metres thick.

Overlying this agglomerate in the north are horizontally bedded basaltic lava flows. These are young, including a one million-year-old Pleistocene sample from 'Cairn Point'. These lavas are the cap-rock of the sequence, and form characteristic bluffs at Metchnikoff Point and elsewhere. At Metchnikoff Point itself there is a series of lavas, 1-5 metres thick, vesicular, fresh, and occasionally showing flow structures. Although reddened by iron-staining and obviously iron-rich, these lavas are not the magnetite noted by the Chileans — indeed no evidence of such rock types was found. Elsewhere the lava flows reach thicknesses of over 80 metres, as at Claude Point. These lavas include no tuffaceous material, indicating quiet flowing phases of volcanic activity. Probable vents were found near Bouquet Bay (at Virchow Hill, Duclaux Point and just south of Roentgen Peak).

Tuffs are however present at 'Pinnacles Spur' and Claude Point. At 'Pinnacles Spur' they are coarse and altered, whereas at Claude Point they are very fine, graded and waterlain. Obviously explosive volcanic activity preceded the young capping lava flows, but the exact relationships are not yet clear.

It is already evident that, as expected, the results from Brabant Island will have more than local significance. They should improve understanding of the mechanisms and timing of the openings of Gerlache Strait and Bransfield Strait, and of related activity in the Peninsula region. Our findings will be correlated with other work being undertaken in the region by several nations. In 1984 this included deep geophysical investigations on the continental shelf west of Brabant Island.

The field data will form the basis of a Ph.D. paper (Nottingham University).

Geomorphology
by Paul Flint

On the west side of the island the north-south mountain chain falls sharply toward the sea, giving rise to high coastal rock- and ice-cliffs, with headlands that become partially snow-free in summer. The eastern side of the island is characterised by gentler gradients and longer glaciers, culminating in a coastline composed almost entirely of ice-cliffs, which typically lie on a rock platform just above present sea-level. The cliffs and few small rocky points on the east coast exhibit no evidence of former sea-levels, and there is very little glacial debris.

It had been hoped that former sea-levels could be determined and related to the heights of platforms described from the South Shetlands.

Stacks and skerries around the north and north-west coasts show two common planation levels above present sea-level. Areas of well-sorted, well-rounded boulders at heights of up to ten metres at Minot Point, Fleming Point and Metchnikoff Point may indicate former sea-levels, but evidence was inconclusive and no datable material was found.

It seems likely that at some time the Pleistocene icecap covering the Peninsula extended across the Gerlache Strait on to Brabant Island, and that a major glacier debouched out of Dallman Bay. However neither hypothesis has been established, and it was hoped that the expedition could find some evidence of previous glacial maxima. No such evidence was found, and there were in fact few phenomena usable to determine events during glacial recession over the last 10,000 years. Glacial tills are most extensive, but nevertheless very localised, on the west and north coasts from Humann Point to Cape Roux. Moraines at Cape Roux, Metchnikoff Point and Claude Point show evidence of three (or four) former 'still-stand' periods of glacial cover, and Humann Point may exhibit similar evidence. No re-exposed moribund mossbanks were found, nor any other datable evidence of recent glacial recessions. The only organic materials found in beach or glacial till deposits that were suitable for radio-carbon dating were in Chiriguano Bay, where elongate, flattened bivalve shells about 8-10 cm long were locally abundant in till at the base of overlying ice. Limpet shells underneath grass swards at 'Astrolabe Point' may be dateable to indicate the minimum length of time this area has been snow-free. Only small rudimentary patches of sorted soil and patterned ground were found.

The first-summer and winter observations, and discussion with Dr Jim Hansom of Sheffield University, suggested that the most profitable investigation for me during the second summer would be a study comparing beach-forming processes on the exposed north and west coasts with those on the more sheltered shores in the Gerlache Strait. Unfortunately, circumstances confined my work to the south-east.

The north and west coasts, south to Fleming Point, are typified by wave-cut rock platforms with some isolated stacks and skerries extending up to 2 km offshore. Extensive flat platforms of mixed rock at low-tide level occur at various sites from Driencourt Point to Cape Cockburn, most impressively just south of Metchnikoff Point. The beaches on this exposed coast are steeper than those in the Gerlache Strait, with storm berms, and they are less affected by brash-ice.

Small isolated beaches on the south-east coast (and probably also in Duperré Bay) are characterised by intertidal boulder barriers, lying across the line of the longest fetch, with patterns of furrows, ridges and hollows caused by brash-ice. In general, sheltered beach areas contain a high proportion of locally derived material (mainly basalts), whereas exposed areas especially on boulder barriers display a wider range of pebble type (many are not locally derived and may have originated across the Gerlache Strait). Sheltered areas are characterised by well-packed mosaics of pebbles, and patterns of circular hollows and ridges, where blocks of ice have settled and ground into the beach. By contrast, exposed areas exhibit patterns of ridges and furrows along the longest fetch, formed by brash-ice bulldozing its way up the beach. Some of these furrows are well established so that ice is channelled into them, whereas others are transitory (particularly in fine beach material, where resorting by subsequent wave and brash-ice action occurs quickly).

Comparison with Hansom's work in the South Shetlands and elsewhere indicates that the ice-formed beach features on south-east Brabant Island are poorly developed. Ice-striated boulders are very rare, packed mosaics of pebbles and boulders are small, many features are transitory, and locally derived material is scarcely smoothed by water or ice, even where closely packed. No direct evidence of frost-shattering within the intertidal zone was found. However, winter air temperatures were usually below the freezing point of sea water and fast ice was absent (at least on the north-west coasts), so frequent tidal freeze-thaw cycles probably did explain the few large boulders and some bedrock in the intertidal zone which appeared to have been frost-shattered in situ.

Results are being worked up with advice from Dr Hansom.

Climate and Meteorology   by Howard Oakley

The climate is harsh polar maritime. Precipitation was high (over twelve metres of snowfall in nine months of records), but most snow was then blown off (as spindrift), reducing overall accumulation. The summers were cool and wet, with frequent depressions, and most big winds from the north-east. Autumn brought a major thaw and gales, settling in May/June to give fine cold spells interspersed with heavy snowfalls. July and August brought the strongest winds at base camp, with south-west winds exceeding 100 knots in clear skies. September was windy, snowy and generally cold despite one spring thaw. October was much better, but November was again windy with both south-west and north-east blizzards. A spring melt early in December heralded the return of summer weather.

The table below summarises records at base camp. Conditions in the field differed considerably. Wind generally increased with height, but strong Föhn winds over the tops and especially through high cols precluded any empirical relationship. A temperature lapse rate of 2°C per 300 metres gave reasonable estimates (e.g. Harvey Heights would be 16°C colder than base camp) though not reliable ones. A major feature was the variation of weather around the island, attributed to orographic effects of the island's mountains and the blocking influence of the Antarctic Peninsula. The north-west coast from 'Astrolabe Point' to Cape Roux often enjoyed clear skies, downstream of Anvers Island in south-west winds, or of the Peninsula in north-east winds. Lister and Paré Glaciers became notorious for trapped cloud and snowfall, whilst Minot Point was a remarkably calm spot. Stable conditions often persisted with stratus up to 300-1,500 metres, producing damp fog at sea-level but sunlit tops. The overall annual mean temperature of −1.2°C was higher than the −3.4°C predicted by regional isotherms.

For people (and other warm-blooded animals) in Antarctica, the effective temperature due to wind-chill is a more realistic measure of cold than actual temperatures. The table below shows wind-chill effective temperatures over the range encountered. For example at the overall mean sea-level temperature of −1°C and overall mean recorded wind-speed of 9 knots, the cold was equivalent to a still-air temperature of −7°C.

Measured Temperature (°C)	Windspeed (knots)				
	9	20	34	60	100
+10	+ 5	− 1	− 4	− 6	(− 7?)
− 1	− 7	−18	−22	−24	(− 26?)
−10	−18	−31	−35	−38	(− 40?)
−20	−29	−46	−50	−54	(− 58?)
−30	−42	−61	−65	−70	(− 75?)
−40	−56	−76	−80	−85	(− 93?)

MONTH	Temperature (°C)			Barometric Pressure (millibars)			Snow-fall (cm)	Number of days when the following were recorded:					
	Abs. min.	Mean	Abs. max.	Abs. min.	Mean	Abs. max.		Rain	Snow	No snow nor rain	Sun	Winds over 34kts	Winds over 60kts
JAN 1984	− 1.0	+1.4	+14.0	986	993	1012	—	7	4	8	10	5	0
FEB	− 3.0	+1.7	+ 6.8	961	993	1013	—	11	5	7	7	4	1
MARCH	− 4.0	+1.1	+10.0	980	997	1018	—	10	6	3	7	4	0
APRIL	− 9.0	−1.6	+14.0	965	986	1005	45	10	18	7	18	13	1
MAY	−13.0	−3.6	+ 5.0	958	979	1018	142	5	22	9	18	8	0
JUNE	−11.0	−4.4	− 0.6	958	1001	1019	119	2	20	10	21	6	0
JULY	−14.6	−4.2	+ 0.5	986	1006	1028	165	9	20	9	15	11	4
AUG	−17.4	−4.5	+ 0.5	936	992	1021	114	7	25	6	22	13	3
SEPT	−14.3	−4.1	+ 9.8	966	994	1017	371	8	27	3	14	20	6
OCT	−13.0	−1.1	+14.5	951	990	1014	67	8	22	9	26	8	4
NOV	− 5.4	+1.0	+20.1	954	983	1009	159	13	22	8	23	10	3
DEC	− 6.0	+2.9	+23.2	968	1001	1023	38	12	12	12	21	8	2
JAN 1985	−21.0	−0.4	+13.1	971	992	1007	—	14	14	11	13	5	1
FEB	− 9.5	?	+11.0	958	980	997	—	1	14	13	7	0	0
MARCH	−16.0	?	+ 7.0	976	985	995	—	0	4	4	3	1	1
Overall percentage of days with these conditions:								30	60	30	57	29	7

No measurement of snowfall was made in January-March of either year.

Vegetation

by Alistair Moffat

The flora of the region has an exactly parallel history to that of the terrestrial invertebrates (p. 216). In Antarctica the main limitation on vegetation is, rather surprisingly, the lack of moisture rather than the direct effects of cold. In the South Shetlands the predominantly cloudy conditions significantly reduce the amount of sunshine available, but in general the conditions of moisture and temperature in the Scotia Arc and down the west side of the Antarctic Peninsula are more favourable than anywhere else in Antarctica, and the vegetation is correspondingly richer. However, compared with most other standards it supports an impoverished flora, confined to scattered small snow-free areas with favourable conditions of moisture and sunshine. Typically these are north-facing or flat areas at low altitude. The macroscopic flora comprises mainly lichens and mosses. Within the region only about 150 species of lichens, 75 mosses, 25 liverworts, 5 macroalgae and 10 macrofungi have been identified. Only 2 species of flowering plants are known: this compares with 90 flowering plants in the north of Greenland at 84°N.

Two main cold-desert ecosystems are represented. The Chaliko system comprises barren gravel with microphytes. We collected some samples of apparently barren material, which will be examined for microfungi by Professor Geoffrey Pugh at Portsmouth Polytechnic. However our main botanical work was concentrated on the richer Bryosystem, comprising more or less open (rarely closed) macrophytic vegetation composed of mosses, lichens and, exceptionally, algal cover. Reference collections of material were made for Professor Pugh (microfungi), for Dr Wyborn of Central London Polytechnic (studying predacious microfungi). Macro-fungi and moulds were collected for Dr Roy Watling at the Royal Botanic Gardens, Edinburgh. Flowering plants, mosses, lichens, liverworts and algae will be identified by Dr Graham Bell and Dr R.I.L. Smith (possibly with assistance on difficult lichens from Dr Orstedal at Tromso). A reference collection will be held in the herbarium of the Institute of Terrestrial Ecology in Edinburgh. Since the species list has not yet been determined, this summary is confined to general descriptions of the main types of plant community.

Fruticose Lichen and Moss Cushion Sub-formations

Various associations of crustose, leafy or bushy lichens, with or without short compact cushions and minute turves of mosses survive on dry stony ground, scree-slopes and rock-faces which remain exposed in winter to desiccating winds and low temperatures. Examples of such communities are common on west and north coast sites from Humann Point to Cape Roux at heights up to 300 metres. The east and south coasts provide far fewer snow-free habitats, but communities of this type were found at a few sites from Chiriguano Bay to Hill Bay, again at up to 300 metres. Surprisingly by far the highest and most 'inland' lichens found were on the east coast, at 810 metres above Freud Passage. Else-where the few inland snow-free areas are remarkably barren, with no lichens at all found on 'Pinnacles Spur', 'First Cache', around 'Claire's Finger', or on 'The Family'.

Crustose Lichen Sub-formations

On sea-cliffs and boulders near birds' nests, favourable habitats for salt and nitrogen-tolerant lichens produce some of the most colourful scenes in the Antarctic, with orange, red, yellow, grey, white and brown crustose or leafy lichens, and occasional other growths. Such communities were found at various coastal sites.

Alga Sub-formations

The only plant that can tolerate the trampling and concentrated guano around penguin colonies is the leafy green alga *Prasiola crispa*. It forms crinkly mats in such wet muddy habitats, and also on some damp cliff-faces below petrel colonies, notably at Metchnikoff Point.

Dense aggregations of pink (or yellow or green) unicellular snow algae occasionally tinge melting snowfields in the Antarctic. However at Brabant Island this was only seen on sea ice.

Moss Turf Sub-formations

The most impressive formation in the Antarctic is the long-term develop-ment by turf-forming mosses of deep banks of moss peat. At Elephant Island one such bank reached 3.4 metres in depth and radio-carbon dating showed material about 2,135 years old. Although that is the deepest known bank, some on Signy Island are older at about 4,800 years. Moss banks do occur as far south as Marguerite Bay, and many have been found on and near Anvers Island, so we hoped to find some on Brabant Island. No banks were found, although we expect some turf-forming species to be identified in our collections from the north and west coasts. Only very few sites appeared suitable for formation of moss banks, but their absence may conceivably reflect very recent emergence of snow-free areas.

Moss Carpet Sub-formations

Moss carpets occur in areas inundated by meltwater during summer and around pools and streams. Sometimes, as at Elephant Island, such carpets may cover extensive areas approaching a hectare. Very few suitable areas occur on Brabant Island, and only one minute pool of fresh water was found (on 'Easter Island' off Metchnikoff Point). No extensive carpets were found, although we expect some carpet-forming species to be identified in our collections from the north and west coasts.

Moss Hummock Sub-formations

Moss cushion communities formed the richest mossy habitats on Brabant Island. These occurred on moist ledges, sloping rock-faces and stable scree-slopes where meltwater trickled down in summer. Cushions were sometimes up to about 15 cm thick, covering areas over a square metre. Such communities were commonest below 120 metres altitude, although smaller moss cushions were found at up to 240 metres in the north-west. Fruiting bodies were seen not infrequently. Moss cushions were commonest on north-facing slopes: this was attributed to greater incidence of meltwater rather than to any direct effects of sunlight and temperature, as they also occurred in some damp south-facing sites, and under snowdrifts persisting into December.

Macrofungi

One species of small brown agaric toadstool was collected from grass at Metchnikoff Point and from mosses at Minot Point.

Herb Tundra Formation

Both the Antarctic flowering plant species (hair grass *Deschampsia antarctica* and pearlwort *Colobanthus quitensis*), were found at Metchnikoff, Claude, 'Astrolabe' and Minot Points, with isolated tillers of grass at two other nearby points. Both species occur also further south to 68°S in Marguerite Bay, but BAS had not expected us to find any, and the richness of their growth at the three more-southerly points was our major botanical discovery. At Claude Point both species grew at 200 metres: this equals the highest previous Antarctic record for pearlwort (on Elephant Island), but an exceptional stand of grass has been recorded at 275 metres (above Marguerite Bay).

In direct contrast to the mosses and lichens, the two flowering plants were absolutely restricted to north-facing slopes, plus a few flat areas with, for example, a sharply defined cut-off line along the east–west crest of the northern promontory at 'Astrolabe Point'. Length of sunshine through the season appeared to be the principle factor controlling growth, and patches of moss communities within grass swards coincided with snowdrifts persisting through November. Freedom from penguins is clearly also a requirement, whilst the richest stands of grass often grew on a substrate of rotted limpet shells presumably deposited by Kelp Gulls long ago.

Neither species flowered at Metchnikoff Point, but both were flowering at the other three main sites, and appeared to have viable setting seed at

'Astrolabe Point'. Both species are known to develop seed while buried under snow through the winter at Signy Island, but the longer summer days and reduced cloud cover at Brabant Island may allow full development in one season. Minot Point is an exceptionally sheltered site, 'Astrolabe Point' sometimes enjoys very localised sunshine, and the main stands on Claude Point are on a sloping sandstone cliff terrace which probably also provides a favourable microclimate.

An M.Sc. paper (UCNW Bangor) on vegetation over environmental gradients is planned using the expedition's field data.

Terrestrial Invertebrates

Although the impoverished terrestrial fauna of the Antarctic is limited to tiny and microscopic invertebrates, studies in the region are interesting on several planes. Specific adaptations to the extreme environment are of intrinsic interest. The very basic ecosystem provides a simple laboratory for quantified studies. The distributions and variations of genera and species interrelate with geological history over the last 200 million years and glaciological history over the last 30 million years, and also provide a data-base for studies of dispersion and colonisation over the last 10,000 years.

Fossil evidence shows a rich terrestrial flora and fauna in Antarctica from the late Palaeozoic Era (over 230 million years ago). The climate then was often subtropical or even tropical, although much of the continent was covered by the Gondwanaland icecap during the Carboniferous and Permian Periods (about 280 million years ago).

Greater Antarctica is the continental shield area stretching from the Transantarctic mountains across the present-day South Pole to the Pacific and Indian Ocean coasts, which were then contiguous with Australia, India and southern Africa. The break-up of Gondwanaland began with the separation of India and southern Africa in the Triassic Period (about 200 million years ago) and it was only at that time that Lesser Antarctica (the Peninsula region) was first formed, by major mountain-building movements. The complex pieces of Lesser Antarctica remained connected with South America and New Zealand, while Greater Antarctica and Australia drifted away together. Greater and Lesser Antarctica thus evolved different terrestrial biota while life flourished through the rest of the Mesozoic Era, still dominated by the dinosaurs. As the new continental areas separated, their terrestrial faunas continued to speciate, rapidly at the evolutionary spearhead of warm-blooded animals, but more slowly among primitive orders such as the invertebrates.

About 100 million years ago the Andean orogen signalled the extension of the Scotia Arc and the parting of Lesser Antarctica from South America, a process which probably continued to the end of the Mesozoic Era/ Cretaceous Period about 63 million years ago.

Various subsequent phases of active volcanism on both sides of the Antarctic Peninsula (including the South Shetlands) reflect spreading of the oceanic floor of Drake Passage and other tectonic movements, which are still continuing. Although minor relative to the earlier episodes, these movements have continued the process of separating parts of the region, with major block-faulting in the Tertiary Period. There have been numerous changes of sea-level so that land bridges have been successively formed or broken. The fauna remaining from the Mesozoic Era was widely distributed over the region, in separated populations; however the invertebrates were late in their evolutionary history, and there was little impetus for change, initially.

The world's climate grew cooler through the Tertiary Period, and icecaps formed first on higher parts of Antarctica in the Miocene Epoch, perhaps 30 million years ago. As glaciation advanced, most terrestrial life was simply wiped out. However a few small areas remained ice-free, in summer at least, acting as isolated oases or refuges: some of these were on high nunataks which divided flowing glaciers; others were on coastal fringes. At the height of glaciation (despite isostatic sinking of the crust), relative sea-levels were lower due to the water locked up as ice, so many of the coastal oases were probably in areas now submerged.

The extent of glaciation fluctuated, but in general reached a maximum in the Quaternary Period/Pleistocene Epoch beginning three million years ago.

The terrestrial fauna surviving in refuges through the Pleistocene glaciation was limited to a few very small invertebrates, all virtually immobile except for very gradual migration over years, or through chance transport by wind, water, or birds. The geographical ranges of various species in the different oases were pruned by the varying (though everywhere severe) environmental pressures. The evolutionary process seems to have been largely confined to eliminating species which were not adaptable to variations of the already hostile conditions in their isolated oases. Little adaptive radiation seems to have occurred to differentiate these isolated populations and indeed there are very few species endemic to the Peninsula region as a whole, let alone parts of the region.

By about 10,000 years ago a definite amelioration of the Antarctic climate had set in, and this interglacial has continued to the present time, as in the Arctic. The glacial cover has receded, and relative sea-levels have risen. During this Recent Epoch some more isolated Antarctic islands (e.g. Bouvet-oya, east of the Weddell Sea) have been successfully recolonised by a few plants and invertebrates. These biota are sometimes collectively termed 'insular', because they are capable of transport by wind or water, usually from temperate mainland areas upwind in the West Wind Drift, or alternatively by birds and seals. Some of the present terrestrial fauna of the Peninsula region has probably arrived in this manner, though most are believed to have spread out from the few oases in the region. Colonisation from outside the region is most likely in the north adjoining Drake Passage. Together with the increasingly cold and dry conditions further south, and the more recent and less extensive areas of ground exposed further south, this has produced a general trend down the Antarctic Peninsula. In the north (e.g. at Elephant Island) the fauna, though impoverished, is comparatively diverse, both diversity of species and density of living organisms then diminish down the length of the Peninsula. Only two species of higher insect (both midges) occur in the region, plus a few macroscopic arthropods and various microscopic organisms, which live in the very limited organic habitats scattered in suitable coastal areas.

Prior to this expedition, arrangements were made to collect specimens for various researchers. Collections totalling some 500 samples were made from various habitats in each of five coastal sites in the north-west (from 'Cairn Point' to Minot Point), and five sites in the south-east (from Pinel Point to Chiriguano Bay). These collections have only recently been returned to Britain: post-expedition analysis has thus scarcely begun, and species lists are not available. Results will be published in the scientific press in due course by the individual researchers listed below.

Arthropods:	Dr Michael Usher, York University and Dr William Block, British Antarctic Survey.
Nematodes:	Dr N.R. Maslen, Tropical Development & Research Institute.
Rotifers:	Dr Herbert Dartnall, ex BAS.
Tardigrades:	Miss Sandra MacInnes, BAS.
Protozoa (amoebae):	Dr Humphrey Smith, Coventry Polytechnic.

Parasites were collected for Dr Ivor Williams of Hull University, Dr Karin Anderson of Oslo University and the British Museum.

The larger arthropods visible to the naked eye gave a rough indication of the richness of the invertebrate fauna. By turning over stones in suitable sites it was easy to find springtails (probably mostly *Cryptopygus antarcticus*, at least three species identified) and mites (at least six species identified, probably including *Alaskozetes antarcticus* and *Gamasellus racovitzae*), and a free-living tick (*Ixodes uriae*) was found thus at Metchnikoff Point. Wingless midges (almost certainly *Belgica antarctica*) were most often seen crawling about on the surface of sun-warmed mosses.

The east and south coasts were largely barren. In contrast the north and west coasts were comparatively rich, and the density and diversity of arthropods at 'Cairn', Metchnikoff, Claude, 'Astrolabe' and 'Minot Points' appeared superficially to rival comparable sites in the Elephant Island group.

Birds
by Chris Furse

Emperor Penguin *Aptenodytes forsteri*. This was the one Antarctic breeding species not recorded.

Chinstrap Penguin *Pygoscelis antarctica*. Only three colonies, two in the north-west. There was a small autumn immigration, but birds were otherwise absent from late April to October.

Gentoo Penguin *Pygoscelis papua*. Scattered non-breeders were regularly present, with minimum numbers in July and August. An autumn influx included reverse migrants from South Shetlands.

Adelie Penguin *Pygoscelis adeliae*. Occasional non-breeders present, in summer only.

Macaroni Penguin *Eudyptes chrysolophus*. Very few non-breeders present, in summer only.

Rockhopper Penguin *Eudyptes chrysocome*. One vagrant ashore in December.

Light-mantled Sooty Albatross *Phoebetria palpebrata*. None were identified from the island although seen from *Endurance* 80 km off Metchnikoff Point.

Black-browed Albatross *Diomedea melanophris*. Regular offshore from January to April, occasionally foraging among the north-west skerries. Some westward movements recorded.

Grey-headed Albatross *Diomedea chrysostoma*. Several probable sightings offshore in summer, but no certain identifications.

Southern Giant Petrel *Macronectes giganteus*. Regular in small numbers throughout the year, but no breeding colonies. Few first-year birds present at any time, and none in winter.

Antarctic Fulmar *Fulmarus glacialoides*. A very localised breeder around the northern end of the island, and frequently seen inshore in summer around all coasts. Through the winter, occasional sightings.

Cape Pigeon *Daption capensis.* A very patchy breeder, in the north only, though present inshore elsewhere. Colonies were used as roosts until mid-winter, but not thereafter by the (reduced) winter population, until returning in September.

Antarctic Petrel *Thalassoica antarctica.* Absent from January to May. Some big coasting movements took place in winter, with a local population present through November.

Snow Petrel *Pagadroma nivea.* A scattered probable breeder, but virtually absent from mid-January to early April and breeding not proven. Large numbers were present through the winter, with frequent occupation of suspected colonies from April to December, and birds were seen overland at up to 2, 450 metres.

Antarctic Prion *Pachyptila desolata.* Wings were found in skua territories at three different north-west sites. A flock of probables in December was the only other record.

Blue Petrel *Halobaena caerulia.* The December flock of whalebirds could have been this species, but the only definite sightings were 150 km offshore, from *Endurance.*

Black-bellied Storm Petrel *Fregetta tropica.* A scarce summer visitor, heard in many sites. Breding was strongly suspected, with adults occupying nests.

Wilson's Storm Petrel *Oceanites oceanicus.* A widespread breeder, numerous in suitable areas. The main departure took place in April, with birds returning in early November.

Blue-eyed Shag *Phalacrocorax atriceps.* Several breeding colonies. Large mobile winter flocks in north-west fished communally offshore, and these exceeded the estimated total breeding population of the island, with sub-adults probably absent.

Brown Skua *Catharacta skua lönnbergi* (also known as Antarctic Skua). Scarce summer visitor, and very few bred. Migration dates thought to be the same as the South Polar Skuas, but not sure.

South Polar Skua *Catharacta maccormicki.* A widespread breeder, in small numbers except for colonies at Minot Point and other west-coast sites. Departed in April and returned in October/November. A total of 2-4 seen over the winter were believed to be this species.

Kelp Gull *Larus dominicanus.* A widespread resident in small numbers. Winter population approximated to breeding population, but there were signs of migration in June and November. Birds fed more offshore from May to October when limpets were unavailable.

Antarctic Tern *Sterna vittata.* A widespread breeder in small numbers. Adults were resident throughout winter, with intermittent territorial behaviour. Winter roosting flocks in the north-west greatly exceeded the local breeding population.

Arctic Tern *Sterna paradisaea.* Several probable sightings in spring and summer.

Sheathbill *Chionis alba.* A very localised breeder, exclusively near Chinstrap and Shag colonies. The only evidence of migration was two ringed birds seen. Winter population approximated to breeding population, but was dispersed and mobile.

Seals and Whales

Elephant Seal *Mirounga leonina.* Brabant Island lies south of their published range, apart from a party reported in Gerlache Strait. However they have recently established a breeding group near Palmer Station, and we sighted singles at several beaches around the island. At Metchnikoff Point, sighted in every month of the year, with maxima of six in April and May and minima of single sightings each month from July to October. Through the summer both cows and bulls came ashore, though very few were full-grown. In late November a pup was born at Metchnikoff Point.

Weddell Seal *Leptonychotes weddelli.* As expected, present in small numbers at most suitable beaches. The largest population was at Metchnikoff Point, where numbers fluctuated widely from day to day making assessment of seasonal variation difficult. The January peak of 54 declined to under 30 from mid-February to mid-April; numbers then rose through May and June to nearly 50, before declining to less than 20 at the end of August; the spring build-up began in September with about 30 present by late October. Two nearly weaned pups were seen at 'Dayglo Point' in early November. However, surprisingly, no pups were actually seen at Metchnikoff Point apart from a dead premature pup in August. In mid-winter, couples were regularly seen circling close to each other in the water: this did not appear to have any sexual context. No other social or sexual behaviour was observed. Three observed deaths from natural causes around Metchnikoff Point seemed a very high mortality rate for such a small population (one carcass was seen at sea, one had been killed by a rockfall and the third had its skull crushed by sea-ice while attempting to land in winter).

Crabeater Seal *Lobodon carcinophagus.* Aerial photographs taken in the summer of 1980–1 showed over 60 resting on sea-ice in a corner of Duperré Bay and larger numbers were expected in winter. It was therefore disappointing to find very few visiting Metchnikoff Point: no more than one was seen there in each summer month, with none between early February and mid-May. There were rather more frequent records in winter but no more than five a day: probably more would occur in years with more pack-ice. No pups were seen, but two pairs with aggressive males stayed ashore at Metchnikoff Point for the second half of October. The boat parties in each summer saw several resting on icefloes in Bouquet Bay, Freud Passage and Gerlache Strait, and observations at 'Dayglo Point' suggested they were commoner on the east coast. A high proportion bore the deep circumferential scars now attributed to Leopard Seals; on some adults these scars were still bleeding.

Leopard Seal *Hydrurga leptonyx.* At Metchnikoff Point very few were seen in summer, but up to four were sighted on many days from July to September, resting on sea-ice or feeding. They were seen on sea-ice around the south and east coasts by the boat parties in each summer, being commonest in Freud Passage and Bouquet Bay. No pups were seen, nor any breeding behaviour.

Ross Seal *Omatophoca rossi.* This pack-ice seal is one of the least-known seals in the world. Only one sighting of a recently born pup has ever been made, in Dallman Bay. Our hopes of seeing some were not realised.

Fur Seal *Arctocephalus gazella*. Based on published information we did not expect to see any of this species. However, large numbers were seen in summer, at many coastal sites: in 1983-4 this could have been part of the unusual emigration from South Georgia following a krill-famine there, but a similar influx in 1984-5 suggested this was a regular occurrence. The largest numbers were at Metchnikoff Point: very few were present there in December but numbers built up steadily through January to a peak of 950 in mid-February, before tapering off to 600 at the end of March, about 80 at the end of April, and under ten at the end of May; numbers recovered through June to about 30, then fell to under ten by the end of July; from August to December they came ashore irregularly, with never more than ten seen in a day. The great majority were males, with few harem bulls and only a very few cows (or possibly first-year animals). No pups were identified. Several pale sandy individuals were seen and one albino; one tagged bull probably came from South Georgia.

Ross Seal *Omatophoca rossi*. This pack-ice seal is one of the least-known seals in the world, and only one sighting of a recently born pup has ever been made, in Dallman Bay. However our hopes of seeing some were not realised.

Humpback Whale *Megaptera novaeangliae*. This was the most frequently identified whale, and most unidentifed sightings were probably of this species. One or two were occasionally seen off all parts of the coast but most commonly in the Gerlache Strait, where up to 13 were seen from *Endurance* in one day. The latest summer sighting was in mid-March; after that a couple visited Metchnikoff Point in late August, but then no more were seen until November.

Sei Whale *Balaenoptera borealis*. Some rorquals in Dallman Bay and the Gerlache Strait in the second summer were though to be this species, but their identity could not be confirmed.

Southern Right Whale *Enbalaena glacialis*. Individuals were sighted twice in Gerlache Strait during the second summer. This species appears to be recovering, and extending its known range southward.

Killer Whale *Orcinus orca*. Parties of Killers are said to frequent bays in the Gerlache Strait in summer and we had expected to see them occasionally. However the only possible sightings were couples off Metchnikoff Point in May and June, and these were not confidently identified.

Index